THREE PLAYS

Heinrich von Kleist

THREE PLAYS

Prince Friedrich von Homburg

The Broken Pitcher

Ordeal by Fire

Translated by Noel Clark

OBERON BOOKS
LONDON

These translations first published in 2000 by Oberon Books Ltd
(incorporating Absolute Classics)
521 Caledonian Road, London N7 9RH
Tel: 020 7607 3637 / Fax: 020 7607 3629
e-mail: oberon.books@btinternet.com

A catalogue record for this book is available from the
British Library.

ISBN 1 84002 123 3

Cover design: Andrzej Klimowski

Typography: Richard Doust

Printed in Great Britain by Antony Rowe Ltd, Reading

Contents

INTRODUCTION

Noel Clark

Recent decades have seen a steady growth in the reputation of Heinrich von Kleist (1777–1811) – dramatist, poet and master of the novella. On the strength of six mould-breaking plays and eight stories – classics of the genre – Kleist is now seen as one of the most original talents of the German Romantic era, though only two of his plays were staged in his life-time, and those with little success. Underrated as a dramatist, even by his compatriots, for almost a century, Kleist remains relatively unfamiliar to English-speaking audiences. Goethe and Schiller? Yes. Lessing? Possibly. Brecht? Of course. But – who did you say?

Kleist was born into a traditional Prussian military family with a score of generals to its credit, as well as a few now largely forgotten poets. For Kleist, a staunch Prussian patriot in a Germany then still no more than a conglomeration of quarrelsome dukedoms, the arch-enemy was Napoleon's France. Kleist, however, was not cut out for army life. After a few years as an officer in the Potsdam Regiment of Guards, he defied family and superiors by resigning his commission in protest against the 'tyranny' of military discipline. Equally, he rejected a civil service post on the grounds that this would involve being obliged to carry out State instructions while forbidden to question their moral validity. 'I cannot do it,' he wrote to his then fiancée, explaining moreover that 'order, exactitude and patience' were qualities which he entirely lacked. He later broke off their engagement.

Retaining faith only in his literary talent, Kleist set out to surpass his already celebrated older contemporaries, Goethe and Schiller. Friends thought he aimed to become the 'Shakespeare of Germany'. But a bout of frenzied study of the philosophers, Kant in particular, left him exhausted, disillusioned and convinced there was no such thing as absolute truth, justice or love. If so – it seemed to Kleist – life would not be worth living. Thereafter, his thoughts seem often to have turned to suicide.

Secretive and given to alternating bouts of elation and despair, Kleist can never have been easy to get along with. Nevertheless, he enjoyed the generous support of his half-sister Ulrike and groups of devoted friends, among them writers and one or two publishers who ensured that most of his work was at least printed. The distinguished older novelist and poet, Christoph Wieland, persuaded Kleist to recite in private a few scraps of his first planned 'masterpiece', *Robert Guiskard*, and was greatly impressed: 'If the shades of Aeschylus, Sophocles and Shakespeare combined to write a tragedy, this would be it,' said Wieland – provided, of course, that the rest was as good as what he had heard. But Kleist, after several futile attempts to finish the play, was shattered to find the task beyond him and abandoned the project in despair. Only a fragment of the work survives.

From the outset, Kleist was an individualist, always on the move, an idealistic genius tortured by self-doubt, unable to reconcile himself to the contradictions which he observed in his own hypersensitive nature and in the world around him. Though increasingly aware of his limitations – 'The truth is, I admire what I imagine, not what I produce' – Kleist went on writing. Plays, stories, poems and articles for literary and patriotic reviews poured from his pen, interrupted only by worsening bouts of despondency and ill-health.

The great Goethe, a sturdy optimist, confessed that, despite his genuine wish to sympathise with the younger writer, Kleist aroused in him only a 'shudder of revulsion'. There were times, however, when the enthusiasm of his friends and a few favourable reviews briefly dispelled his depression. In 1808, one of his most prolific and truly happy years, Kleist wrote: '…my dearest hopes are being fully realised.' But fresh disappointments lay ahead. Theatre directors continued to turn down his plays; the censors were implacable; the public indifferent.

In 1812, poverty-stricken and broken in health and spirit by literary setbacks and by Napoleon's humiliation of his beloved Prussian Fatherland, Kleist, aged only 34, perished in a suicide pact with a woman friend who was convinced that she was terminally ill. After shooting her, as she requested, Kleist shot himself. They left a joint letter addressed to mutual friends which said: 'Remember us in joy and sadness: two strange mortals about to embark on their great voyage of discovery.'

Kleist's contemporaries were often shocked, even revolted by the violent emotions, abrupt switches in mood and the cruelties depicted in some of his plays. As one German critic observed, earlier Romantic writers of the *Sturm und Drang* era had 'played' with the 'forces of darkness' in their work, but in Kleist's case, such forces seemed to 'spring from the very core of his spirit.' To us, on the threshold of the twenty-first century, with two world wars and the Holocaust behind us (not to mention Freud and Jung) the explosive inner conflicts and dilemmas which Kleist experienced so acutely and projected with such brutal passion in some of his works are less mystifying. Nowadays, Kleist might well have been offered 'counselling'.

Some of his friends, indeed, detected what they feared were signs of mental derangement in his behaviour and in his writing. Perceptive critics, however, such as the poet and dramatist Ludwig Tieck (1773–1853), recognised that the strength and originality of Kleist's work – despite artistic flaws – sprang from the sheer depth and power of his emotions.

The three plays in this volume, those best loved by German audiences, illustrate the most enduring facets of Kleist's genius, not least his versatility. *The Broken Pitcher* (1808) originally won a prize for the youthful author in a competition for members of his writers' circle. Ingenious plotting, skill in character-portrayal, robust humour and crisp dialogue gave promise of great things to come. Alas, the first important stage performance was a fiasco, largely thanks to Goethe, then director of the Weimar Theatre, who destroyed the unity and comic impact of the play by splitting it into three acts. The infuriated Kleist launched a public attack on

Germany's most revered author. This ill-considered action, described by Schiller as an aberration, was ignored by Goethe. But years elapsed before Kleist's little masterpiece was at last revived and played in Berlin to great acclaim.

Kleist's most enigmatic drama, the sprawling Gothic dream-play *Ordeal by Fire* (*'Das Kätchen von Heilbronn'*), was published in 1810 and performed the same year at the Wiener Theatre in Vienna. The public enjoyed it hugely for its colour, atmosphere and extravagant action. Not so the critics. Kleist then offered his play to the Berlin National Theatre whose director, August Iffland, returned the manuscript, wrapped in blotting paper, with the comment that it was unstageable. Kleist replied with a bitterly sarcastic letter, apologising for the fact that the heroine was a girl. He added waspishly: 'It would have pleased you better had she been a boy.'

It was not until 1905 at the Deutsches Theatre in Berlin that the celebrated Austrian director Max Reinhard (1873–1943) first revealed the true stage potential of this challenging fantasy. Part fairy tale for adults, part psychodrama with medieval trappings, the play was later performed several times with notable success, both in Germany and at the Vienna Burg Theatre. The lasting popular appeal of the drama – inspired by an old Scottish ballad known to Kleist in translation – was reflected as recently as 1994, when it was performed for the first time in a new Polish translation, at the Teatr Polski in Wrocław. Critics these days show greater appreciation of Kleist's skill in handling the dream motifs and magical elements in this strange saga of a primevally innocent young girl, obsessed by a passion she does not understand for the charismatic knight, Count vom Strahl.

If neither of these plays is wholly *typical* of Kleist's varied output, both bear the hallmarks of his struggle to reach the public with a stimulating weave of Classic, Romantic and realistic strands. This he comes closest to achieving in *Prince Friedrich von Homburg* (1810) – a tautly plotted, deeply moving exploration of the complex relationship between love, honour, obedience to the State, sin, forgiveness and redemption. Here is Kleist at his most passionate and poetic, writing from the fullness of his heart and for once positively resolving in literature, as he failed to do in life, the clash between harsh reality and the idealistic dreams of the spirit.

Sadly, Kleist's last and greatest drama at once fell foul of the authorities. Prussian military and court circles were aghast at what they saw only as an insulting and demoralising portrayal of a young Prussian officer of noble birth, reduced by fear of death to begging for his life. The play could not even be published until ten years after Kleist's own death and was not performed in Berlin till 1828 – in a carefully censored version. Decades passed before it was hailed not only as a great patriotic drama but, more importantly perhaps, as a noble and humane masterpiece of German, indeed European, theatre.

It has been suggested that Kleist was too idiosyncratic a writer to found a school of imitators. But his influence on German literature has been profound. He is often described as the 'first of the moderns'. It is not altogether surprising that the novelist Franz Kafka (1883–1924) was among Kleist's greatest admirers, while various critics have drawn attention to 'Kleistian' echoes in the works of – among others – Friedrich Hebbel (1813–63), Georg Büchner (1813–37), Gerhart Hauptmann (1862–1946), Franz Wedekind (1864–1918), Bertolt Brecht (1898–1956) and Fritz von Unruh (1855–1970).

Noel Clark
London, 2000

PRINCE FRIEDRICH
VON HOMBURG

Characters

THE ELECTOR OF BRANDENBURG
Friedrich Wilhelm

THE ELECTRESS
Elisa, his wife

PRINCESS NATALIA OF ORANGE
niece and foster-daughter of Electress; Colonel-in-Chief
of Princess of Orange Regiment

FIELD MARSHAL DÖRFLING

PRINCE FRIEDRICH ARTHUR VON HOMBURG
General-in-Command of Cavalry

COLONEL KOTTWITZ
Commanding Officer of Princess of Orange Regiment

HENNINGS
Infantry Colonel

COUNT TRUCHSS
Infantry Colonel

COUNT HEINRICH HOHENZOLLERN
member of the Elector's suite

CAPTAIN VON DER GOLZ

CAPTAIN COUNT GEORG VON SPARREN

CAPTAIN STRANZ

CAPTAIN SIEGFRIED VON MÖRNER

CAPTAIN COUNT REUSS

A SERGEANT-MAJOR

OFFICERS, CORPORALS, TROOPERS, COURT
CHAMBERLAIN, LADIES- AND GENTLEMEN-IN-
WAITING, PAGES, FOOTMEN, GROOMS, SERVANTS

PEOPLE OF ALL AGES AND BOTH SEXES

Note

The Battle of Fehrbellin in which the Prussians defeated the Swedish forces under General Wrangel was fought in 1675.

The play was probably written in the winter of 1809-10. It was first published in the 1820 posthumous edition of Kleist's works. The same year it was performed in Vienna, on 30 October, and the following year in Breslau, Frankfurt am Main and Hamburg. It was first seen in Berlin at the Royal Theatre in July 1828 in a version carefully expurgated to avoid giving offence to the army. By the end of the century *Prince Friedrich von Homburg* – belatedly recognised as a masterpiece – was firmly established in the repertoire of the country's leading theatres.

ACT ONE

Scene 1

The scene is Fehrbellin. A garden in the old French style. Castle in the background, with a ramp leading down. It is night.

PRINCE FRIEDRICH VON HOMBURG, bare-headed and with an open-necked shirt, is seated half-waking, half-sleeping under an oak tree, plaiting a wreath.

The ELECTOR and the ELECTRESS, with PRINCESS NATALIA, COUNT HOHENZOLLERN, CAPTAIN VON DER GOLZ and OTHERS quietly emerge from the castle and stand looking down at him from the balustrade of the ramp. PAGES with torches in attendance.

HOHENZOLLERN: Our gallant cousin Friedrich, Prince
von Homburg,
    Leading our cavalry, these past three days,
    Has kept the Swedish forces on the run;
    It wasn't till this evening, breathless still,
    He reappeared at Fehrbellin headquarters.
    Did you, though, not command him tarry here
    Three hours – no more – to fodder, then renew
    His drive on Wrangel to prevent the Swedes
    From digging in along the River Rhyn
    And drive them on as far as Hackelberge?
ELECTOR: I did!
HOHENZOLLERN: Well, having briefed his squadron
leaders –
    According to your grace's strategy –
    To ride again at ten o'clock tonight,
    He flung him in the straw, like a panting hound,
    Intent on resting his exhausted limbs
    Before the battle which, we're all aware,
    Is waiting for us at the crack of dawn.
ELECTOR: Yes, so I heard. Well then?
HOHENZOLLERN: The hour has struck –
    All riders mounted and the turf stamped flat

Outside the city gates – but who's still missing?
The Prince himself, who should be at their head!
With torches, lanterns, lights, they seek the hero
And come upon him – where? I ask you – where?
(*Taking a torch from one of the PAGES.*)
Sleepwalking, if you please! Look – on that bench –
Where, in such slumber as one wouldn't credit,
The moonlight's lured him forth and busies him –
Dreaming, no doubt, of his posterity –
With plaiting a wreath to celebrate his fame!

ELECTOR: What?

HOHENZOLLERN: It's a fact! Look down! See, where he sits!
(*Shining light down on HOMBURG.*)

ELECTOR: Still fast asleep? Impossible!

HOHENZOLLERN: Yet so!
Call him by name and he'll collapse at once!
(*Pause.*)

ELECTRESS: The young man's ill, as true as I'm alive.

NATALIA: He needs a doctor–

ELECTRESS: Hasten to his aid,
Don't squander precious moments making mock!

HOHENZOLLERN: (*Handing back the torch.*)
He's well enough, you tender-hearted ladies;
No less robust than I! The Swedes, by God,
Will find that out tomorrow when we meet.
It's no more – you can take my word for it –
Than some queer trick of his unruly spirit!

ELECTOR: I'd never have believed it! Come, my friends,
Let's all go down and take a closer look!
(*They follow the ELECTOR down the ramp.*)

COURTIER: (*To the PAGES.*)
Stand back, torch-bearers!

HOHENZOLLERN: No friends, let them be!
The place could all go up in flames and he'd
Be no more conscious of it than that diamond
Ring he's wearing on his princely finger!
(*They surround him by the light of the torches.*)

ELECTOR: (*Bending over HOMBURG.*)
What is that foliage he's plaiting? Willow?

HOHENZOLLERN: A wreath of willow? God forbid!

That's laurel:

    The like he's seen on many a hero's brow,

    Depicted in the Berlin Hall of Fame.

ELECTOR: Where did he find it in my sandy soil?

HOHENZOLLERN: The gods above alone could answer that!

COURTIER: Perhaps he found it in that plot back there,

    Where the gardener grows his more exotic plants.

ELECTOR: It's very odd! No matter. Well I know

    What's stirring in the breast of this young fool!

HOHENZOLLERN: Indeed! Tomorrow's battle, mark

my words!

    Star-gazing, as he's wont, I'll bet he sees

    A victor's crown of sunbeams ready spun!

    (*HOMBURG eyes the wreath.*)

COURTIER: He's finished it.

HOHENZOLLERN: Oh, what a shame it is,

    We haven't got a looking-glass to hand!

    As vain as any maiden, he'd draw near,

    Admiring the effect, this way and that,

    Like trying on a bonnet, girt with flowers.

ELECTOR: God's teeth! I must just see how far he'll go!

    (*The ELECTOR takes the crown from the hands of HOMBURG,*

    who looks at him and blushes. The ELECTOR winds his

    neck-chain into the wreath and hands it back to NATALIA.

    HOMBURG jumps to his feet. The ELECTOR shrinks back

    with NATALIA, who raises the crown. HOMBURG follows

    her with outstretched arms.)

HOMBURG: (*In a whisper.*)

    Natalia! My dearest! My own bride!

ELECTOR: Quick, let's away!

HOHENZOLLERN: The fool!

COURTIER: What's that he said?

    (*ALL mount the ramp.*)

HOMBURG: Friedrich! My Lord! My father!

HOHENZOLLERN: God almighty!

ELECTOR: (*Shrinking back out of the way.*)

    Open the gate for me!

HOMBURG: O mother mine!

HOHENZOLLERN: The lunatic! He's—

ELECTRESS: Whom is he addressing?

HOMBURG: (*Reaching for the crown.*)
Why flee from me, dear heart? Natalia!
(*He snatches a glove from NATALIA's hand.*)

HOHENZOLLERN: God help us! What on earth was that
he snatched?

COURTIER: The crown?

NATALIA: No, no!

HOHENZOLLERN: (*Opens the gate.*)
Come swift inside, my lord,
And let the scene be banished from his mind!

ELECTOR: Back to obscurity with you, master Prince –
Obscurity! And on the battlefield,
If so it please you, let us meet again!
Such peaks are not for scaling in a dream!
(*Exeunt ALL except HOMBURG. Gate slams shut in front
of him. He pauses for a moment in front of the gate, with an
expression of bewilderment, then walks down the ramp, with
the hand in which he holds NATALIA's glove pressed to his
forehead, as though deep in thought. At the bottom of the
ramp, he turns and stands gazing up at the gate.
Enter HOHENZOLLERN from below, through a wrought-
iron gate, followed by a PAGE.*)

PAGE: (*Softly.*)
Listen, your excellency! Hear me, Count!

HOHENZOLLERN: (*Irritated.*)
Quiet, you cricket! What's the matter?

PAGE: I've –

HOHENZOLLERN: Don't rouse His Highness with your
idle chirping!
What is it?

PAGE: The Elector sent me back
And bade me tell you, when the Prince wakes up,
To breathe no word to him about the joke
Which he allowed himself to play on him!

HOHENZOLLERN: (*Softly.*)
Back to your hayfield, cricket! Sleep your fill!
As if I needed telling! Off you go! (*Exit PAGE.*)

(*HOHENZOLLERN positions himself some distance behind
HOMBURG who is still standing motionless, staring up at
the gate.*)

HOHENZOLLERN: Friedrich! (*HOMBURG collapses.*)
    That's laid him out – as neatly as a bullet!
    (*Approaches him.*)
    I'm more than curious to hear the yarn
    He'll spin in order to explain what made
    Him choose so strange a spot to fall asleep!
    (*Bending over him.*)
    Friedrich! What the devil are you up to?
    What are you doing out here in the dark?

HOMBURG: Good God, where am I?

HOHENZOLLERN: Where, you may well ask!
    The troopers you're supposed to be commanding
    Rode out of camp an hour since, on their way,
    And you're here in the garden still asleep!

HOMBURG: What troopers?

HOHENZOLLERN: (*Ironically.*)
                      Mamelukes, for all you know!
    As sure as I'm alive, he's quite forgotten
    That he's the Colonel of the Brandenburgers!

HOMBURG: (*Standing up.*)
    Quick! My helmet! Weapons!

HOHENZOLLERN: Yes – where *are* they!

HOMBURG: There, to your right, look! Lying on the stool!

HOHENZOLLERN: Where? What stool?

HOMBURG: I think that's where I laid them –

HOHENZOLLERN: (*Looking at him.*)
    If so, then go and take them from the stool!

HOMBURG: Whose is this glove? (*Staring at it in his hand.*)

HOHENZOLLERN: How'm I supposed to know?
    (*To himself.*)
    Oh, damn and blast! That's what he must have snatched
    From the Elector's niece, without her seeing!
    (*Breaking off.*)
    Come on! What's keeping you?

HOMBURG: (*Throwing the glove away.*)
                I'm coming now!
    Hey, Franz! That ruffian was supposed to wake me!

HOHENZOLLERN: (*Observing him.*)
  He's raving mad!
HOMBURG: Upon my oath, I'm lost!
  I just don't know, dear Heinrich, where I am!
HOHENZOLLERN: In Fehrbellin, you scatterbrain!
                                 You're dreaming!
  This is a side-path leading through the gardens
  That stretch away behind the castle-keep.
HOMBURG: (*To himself.*)
  I wish the night would swallow me! Again,
  By moonlight, I've been walking in my sleep!
  (*Pulling himself together.*)
  Forgive me! But you know the heat in bed
  Was practically unbearable last night.
  I crept into the gardens, quite exhausted,
  And so beguiling was the night's embrace –
  Blond hair, all redolent of perfume – that,
  Like some young Persian groom beside his bride,
  I laid me down to slumber in her lap.
  What time is it?
HOHENZOLLERN: Eleven-thirty now.
HOMBURG: You say the squadrons have already left?
HOHENZOLLERN: Of course! They set off sharp at ten
                                as planned.
  The Princess of Orange Regiment, I'd say –
  At least the van – by now has surely reached
  The heights of Hackelwitz where, at first light,
  They'll cover the deployment of the army
  Against the Swedish forces under Wrangel.
HOMBURG: No matter! They've old Kottwitz in command;
  He's fully briefed concerning our objective.
  Besides, I was due here at Fehrbellin by two
  To hear the final order of the day.
  It's therefore just as well I stayed behind.
  Come, let's go in! The Elector doesn't know?
HOHENZOLLERN: Don't worry! He's in bed and
                             sleeping sound.
  (*They are about to go in when HOMBURG pauses and turns*
  to pick up the glove.)

HOMBURG: I had a most extraordinary dream!
    It was as if I saw the royal castle,
    Gleaming with gold and silver, open up
    And down the marble ramp in state there came
    A train of noble persons dear to me:
    First, the Elector and his lady; then –
    What is her name?
HOHENZOLLERN: Who?
HOMBURG: Why – the one I mean!
    (*Seeming to search for the name.*)
    A man born dumb could hardly fail to name her!
HOHENZOLLERN: Platen?
HOMBURG: No, not her!
HOHENZOLLERN: Ramin, perhaps?
HOMBURG: Good heavens, no!
HOHENZOLLERN: Bork? Winterfeld?
HOMBURG: My dear man, no! You've overlooked the pearl,
    So dazzled are you by the lustrous setting!
HOHENZOLLERN: Her name! Am I to guess it from
                        your face?
    Which lady do you mean?
HOMBURG: It doesn't matter.
    The name escapes me now that I'm awake
    In any case, you'll understand without it.
HOHENZOLLERN: Alright! Go on –
HOMBURG: But please don't interrupt!
    Then the Elector, with the brow of Zeus,
    Holding a crown of laurels in his hand,
    Came face to face with me and fired my soul –
    Draping his neck-chain round the wreath, which he
    Then handed her to crown me –
HOHENZOLLERN: Who?
HOMBURG: Lord!
HOHENZOLLERN: Speak!
HOMBURG: The Platen, I suppose, it would have been.
HOHENZOLLERN: The Platen, eh? The one who's now
                       in Prussia?
HOMBURG: Oh, is she really? Then, perhaps – Ramin?

HOHENZOLLERN: Ah, the Ramin! The one with bright
                                           red hair?
   The Platen has those roguish, violet eyes –
   We know you fancy her –
HOMBURG: Well, yes – I do.
HOHENZOLLERN: Then it was she who handed you
                                           the wreath?
HOMBURG: Like glory's goddess, raised the wreath aloft
   From which the Elector's chain of office hung,
   As though she were about to crown a hero.
   A prey to inexpressible emotion,
   I stretched my arms, my hands reached out to seize it,
   I meant to sink upon my knees before her;
   When suddenly, like morning mist dispersed
   By a fresh breath of wind, the Court entire
   Eluded me, retreating up the ramp
   Which, as I climbed it, seemed to stretch ahead,
   Unending, to the very gates of Heaven.
   To left and right, I cast about me blindly,
   Strove in my fear to seize some well-loved hand:
   In vain! The castle gate flew open wide;
   A flash of light engulfed them from within
   And, with a clang, the gate once more slammed shut.
   Only a glove I snatched in wild pursuit,
   From the sweet phantom-figure of my dream –
   And sure enough, ye gods, it is a glove
   Which, as I wake, I'm holding in my hand!
HOHENZOLLERN: Upon my oath! And you believe
                                           this glove
   Belongs to her?
HOMBURG: To whom?
HOHENZOLLERN: Why? To the Platen!
HOMBURG: The Platen. Yes, indeed. Or the Ramin?
HOHENZOLLERN: (*Laughing.*)
   You and your visions! What a rogue you are!
   Who knows from what idyllic lovers' tryst –
   A flesh and blood affair, with both awake –
   This glove you're holding is a souvenir?

HOMBURG: What? For me? By all I love –
HOHENZOLLERN: Who cares?
    For my part, be it Platen or Ramin!
    On Sunday there's a mail coach bound for Prussia:
    So you can very quickly ascertain
    Whether your beauty has mislaid her glove.
    Come on! It's midnight. No more gossiping!
HOMBURG: (*Dreamily, to himself.*)
    You're right enough. Come on, let's go to bed.
    Something I meant to ask you, my dear fellow:
    The Elector's charming niece – the young Princess
    Of Orange – who was recently in camp –
    Is she still here with the Elector's wife?
HOHENZOLLERN: Why ask? I do believe the fool is –
HOMBURG: Why?
    You know I had to earmark thirty troopers
    For their safe conduct from the scene of action.
    I put Ramin himself in charge of that.
HOHENZOLLERN: Long gone – or else about to take
                               the road!
    At least, Ramin was standing by all night ·
    Outside the palace portals with his men.
    Come on! It's midnight and before this battle
    I, for one, would like to get some sleep.
    (*Exeunt.*)

Scene 2

A hall in Fehrbellin Castle. Gunfire can be heard in the distance. Enter the ELECTRESS and PRINCESS NATALIA dressed for a journey and escorted by a COURT CHAMBERLAIN. They take seats at the side, with LADIES-IN-WAITING. Next come the ELECTOR, FIELD MARSHAL DÖRFLING, HOMBURG with NATALIA's glove in his jacket, HOHENZOLLERN, COUNT TRUCHSS, COLONEL HENNINGS, CAPTAIN VON DER GOLZ and several other GENERALS, COLONELS and other OFFICERS.

ELECTOR: What's all that shooting? Is it Götz?
DÖRFLING: It is, your Excellency – Colonel Götz
    Who took the vanguard with him yesterday.

He's sent an officer back to base already
To give you reassurance in advance.
A Swedish force a thousand strong, it seems,
Is now established on the Hackelberge.
Götz pledges to secure those hills for you,
Advising that your Excellency proceed
As though his vanguard held the heights already.

ELECTOR: (*To the OFFICERS.*)
The Marshal knows the detailed battle-plan;
So take your pencils, please, and note it down!
(*The OFFICERS gather round DÖRFLING on the other
side of the hall and take out their notepads. The ELECTOR
turns to the CHAMBERLAIN.*)
Ramin has left already with the carriage?

CHAMBERLAIN: About to leave, my lord. They're
harnessing.

ELECTOR: (*Seating himself in a chair behind the ELECTRESS
and NATALIA.*)
Ramin is to escort you, dear Eliza,
Together with a troop of thirty horsemen.
You're staying at my Chancellor's castle, Kalkhuhn,
Near Havelberg, across the Havel river.
You'll see no Swedish faces over there!

ELECTRESS: But is the ferry now in working order?

ELECTOR: At Havelberg? All measures have been taken.
Besides, it will be light before you're there. (*Pause.*)
Natalia, you're very quiet, dear girl.
Is something wrong?

NATALIA: I'm feeling nervous, uncle.

ELECTOR: But you'll be absolutely safe, my dear –
You'd not be safer in your mother's lap.
(*Pause.*)

ELECTRESS: When do you think that we'll be reunited?

ELECTOR: Once God grants victory, as I do not doubt –
Perhaps within the next few days, at most.
(*PAGES serve the LADIES with breakfast. DÖRFLING
dictates. HOMBURG, pencil and notepad in hand, keeps his eyes
fixed on the LADIES.*)

DÖRFLING: The plan of battle, gentlemen, devised
By his Excellency, aims to decimate

The fleeing Swedish forces, having driven
A wedge between them and the bridgehead they've
Established on the Rhyn, to guard their rear.
You, Colonel Hennings –
HENNINGS: Sir! (*Writing.*)
DÖRFLING: Will take command
Today of our right wing by his grace's order.
Your task: to skirt the enemy's left flank
And, unobserved, between him and bridges
Thrust, so joining forces with Count Truchss –
Count Truchss!
TRUCHSS: Sir! (*Writing.*)
DÖRFLING: – joining forces with Count Truchss...
(*He pauses.*)
Who'll meanwhile take position with his guns
Upon the high ground overlooking Wrangel –
TRUCHSS: (*Writing.*)
Overlooking Wrangel...
DÖRFLING: Got that down?
Then you will strive to chase the Swedish force
Into the swamps behind them, to their right.
(*Enter a FOOTMAN.*)
FOOTMAN: Your carriage, Ma'am, is waiting down below.
(*The LADIES rise.*)
DÖRFLING: The Prince von Homburg –
ELECTOR: (*Also rising.*)   Is Ramin prepared?
FOOTMAN: He's mounted ready by the palace gate.
(*LADIES and GENTLEMEN take leave of one another.*)
TRUCHSS: (*Writing.*)
Into the swamps behind them, to their right...
ELECTOR: The Prince von Homburg –
Where's the Prince von Homburg?
HOHENZOLLERN: (*Quietly.*) Friedrich!
HOMBURG: (*With a start.*)   Sir!
HOHENZOLLERN: Are you awake?
HOMBURG: Your orders, Marshal?
(*He blushes, seizes pencil and paper and writes.*)
DÖRFLING: To you his grace has once again entrusted –
Just as at Rathenow – illustrious command

Of all the cavalry of Brandenburg;
That's without prejudice to Colonel Kottwitz
Who'll be on hand to offer his advice.
(*Softly to GOLZ.*)
Is Kottwitz here?

GOLZ: No, Marshal – as you see,
He sent myself with orders, in his stead,
To hear you brief us on the battle-plan.
(*HOMBURG again looks towards the LADIES.*)

DÖRFLING: (*Continues.*)
You will be stationed on the plain near Hackelwitz,
Facing the right wing of the Swedish forces,
But well beyond the range of cannon-shot.

GOLZ: (*Writing.*)
But well beyond the range of cannon-shot...
(*The ELECTRESS ties a scarf round NATALIA's neck.
NATALIA, about to draw on her gloves, looks around her as
though searching for something.*)

ELECTOR: (*Going towards her.*)
What have you lost, my dear?

ELECTRESS: You're missing something?

NATALIA: I don't know, aunt. I cannot find my glove...
(*ALL start looking.*)

ELECTOR: (*To the LADIES-IN-WAITING.*)
Come, ladies, would you kindly hurry up!

ELECTRESS: You have it, child.

NATALIA: The right one; but the left?

ELECTOR: Perhaps you left it somewhere in your bedroom?

NATALIA: (*To 1ST LADY-IN-WAITING.*)
Dear Bork!

ELECTOR: Be quick!

NATALIA: Look on the mantlepiece!
(*Exit 1ST LADY.*)

HOMBURG: (*Aside.*)
Good Lord above! I can't believe my ears!
(*Removing the glove from his jacket.*)

DÖRFLING: (*Looking at the paper in his hand.*)
But well beyond the range of cannon-shot. (*Goes on.*)
Your Highness must –

HOMBURG: She's searching for her glove –
(*He looks alternately at the glove and NATALIA.*)
DÖRFLING: By the Elector's most express command –
GOLZ: (*Writing.*)
   By the Elector's most express command…
DÖRFLING: Regardless how the tide of battle flows,
   You must not move from your appointed place!
HOMBURG: Quick! I must see if it's the one she lost!
   (*He drops a handkerchief as well as the glove, picks up the
   handkerchief but leaves the glove lying where everyone can
   see it.*)
DÖRFLING: (*Irritated.*)
   What now, your Highness?
HOHENZOLLERN: (*Quietly.*)
                       Friedrich!
HOMBURG: Yes?
HOHENZOLLERN: You must
   Be off your head!
HOMBURG: Your orders, Marshal?
   (*Again readies his pencil and notepad. DÖRFLING throws
   him a questioning look. A pause.*)
GOLZ: (*After writing.*)
   You must not move from your appointed place –
DÖRFLING: (*Going on.*)
   Until, hard-pressed by Hennings and by Truchss –
HOMBURG: (*To GOLZ, quietly, peering at his notes.*)
   Who, Captain Golz, who? What? Me?
GOLZ: You! Who else?
HOMBURG: The place – I'm not – ?
GOLZ: Of course not!
DÖRFLING: Got all that?
HOMBURG: I must not move from my appointed place.
   (*He writes.*)
DÖRFLING: Until, hard-pressed by Hennings and
                            by Truchss –
   (*Pause.*)
   The enemy's left flank in disarray
   Collapses towards the right, and all his troops
   Pour panic-stricken back across the marsh,

Criss-crossed by ditches. There, our battle-plan
Envisages his ultimate destruction.

ELECTOR: Pages, light our way! Your arm, my dears!
(*Exeunt the ELECTOR with the ELECTRESS and NATALIA.*)

DÖRFLING: And then he'll bid the buglers sound the charge.

ELECTRESS: (*As a number of OFFICERS bow in her direction.*)
Farewell, gentlemen! Let's not disturb you!
(*DÖRFLING also bows to her.*)

ELECTOR: (*Suddenly stands still.*)
Look! My niece's glove! Quick, over there!

CHAMBERLAIN: Where is it?

ELECTOR: By the Prince, our cousin's feet!

HOMBURG: At my – What? Does this glove belong to you?
(*Picks it up and takes it to NATALIA.*)

NATALIA: I thank you, noble Prince.

HOMBURG: (*Confused.*)   It's really yours?

NATALIA: It's mine! The very one I thought I'd lost.
(*Accepts it and draws it on.*)

ELECTRESS: (*To HOMBURG as she departs.*)
Farewell! Good fortune, health and blessings, Prince!
Make sure we see you soon again and happy!
(*Exeunt the ELECTOR and LADIES followed by COURTIERS, CHAMBERLAIN and PAGES.
HOMBURG stands still a moment, as though thunderstruck, then turns and rejoins the other OFFICERS with triumphant steps.*)

HOMBURG: And then he'll bid the buglers sound

                           the charge.
(*Pretending to write.*)

DÖRFLING: (*Studying his notes.*)
And then he'll bid the buglers sound the charge.
But he'll be sent an officer to confirm it,
Lest error cause the blow to fall too soon...
(*Pause.*)

GOLZ: (*Writing.*)
Lest error cause the blow to fall too soon...

HOMBURG: (*To HOHENZOLLERN with great emotion.*)
Oh, Heinrich!

HOHENZOLLERN: (*Reluctantly.*)
>What now? What have you in mind?

HOMBURG: You didn't see?

HOHENZOLLERN: No, nothing. Quiet, can't you!

DÖRFLING: (*Going on.*)
>An officer from his excellency's staff –
>Mark well – will bring him an express command
>To launch the final onslaught on the Swedes.
>Until he does, the bugles must not sound!
>(*HOMBURG stands there dreaming.*)
>Quite clear?

GOLZ: (*Writing.*) Until he does, the bugles must not sound.

DÖRFLING: (*Raising his voice.*)
>Is that quite clear, Your Highness?

HOMBURG: Sorry, sir?

DÖRFLING: You've got that down?

HOMBURG: The bit about the bugles?

HOHENZOLLERN: (*Aside, with angry emphasis.*)
>Bugles be damned! Until he does, they mustn't –

GOLZ: (*Similar tone.*)
>Till he himself –

HOMBURG: (*Interrupting them.*)
>   Yes, yes – of course! Not till –
>But then, he will command the buglers blow.
>(*He writes. After a pause.*)

DÖRFLING: Captain Golz, will you please note, I wish,
>If possible, to talk to Colonel Kottwitz
>Privately, before the battle starts.

GOLZ: (*Meaningfully.*)
>I'll make a point of it, you may be sure!
>(*Pause.*)

ELECTOR: (*Returning.*)
>Now, Generals and Colonels, gentlemen, grey dawn
>Is in the sky! You're fully briefed?

DÖRFLING: It has been done, my lord; your battle-plan
>Has been explained precisely to all here!

ELECTOR: (*Picking up his hat and gloves, to HOMBURG.*)
>You – Prince von Homburg – I advise, keep calm!

Not long since, on the Rhine, as you're aware,
Your folly robbed me of two victories!
This time, take care! Don't cheat me of a third,
Which could well cost me both my throne and kingdom!
(*To the other OFFICERS.*)
Follow me! Franz!
(*Enter a GROOM.*)

GROOM: Sir!

ELECTOR: Quickly! My white charger!
I must be in the field before sunrise!
(*Exit the ELECTOR followed by all OFFICERS.*)

HOMBURG: (*Stepping forward.*)

So then, O mighty goddess, on your globe,
Whose veil is lifted, like a sail, by breath
Of morning wind – roll on, Fortuna!
Have you not already stroked my locks
And, from your cornucopia in passing,
Tossed me a favour with a gracious smile?
Today, you fleeting offspring of the gods,
I'll seek you, seize you on the battlefield;
Your blessings all shall tumble at my feet,
Be you, with seven-fold chains of iron-link,
Bound fast to Sweden's victory chariot!
(*Exit HOMBURG.*)

End of Act One.

ACT TWO

Scene 1

The battlefield near Fehrbellin. KOTTWITZ, HOHENZOLLERN, GOLZ and other SENIOR OFFICERS in command of the cavalry.

KOTTWITZ: (*Off.*)
  Cavalry, halt here and all dismount!
HOHENZOLLERN/GOLZ: Halt! Halt!
KOTTWITZ: (*Off.*)   Who's going to help me down,
                                              my friends?
HOHENZOLLERN/GOLZ: We're coming ,sir!
  (*They go to help him, off-stage.*)
KOTTWITZ: (*Off.*)
                          Thanks! Ouch! God rot this gout!
  I wish you both fine sons who'll do the same
  For each of you, when you begin to crumble!
  (*Enter KOTTWITZ followed by HOHENZOLLERN,
  GOLZ etc.*)
  On horseback, I feel full of youthful vigour.
  But, soon as I dismount, the trouble starts –
  With flesh and spirit parting company! (*Looks about.*)
  What's become of His Highness, our commander?
HOHENZOLLERN: He'll be back directly –
KOTTWITZ: But where *is* he?
HOHENZOLLERN: He stopped to see that village which
                                              you passed –
  Hidden by bushes. He'll be back at once.
OFFICER: I hear his horse fell with him in the dark?
HOHENZOLLERN: So I believe.
KOTTWITZ: He fell?
HOHENZOLLERN: It wasn't serious.
  His horse took fright beside the mill and shied,
  But, happily, the Prince slid off in time
  To save himself from suffering any hurt.
  No reason whatsoever for concern.

KOTTWITZ: (*Standing on a rise.*)
    A lovely day, as sure as I'm alive!
    A day the Lord God made for better things
    Than slaughtering each other in a battle.
    The sun looks rosy, shining through the clouds
    And feelings flutter skyward with the lark,
    Rejoicing in the heavens' fragrant haze.
GOLZ: Did you succeed in finding Marshal Dörfling?
KOTTWITZ: (*Stepping forward.*)
    Damned if I did! What was he thinking of?
    Am I a bird, an arrow or a thought,
    That I should scour the battlefield entire?
    I tried the vanguard on the Hackel heights,
    The rearguard, too, along the Hackel valley –
    No sight or sound of Dörfling anywhere!
    So back I came to join my cavalry.
GOLZ: That will upset him greatly, for it seemed
    He'd something special to confide to you.
1ST OFFICER: Excuse me, sir, here comes the Prince, our
leader!
    (*Enter HOMBURG, wearing a black bandage on his left
    hand.*)
KOTTWITZ: Greetings, my young and noble Prince! See how,
    While you were in the village, I disposed
    Our troopers. They're strung out along the valley:
    I hope you're satisfied with what I've done?
HOMBURG: Good morning, Colonel Kottwitz!
                              Morning, friends!
    You know that I approve of all you do.
HOHENZOLLERN: Friedrich, what were you doing in
                                the village?
    You look so solemn!
HOMBURG: I – was in the chapel,
    Whose walls shone white amid the silent bushes;
    I heard the bell as we were riding past,
    Calling to worship, and I felt impelled
    To kneel and pray, myself, before the altar.
KOTTWITZ: A most devout young man, that I will say!
    A task begun with prayer will surely be
    Crowned in the end with victory, fame and fortune.

HOMBURG: (*To HOHENZOLLERN, taking him aside.*)
    I meant to ask you, Heinrich, what precisely
    Did Dörfling say last night regarding me,
    When he was giving out the battle orders?
HOHENZOLLERN: Your mind was wandering, as
                                       I could see.
HOMBURG: Wandering – divided. No idea what ailed me.
    I always find dictation most confusing.
HOHENZOLLERN: Well, luckily, there wasn't much for you.
    Truchss and Hennings with the infantry
    Will carry out the first direct assault;
    You are to wait with your riders in this glen,
    Till you are sent the order to attack.
HOMBURG: (*After a pause, dreamily.*)
    A curious occurrence!
HOHENZOLLERN: Which was that?
    (*He looks at him sharply. Noise of gunfire.*)
KOTTWITZ: Hey there, look lively! Mount your horses!
    That's Hennings now! A sign the battle's starting.
    (*ALL climb a hillock.*)
HOMBURG: Who is it? What?
HOHENZOLLERN: It's Colonel Hennings, Friedrich;
    He's crept round Wrangel's flank to strike his rear.
    Come here, where you can see what's going on!
GOLZ: (*On the hillock.*)
    He's giving them what for along the Rhyn!
HOMBURG: (*Hand shading his eyes.*)
    That's Hennings on our right flank, is it not?
1ST OFFICER: It is, Your Highness.
HOMBURG: What's he think he's doing?
    Why, yesterday his station was the left!
    (*Gunfire in the distance.*)
KOTTWITZ: Hell's bells! Now Wrangel's guns have opened up:
    Twelve of them pounding Hennings and his lads!
1ST OFFICER: Those Swedes know how to build
                            a good redoubt!
2ND OFFICER: Stacked up as high's the bloody steeple
    In that small village, slightly to their rear!
    (*Noise of firing close by.*)

GOLZ: Truchss!

HOMBURG: Is it?

KOTTWITZ: Yes, it's Truchss! He's linking up
    With Hennings' lot, so he can help him out!

HOMBURG: But how is it today he's in the centre?
    (*Heavy cannon-fire.*)

GOLZ: Oh heavens, look! The village is alight!

3ᴿᴰ OFFICER: On fire, as I'm alive!

1ˢᵀ OFFICER: It's all ablaze!
    The flames already leaping up the tower!

GOLZ: Look! Swedish runners darting left and right!

2ᴺᴰ OFFICER: They're falling back!

KOTTWITZ: Where?

1ˢᵀ OFFICER: On the right flank, see?

3ᴿᴰ OFFICER: Dispersing by platoons – three regiments!
    I think they're trying to reinforce the left.

2ᴺᴰ OFFICER: Well, I'll be damned! The cavalry's advancing
    To give the right flank cover on the march!

HOHENZOLLERN: (*Laughs.*)
    They'll beat a quick retreat once they discover
    Ourselves in hiding, all along the glen!
    (*Musket-fire.*)

KOTTWITZ: Look, brothers, look!

2ᴺᴰ OFFICER: And listen!

1ˢᵀ OFFICER: Musket-fire!

THIRD OFFICER: They're fighting hand-to-hand for
                                        the redoubt!

GOLZ: I swear to God, in all my born days –
    I never heard such thundering of cannon!

HOHENZOLLERN: Fire! Fire away! And split earth's
                                        womb apart!
    The cleft shall serve to sepulchre your corpses!
    (*A pause – then distant shouts of jubilation.*)

1ˢᵀ OFFICER: O Lord above who grantest victory:
    Wrangel has turned about!

HOHENZOLLERN: Is that a fact?

GOLZ: By heaven! On the left flank! Look, my friends!
    They're fleeing the redoubt – both troops and guns!

ALL: Hurrah! We've won! Hurrah! The victory's ours!

HOMBURG: (*Coming down from the hillock.*)
  Follow me, Kottwitz!
KOTTWITZ: Now then, easy does it!
HOMBURG: Charge! Let the bugles sound – and follow me!
KOTTWITZ: Steady, I say!
HOMBURG: By heaven, earth and hell!
KOTTWITZ: His excellency, at last night's battle-briefing,
  Commanded us to wait here for the order.
  Golz, read out precisely what was said!
HOMBURG: Await the order? Kottwitz, you're a slowcoach!
  Hasn't your heart already ordered you?
KOTTWITZ: Ordered?
HOHENZOLLERN: For God's sake!
KOTTWITZ: Ordered – by my heart?
HOHENZOLLERN: Friedrich! Have some sense!
GOLZ: Be careful, sir!
KOTTWITZ: (*Insulted.*)
  You dare to take that tone with me, young sir?
  That dray-horse there on which you prance about,
  My own could drag, if need be, by its tail!
  Then, into action! Buglers sound the charge!
  Let's on to battle! Kottwitz in the lead!
GOLZ: (*To KOTTWITZ.*)
  No, Colonel, no! An order is an order!
2ND OFFICER: See, Hennings' men have still to
                              reach the Rhyn!
1ST OFFICER: Remove his sword!
HOMBURG: My sword? Are you quite mad?
  (*Pushes him away.*)
  You impudent stripling, you have still to learn
  The meaning of the Brandenburg commandments!
  I'm taking yours – the sword and scabbard both!
  (*Tears off his sword and sword belt.*)
1ST OFFICER: (*Staggering.*)
  That action, Prince – by God!
HOMBURG: (*Takes a step towards him.*)
                          You dare say more?
HOHENZOLLERN: (*To the OFFICER.*)
  Be silent! Are you crazy?

HOMBURG: (*Handing over the sword.*)
>   Orderlies,
>   Look sharp! Escort the prisoner to headquarters!
>   (*To KOTTWITZ and the other OFFICERS.*)
>   Now, hear me, all! A rogue is he who fails
>   To follow his commander into battle!
>   Who lags behind?
KOTTWITZ: You heard me! Why insist?
HOHENZOLLERN: (*Placating.*)
>   He's only giving you advice, that's all!
KOTTWITZ: Then be it on your head! I'll follow you.
HOMBURG: On my head be it, brothers! Follow me!
>   (*Exeunt ALL.*)

Scene 2

A room in the village.

A FARMER and his WIFE are seated at a table, working. Enter a COURTIER, in boots and spurs.

COURTIER: Greetings, good people! Have you in your home
>   Space enough to shelter a few guests?
FARMER: Right willingly.
WIFE: But may we know who 'tis?
COURTIER: None other than first lady of the land!
>   Her carriage broke an axle at the village;
>   Since we've just heard the battle has been won,
>   No need for her to journey any further.
>   (*FARMER and WIFE stand up.*)
FARMER: A battle won? Heavens!
COURTIER: You didn't know?
>   The Swedish army has been soundly thrashed.
>   If not for ever – for a year at least –
>   Our land's secure against their fire and sword!
>   But look! Here comes our ruler's lady now.
>   (*Enter the ELECTRESS, pale and distraught, followed by
>   NATALIA and LADIES-IN-WAITING.*)
ELECTRESS: (*In the doorway.*)
>   Bork! Winterfeld! Come, let me lean on you!

NATALIA: (*Hurrying towards her.*)
Oh, mother!
LADIES:　　　Lord! How pale she is! She's swooning!
(*They support her.*)
ELECTRESS: Lead me to a chair! I must sit down.
Dead, did he say? Not – dead!
NATALIA:　　　　　　　O dearest mother!
ELECTRESS: I wish to see the messenger himself.
(*Enter CAPTAIN VON MÖRNER, wounded, supported by
two CAVALRYMEN.*)
What can you tell me, herald of my dread?
MÖRNER: Alas, dear lady, what with my own eyes
I saw myself to my eternal grief –
ELECTRESS: I pray you speak!
MÖRNER:　　　　　　The Elector is no more!
NATALIA: Heaven! Must we endure so great a blow?
(*Covers her face.*)
ELECTRESS: Give me a full report of how he died!
As lightning bolt that strikes the wanderer,
The world about him bathes in purple light,
So let your speech illuminate –
And when you've spoken, night once more descend!
(*MÖRNER, supported by CAVALRYMEN, stands before her.*)
MÖRNER: No sooner did the Swedes, hard-pressed
　　　　　　　　　　　　　　　　　by Truchss,
Fall back, than Prince von Homburg, on the plain
Set about Wrangel, with his cavalry;
Two ranks the Prince had slain in flight,
When he came up against a strong redoubt
Where such a murderous rain of musket-balls
Descended on his men that down they went,
Like corn before the scythe, and he was forced
To call a halt between the wood and hills
In order to regroup his scattered troops.
NATALIA: (*To the ELECTRESS.*)
Courage, dear aunt!
ELECTRESS:　　　Just let me be, my love!
MÖRNER: That moment, as the smoke of battle lifted,
We saw the Elector with his standard-bearers,

Galloping towards the Swedes – majestic sight –
On his white stallion, upright in the saddle,
Lit by a sunbeam, pointing victory's path.
At sight of him, we gathered on a slope,
All of us deep dismayed to see our leader
Exposed to fire; and then, quite suddenly,
We saw the Elector, steed and rider, sink
Before our very eyes into the dust.
Two standard-bearers threw themselves upon him
And wrapped their flags about him where he lay.
NATALIA: Oh, my dear aunt!
1ST LADY: Heavens!
ELECTRESS: Go on! Go on!
MÖRNER: At this appalling spectacle, the Prince
Was overwhelmed by grief beyond all measure;
Spurred, like a bear, by rage and lust for vengeance,
He charged with us against the Swedes' redoubt.
In our mad onslaught, trench and barricade
We overran, the occupants cut down –
Scattered them far and wide, all done to death;
Flags, cannon, kettle-drums and standards seized –
The Swedes' whole battle-kit our booty made:
Had not their bridgehead on the Rhyn restrained
Our massacre, no Swede had lived to tell
His sons: 'I saw that hero fall at Fehrbellin!
ELECTRESS: A victory bought too dearly for my liking!
Oh, give me back the price that we have paid!
(*Collapses in a faint.*)
1ST LADY: Help, quick – for heaven's sake! She's fainted!
(*NATALIA weeps.*)
(*Enter HOMBURG.*)
HOMBURG: Natalia, my dearest!
(*Places her hand on his heart.*)
NATALIA: Then it is true?
HOMBURG: Would I could tell you no!
I only wish my loyal heart could spill
Its blood and bring his own once more to life!
NATALIA: (*Drying her tears.*)
But has my uncle's body been recovered?

HOMBURG: My sole preoccupation until now
    Has been to wreak a just revenge on Wrangel;
    How could I turn my mind to other cares?
    But I at once dispatched a strong detachment
    To search for him upon the field of death;
    I doubt not they will bring him home by dusk.
NATALIA: Now who, in this most terrifying struggle,
    Will hold the Swedes at bay? And from a world
    Of enemies afford us all protection?
    His valour 'twas that won our fame and fortune!
HOMBURG: (*Taking her hand.*)
    I, dear Princess, will champion your cause!
    An angel with a flaming sword, I'll stand
    To guard the steps of your defenceless throne!
    His excellency wished, before year's end,
    To see our borders freed; executor
    Of this last wish of his, Homburg shall be!
NATALIA: My dear, good cousin! (*She draws her hand away.*)
HOMBURG: O Natalia!
    (*A moment's silence.*)
    What think you now, dear one, of your own future?
NATALIA: After this bolt of lightning that has rent
    The ground beneath me, what am I to do?
    Father and mother, dearly loved, lie buried
    In Amsterdam. Doordrecht, the family seat,
    Is now reduced to heaps of ash and rubble;
    Oppressed by the tyrant regiments of Spain,
    My cousin, Maurice of Orange, scarcely knows
    Where his own children can be safely housed.
    And now the final prop is lost to me
    On which my happiness depended like a vine.
    Today, I have been orphaned yet again!
HOMBURG: (*Putting his arm round her.*)
    O dearest friend, were not this hour of grief
    To mourning dedicated, I would say:
    Let your sweet tendrils twine about this breast
    Which, lonely thriving for so many years,
    Has yearned to breathe the fragrance of your blooms!

NATALIA: My dear, good cousin!
HOMBURG: Will you? Will you, please!
NATALIA: If I might grow into its very core…
   (*Rests her head on his breast.*)
HOMBURG: (*Noise of footsteps approaching.*)
   Who's coming now?
NATALIA: Let go!
HOMBURG: (*Holding her.*)

                …its very kernel!
   Into the kernel of my heart, Natalia!
   (*He kisses her; she tears herself away.*)
   O God, if only he for whom we weep were here
   To see our union! Oh, if only we
   Could beg him shyly: 'Father, bless us both!'
   (*He covers his face with his hands. NATALIA turns round
   again to face the ELECTRESS.*)
   (*Enter a SERGEANT MAJOR hurriedly.*)
SERGEANT MAJOR: Highness, I hardly dare – as God's
                        my judge –
   Acquaint you with the rumour going round:
   The Elector is alive!
HOMBURG: Alive!
SERGEANT MAJOR: I swear!
   Count Sparren's on his way here to report!
NATALIA: Oh Lord above us! Mother, did you hear?
   (*Falls to her knees, embracing the ELECTRESS.*)
HOMBURG: No – what? Who's coming here?
SERGEANT MAJOR: Count Georg von Sparren
   Saw him, with his own eyes, in Hackelwitz:
   Saw him with Truchss' men – alive and well!
HOMBURG: Quick, fetch him, Sergeant Major! Bring him in!
   (*Exit SERGEANT MAJOR.*)
ELECTRESS: Don't plunge me twice into the same abyss!
NATALIA: Oh no, dear aunt!
ELECTRESS: My husband is alive?
NATALIA: (*Helping her to her feet with both hands.*)
   Life's summit once more beckons you to rise!
   (*Enter SERGEANT MAJOR.*)
SERGEANT MAJOR: Here is the officer!

HOMBURG: Count Georg von Sparren!
You saw the Elector, Count, alive and well
In Hackelwitz, with Truchss' infantry?
SPARREN: I did, Your Highness, in the churchyard. There
He stood, his staff about him, giving orders
For burying the dead on either side.
LADIES: Thank God! Oh, what a mercy!
(*They embrace one another.*)
ELECTRESS: Dearest child!
NATALIA: Such sudden bliss is almost past enduring!
(*Buries her face in her aunt's lap.*)
HOMBURG: Did I not, leading my own squadrons see,
Caught in a distant hail of fire, my lord,
The Elector, and his white stallion go down?
SPARREN: It's true, the white horse fell, the rider, too;
But he who rode was not our lord, in fact.
HOMBURG: Not him, you say?
NATALIA: Oh, joy!
(*She stands up, beside the ELECTRESS.*)
HOMBURG: Speak! Tell us all!
Your every word's more dear to me than gold!
SPARREN: Then be apprised of an event more moving
Than any yet to charm the ear of man.
Our noble ruler, deaf to every warning,
Once more astride that charger, gleaming white,
Which Froben brought him recently from England,
Today, as usual, became the target
Most favoured by the Swedish shot and shell.
The members of his entourage, indeed,
Could scarce draw closer than a hundred paces;
Around him, cannonball, grenade and bullet
Flowed like an ever-rolling stream of death,
To whose far banks all living mortals clung,
While he alone, brave swimmer undeterred,
Forged calmly on, encouraging his friends,
Towards the heights, from which the torrent sprang.
HOMBURG: By heaven, yes! I shuddered at the sight!
SPARREN: His equerry, Froben, closest to him, then
Called out to me: 'Today, I'll curse the gleam

Of that white stallion which no time ago
Cost such a heap of gold to buy in London!
I'd gladly part with fifty ducats more,
If only I could turn his coat mouse-grey!'
Full of concern, he halted him and said:
'Highness, your horse is shy, you must allow me
To take him back to school for more instruction.'
So saying he dismounted from his bay
And seized the reins of the Elector's horse.
Our lord, dismounting, with a smile retorted:
'The art you mean to teach him, he'll not learn
While still 'tis daylight, so remove him, pray,
And take him right away behind those hills,
Where Swedish eyes can't see his misdemeanours.'
The Elector, having mounted Froben's bay,
Rode off about his duties in the field.
No sooner though did Froben mount the white,
Than from the Swedes' redoubt a deadly rain
Of lead laid horse and rider in the dust.
Poor Froben, victim of his loyalty, fell
And not another sound was heard from him.
(*Short pause.*)

HOMBURG: He's compensated! If I had ten lives,
  I couldn't lose them in a better cause!
NATALIA: Gallant Froben!
ELECTRESS: What a splendid man!
NATALIA: A lesser one would still deserve our tears!
  (*Both weep.*)
HOMBURG: Enough! To business! Where is the Elector?
  Has he made Hackelwitz his new headquarters?
SPARREN: Beg pardon, but my lord has left already
  For Berlin. All members of the general staff,
  So he commands, should follow him at once.
HOMBURG: What? To Berlin? Then, is the campaign over?
SPARREN: Yes, indeed! Amazed, you haven't heard!
  The Swedish General, Count Horn, arrived
  In camp and – straight away – an armistice
  Between the warring parties was proclaimed.

If I correctly understood the Marshal,
Negotiations have been set in train
And peace itself could easily ensue.
ELECTRESS: Thank God! All problems wonderfully resolved!
(*Stands up.*)
HOMBURG: Let us then follow him to Berlin at once!
To save time, could you possibly find room
For me to travel with you in your coach?
I'll scribble just a line or two for Kottwitz
And join you in the carriage presently.
(*Sits down and writes.*)
ELECTRESS: By all means, come with us!
HOMBURG: (*Folds the letter, hands it to the SERGEANT MAJOR,
then turns to the ELECTRESS and gently places an arm round
NATALIA's waist.*)
I've one more wish
Which I will timidly confide to you,
Unburdening myself upon the journey.
NATALIA: (*Freeing herself from him.*)
My scarf, Bork, quickly!
ELECTRESS: You? A wish for me?
1ST LADY: You're wearing it, Princess, about your neck!
HOMBURG: (*To the ELECTRESS.*)
Can you not guess?
ELECTRESS: Why, no!
HOMBURG: You've no idea?
ELECTRESS: No matter! There's no suppliant on earth
Whom I'd refuse today, whate'er his plea:
You least of all, victorious in battle!
Now let's away!
HOMBURG: What words were those you spoke?
May I interpret them as I would wish?
ELECTRESS: Let's go, I say! More later, in the coach!
Now come, give me your arm!
HOMBURG: O Caesar *divus*!
I'll scale the ladder to your mighty star!
(*He leads the LADIES outside; ALL follow.*)

Scene 3

Berlin.

Garden in front of the old castle. In the background, the chapel of the castle and a staircase. Bells ringing. The church is brightly lit. We see the corpse of FROBEN being carried past and deposited on a magnificent catafalque. Enter the ELECTOR, DÖRFLING, HENNINGS, TRUCHSS, a number of COLONELS and other OFFICERS, some bearing dispatches.

In the church and on the square, MEN and WOMEN of all ages.

ELECTOR: Whoever it was who led the cavalry
    While battle raged and who, ere Colonel Hennings
    Had time to utterly destroy the Swedish bridges,
    Advanced, unbidden, reckless to the charge –
    Forcing the foe to flee, before I ordered –
    Is guilty of a capital offence,
    And I shall have him dealt with by court martial.
    The Prince von Homburg, was it not, who led them?
TRUCHSS: No, your excellency.
ELECTOR: Who says it wasn't?
TRUCHSS: The troopers will confirm for you, my lord,
    What they told me before the battle started:
    The Prince, it seems, had fallen with his horse;
    They saw him in a church being bandaged up –
    His head and thigh-bones seriously hurt.
ELECTOR: No matter! True, our victory was brilliant;
    Tomorrow, I'll thank God before the altar.
    But, ten times greater, it would not excuse
    The one who brought me victory by chance!
    Many a battle still I have to fight
    And I insist that orders be obeyed.
    Whoever led our horsemen into battle,
    I say again, deserves to lose his life:
    I'll have him brought before a field court martial.
    Come now, my friends, let's all go into church!
    (*Enter HOMBURG, carrying three Swedish flags, KOTTWITZ,
    bearing two more, HOHENZOLLERN, GOLZ, REUSS, each*

*bearing a flag, and several other OFFICERS, CORPORALS
and TROOPERS with flags, drums and standards.)*

DÖRFLING: (*At sight of HOMBURG.*)

Prince Homburg! Truchss! Your story's balderdash!

ELECTOR: (*Taken aback.*)

Where have you come from, Prince?

HOMBURG: From Fehrbellin,

With battle trophies to present my lord.

(*He lays the three flags at his feet and the others, in turn,
follow suit.*)

ELECTOR: (*Perplexed.*)

I heard that you were wounded – dangerously?

Count Truchss!

HOMBURG: (*Light-heartedly.*)

No, sir – I'm sorry.

TRUCHSS: I'm astounded!

HOMBURG: My chestnut tripped and fell before the fight;

A doctor dressed my hand – a scratch, that's all –

Unworthy to be dubbed a wound, my lord.

ELECTOR: You led them into battle, after all?

HOMBURG: I did indeed! But must I tell you so?

The proof of it is lying at your feet.

ELECTOR: Remove his sword! He's under close arrest!

DÖRFLING: (*Startled.*)

Who?

ELECTOR: (*Walking among the flags.*)

I'm glad to see you, Kottwitz!

TRUCHSS: (*Aside.*)

Hell!

KOTTWITZ: By heaven, I'm completely–

ELECTOR: What was that?

Look at this harvest, reaped for our renown!

Aren't these the colours of the Swedish life-guards?

(*He picks up a flag, unfurls it and studies it closely.*)

KOTTWITZ: Elector?

DÖRFLING: My lord?

ELECTOR: They are, indeed!

A relic of King Gustav Adolf's days.

What is the motto?

KOTTWITZ: Er –
DÖRFLING: *Per aspera ad astra.*
ELECTOR: It didn't see them through at Fehrbellin...
   (*Pause.*)
KOTTWITZ: (*Nervously.*)
   My lord, a word, I pray –
ELECTOR: What's on your mind?
   Collect these banners, standards, flags and drums
   And hang them on the pillars in the church!
   We'll need them at the victory celebration.
   (*The ELECTOR turns to OFFICERS bringing dispatches,*
   which he opens and reads.)
KOTTWITZ: (*Aside.*)
   So help me, God! This is too much to bear!
   (*After some hesitation, KOTTWITZ picks up his two flags.*
   The OTHERS follow suit. Finally, since HOMBURG's three
   flags are left lying on the ground, KOTTWITZ picks up these
   as well, so that he now has five to carry.)
OFFICER: (*Confronting HOMBURG.*)
   Your sword, Prince, if you please!
HOHENZOLLERN: (*Standing beside him, flag in hand.*)
             Keep calm, my friend!
HOMBURG: I'm dreaming! Am I awake? Alive and sane?
GOLZ: I'd let him have your sword. You'd best not speak!
HOMBURG: Am I a prisoner?
HOHENZOLLERN: Yes.
GOLZ: You heard the Elector!
HOMBURG: May one inquire the reason?
HOHENZOLLERN: (*Emphatically.*)
             Not just now!
   You moved too soon – we told you at the time –
   Charged into battle when the orders were
   Not to advance till called upon to act!
HOMBURG: Oh, help me, friends! I'm mad!
GOLZ: Shush! Say no more!
HOMBURG: But were our forces beaten then – or what?
HOHENZOLLERN: (*Stamping his foot.*)
   That's not the point! Commands must be obeyed!

HOMBURG: (*Bitterly.*)

    I see…I see…

HOHENZOLLERN: (*Moving away from him.*)

               You won't be shot for this –

GOLZ: No, like as not, they'll free you by tomorrow.

    (*The ELECTOR gathers his papers together and rejoins the
    circle of OFFICERS.*)

HOMBURG: (*After unfastening his sword.*)

    So cousin Friedrich wants to play at Brutus –
    Seeing himself, roughed out in chalk on canvas –
    Sitting in judgement, with the Swedish banners
    Ranged in front, and – open on his desk –
    The military code of Brandenburg!
    By heaven, he'll not find in me a son
    To sing his praises as the axe descends!
    A German, of the good old-fashioned school,
    I'm used to magnanimity and love;
    If he confronts me at this juncture with
    The grim severity of ancient Rome,
    I'm sorry for him and he has my pity!

ELECTOR: Take him back to base at Fehrbellin

    And summon a court martial there to try him.

    (*The ELECTOR leads the way into the church, followed by
    the OFFICERS bearing flags. While the ELECTOR and
    his staff kneel in prayer by FROBEN's coffin, the flags are
    suspended from the pillars. Funeral music.*)

End of Act Two.

ACT THREE

Scene 1

Fehrbellin. A prison. HOMBURG under arrest. In the background, two TROOPERS guarding him. Enter HOHENZOLLERN.

HOMBURG: It's good to see you, Heinrich! You are welcome!
　　You've come to tell me that I'm free again?
HOHENZOLLERN: (*Astonished.*)
　　For heaven's sake!
HOMBURG:　　　　　What's that you say?
HOHENZOLLERN:　　　　　　　　How? Free!
　　Has he returned your sword to you, my friend?
HOMBURG: Why, no.
HOHENZOLLERN:　No?
HOMBURG:　　　　　No!
HOHENZOLLERN:　　　　How then could you be free?
HOMBURG: (*After a pause.*)
　　I thought you might have brought it. Never mind!
HOHENZOLLERN: I have no news!
HOMBURG:　　　　　　　　I said, it doesn't matter!
　　He'll send a messenger to let me know.
　　(*Turns to bring chairs.*)
　　Sit down and tell me what's been going on.
　　Elector's back already from Berlin?
HOHENZOLLERN: (*Vaguely.*)
　　Came back last night.
HOMBURG:　　　　The victory celebration
　　Took place as planned? Of course – I know it did!
　　I take it he was present in the church?
HOHENZOLLERN: Together with the Electress and Natalia.
　　The chapel was magnificently lit;
　　Guns on the castle square in solemn pomp
　　Accompanied the *Te Deum* with salutes;
　　The Swedish regimental flags and colours –
　　Our battle-trophies – from the pillars hung
　　And, at my lord's express command, your name –

As he who led our troops to victory –
Was given special mention from the pulpit.
HOMBURG: So I heard! What else have you to tell me?
Your face, my friend, looks anything but cheerful!
HOHENZOLLERN: Who's talked to you already?
HOMBURG: Golz – just now –
While I was being questioned at the castle. (*Pause.*)
HOHENZOLLERN: (*With a serious expression.*)
Friedrich, how do you see your situation,
Now that it's altered in so strange a way?
HOMBURG: I? The same as you, Golz and the judges!
My lord has done what duty bade him do,
But now he will obey his heart in turn.
You were at fault, he'll tell me solemnly –
Perhaps refer to death or long confinement –
'However, I shall now restore your freedom,'
And on my sword, which won the victory for him,
Perhaps confer some token of his grace –
If not – no matter, for I don't deserve it!
HOHENZOLLERN: Oh, Friedrich! (*He falls silent.*)
HOMBURG: Well?
HOHENZOLLERN: How can you be so sure?
HOMBURG: I feel it in my bones! He loves me dearly –
As dearly as a son. Since early childhood
He's proved it to me time and time again.
I cannot see why you should harbour doubts.
His joy seemed almost greater than my own
Each time I added to my youthful fame.
All that I am, do I not owe to him?
How could he, unfeelingly, the plant
That he himself so lovingly has nurtured,
Now trample in the dust with jealous spite –
For flowering all too richly and too soon?
I doubt his vilest foes could think it of him;
Far less yourself, who know and love the man.
HOHENZOLLERN: You've been court martialled,
                              Friedrich, you've been tried!
Yet you have faith?
HOMBURG: But that's precisely why!
Who'd go that far, as sure as God's above us,

Unless already set on granting pardon?
Indeed, it was while standing there in court
That I regained my total confidence.
Was it a crime deserving execution,
To grind the might of Sweden in the dust
A moment or two before he ordered it?
What other fault have I to answer for?
How could he summon me before those judges
Who, heartless and ill-omening as owls,
Sang me their song of death by firing-squad,
Unless he meant at last to join their circle
And, god-like, overrule them with a word?
No, friend, he's massed the storm clouds round my head
Only that I may see him, like the sun,
Rise, all the more resplendent from the gloom!
I can afford to grant my lord that pleasure.
HOHENZOLLERN: I understand the court has sentenced you.
HOMBURG: Yes – so I've heard: to death.
HOHENZOLLERN: (*Astonished.*)

                    You know already?
HOMBURG: Golz, who was there when sentence

                      was pronounced,
Called in to let me know how things had gone.
HOHENZOLLERN: For God's sake! Did that leave you

                     quite unmoved?
HOMBURG: Me? Moved? Not in the least!
HOHENZOLLERN: You must be mad!
What grounds have you for feeling so secure?
HOMBURG: My trust in him! (*Stands up.*)

             Now, leave me, if you please!
Why let myself be plagued by needless doubts?
(*Reflects for a moment, then sits down again. Pause.*)
Death was the only sentence they could pass,
According to the law that rules the court.
But sooner than approve its execution –
At the drop of a handkerchief expose a heart
That loves him truly, to a hail of lead –
The Elector'd sooner tear his breast apart
And sprinkle his own blood upon the dust.

HOHENZOLLERN: But Friedrich, I assure you –
HOMBURG: (*Annoyed.*)

          No more, please!
HOHENZOLLERN: The Marshal –
HOMBURG: Go, friend!
HOHENZOLLERN: Listen, two words more!
 If they don't change your mind, then I give up!
HOMBURG: (*Turns towards him again.*)
 I've told you, I know all! What's left to say?
HOHENZOLLERN: Something quite unusual: the Elector,
 Informed by the Marshal of the sentence passed,
 Far from acting as the law permits
 And granting pardon, ordered it be brought
 To him without delay for signature.
HOMBURG: What of it!
HOHENZOLLERN: You don't care?
HOMBURG: For signature?
HOHENZOLLERN: Upon my honour! You may rest assured.
HOMBURG: The sentence? No! The record – ?
HOHENZOLLERN: Sentence of death!
HOMBURG: Who told you that?
HOHENZOLLERN: The Marshal did, himself!
HOMBURG: When?
HOHENZOLLERN: Just now.
HOMBURG: He'd spoken to the Elector?
HOHENZOLLERN: We talked as he came down the
          palace stairs,
 And, seeing I was thunderstruck, he added
 That all was not yet lost; tomorrow was
 Another day, when you might yet be pardoned.
 But ashen lips belied the words they spoke,
 Seeming to say: 'We fear it will not happen.'
HOMBURG: (*Standing up.*)
 Could he – but, no! So monstrous a resolve
 He surely couldn't nourish in his bosom!
 So slight a flaw, unseen by naked eye,
 In such a diamond, only just received,
 Could never move him to destroy the donor!
 Such deed would bleach the Dey of Algiers white

As snow, with wings like those of cherubim;
Would sweeten Sardanapalus and the ranks
Of Roman tyrants would make innocent
As babes that perished at their mother's breast –
Inviting all to stand at God's right hand!

HOHENZOLLERN: (*Also stands up.*)
My friend, you must convince yourself, it's so.

HOMBURG: The Marshal stood there, saying nothing more?

HOHENZOLLERN: What could he say?

HOMBURG: Great heaven! Where's my hope?

HOHENZOLLERN: Did you perhaps, at some time, step
                       too close –
On purpose or unwittingly – encroach
Upon our lord Elector's proud domain?

HOMBURG: Not once!

HOHENZOLLERN: Think back!

HOMBURG: I never did, I swear!
For me, the shadow of his head was sacred.

HOHENZOLLERN: Friedrich, forgive me, if I have
                    my doubts.
Count Horn, the Swedish envoy, has arrived
And I'm assured his business here concerns
Not least, Natalia, Princess of Orange.
Something her aunt, the Electress, chanced to say
Upset the gentleman exceedingly.
It seems the Princess has already chosen.
Are you quite sure that you are not involved?

HOMBURG: Oh God! What's that you say?

HOHENZOLLERN: Are you? Are you?

HOMBURG: I am, my friend; now all is clear to me.
I'm being destroyed because of his proposal!
If she's refused him, I'm the one to blame:
The Princess is engaged to marry me!

HOHENZOLLERN: You reckless idiot! What have you done?
No end of times I've warned you as a friend!

HOMBURG: Then, help me now, my friend, for I am lost!

HOHENZOLLERN: There must be some way out of
                  this dilemma!
Perhaps you ought to go and see her aunt?

HOMBURG: Hey, guard!

GUARD: (*In the background.*)

                Here, sir!

HOMBURG: Go call your officer!

   (*Takes down his coat which is hanging on the wall and picks up his hat from the table.*)

HOHENZOLLERN: (*Helping him dress.*)

   You might just save your neck, if you are clever.

   For peace with Sweden's King, it seems the Elector

   Must pay the price we know; it's up to you

   To make *your* peace with him. If all goes well,

   Within the next few hours, you could be free.

   (*Enter CAPTAIN STRANZ.*)

HOMBURG: Stranz, officially, I'm in your charge!

   Allow me, for the sake of urgent business,

   If you would, to leave you for an hour.

STRANZ: I'm not in charge of you, Your Highness.

   According to the orders I was given,

   You're free to come and go as you desire.

HOMBURG: That's odd! Then, I am not a prisoner?

STRANZ: Excuse me, sir, your word remains your bond.

HOHENZOLLERN: (*Leaving.*)

   That's fair enough –

HOMBURG: So be it then, farewell!

HOHENZOLLERN: That bond will trail His Highness all

                        the way.

HOMBURG: I'm going to see the Electress at the castle –

   I won't be long and I shall come straight back.

   (*Exeunt ALL.*)

Scene 2

The ELECTRESS' room in the castle. The ELECTRESS and NATALIA.

ELECTRESS: Come, daughter, come! Your moment is at hand.

   Sweden's ambassador, Count Gustav Horn,

   And his associates have left the palace.

   But light's still burning in your uncle's study:

   Put on your kerchief and slip in, my dear!

   See whether you can save the Prince's life.

(Enter a LADY-IN-WAITING.)

LADY: The Prince von Homburg, ma'am, is at the door!

    I hardly knew if I dared trust my eyes!

ELECTRESS: *(Surprised.)*

    Heavens!

NATALIA: The Prince?

ELECTRESS: He's not in close arrest?

LADY: He's standing there in coat and feathered hat,

    Distraught and pleading urgently to see you!

ELECTRESS: *(Angrily.)*

    The reckless youth! To break his solemn word!

NATALIA: Who knows what stress he's under!

ELECTRESS: *(After some consideration.)*

                              Let him in!

(Takes a seat. Enter HOMBURG.)

HOMBURG: O mother mine! *(Falls on his knees before her.)*

ELECTRESS: What are you doing here?

HOMBURG: O hear me, mother! Let me kneel to you!

ELECTRESS: *(With suppressed emotion.)*

    Prince, you're a prisoner, yet you dare come here?

    Why heap fresh guilt on what you bear already?

HOMBURG: *(Urgently.)*

    You know what's happened to me?

ELECTRESS: I know all.

    But how can I – poor woman – help you now?

HOMBURG: O mother, you would never speak such words

    If death were haunting you, as death haunts me!

    To me, you're rich with heavenly power to save –

    You, the Princess, your ladies, all about me;

    The merest stable-lad who tends your horses,

    I could embrace, beseeching him to save me!

    I alone of all in God's wide world,

    Am helpless and abandoned – powerless!

ELECTRESS: What is it, Prince? You're quite beside yourself!

HOMBURG: As I was coming here to visit you,

    I caught a glimpse by torchlight of the tomb,

    Being opened to receive my corpse tomorrow.

    Aunt, these eyes which see you now, they'll shade

In darkness and this breast pierce through
With murderous bullets! On the market square,
Already, window-seats have been reserved,
For sight of that appalling spectacle
And he, for whom today the future gleams –
Viewed from life's pinnacle – like fairyland,
Shall lie tomorrow, rotting, in a box –
With just a stone to tell you he once lived!
(*At these words, NATALIA, who up to now has been leaning
on the shoulder of a LADY-IN-WAITING, sinks into a chair,
weeping.*)

ELECTRESS: My son! If that is heaven's will, then you
Must arm yourself with courage and composure!

HOMBURG: Oh, mother, God's world is so beautiful!
Don't let me, I beseech you – ere my time –
Descend into the shadowy realm of death!
If I've offended, let him punish me.
Why must it be a bullet? Why, oh why?
Let me be stripped of all my offices,
Cashiered, if that is what the law demands –
Dismissed the army – Oh, dear God in heaven!
Since I beheld my tomb, life's all I want –
To live! Be hanged to fame and honour!

ELECTRESS: Stand up, my son! Stand up! What are
you saying?
You're thoroughly unmanned! Compose yourself!

HOMBURG: Not till you've promised me, dear aunt,
you'll take
That one short step required to save my life
And plead for me in his majestic presence!
My mother, Hedwig, just before she died,
Entrusted me to you – her childhood friend –
Begging you be my mother in her place.
You, deeply moved, and kneeling by her bed,
Bent to her hand and earnestly replied:
'He'll be to me, as though my own begotten!'
I now remind you of that solemn pledge.
Go speak to him, as for your child, and say:

'I beg for mercy! Mercy! Set him free!'
And then, come back to tell me that I am!
ELECTRESS: (*Weeping.*)
My own dear son! I have already tried!
But all my tearful pleading was in vain!
HOMBURG: I am resigned to forfeit happiness.
Please make a point of telling him that I
No longer wish to wed Natalia –
The love I felt for her is past and done.
She's free, as any doe upon the heath,
In thought and act – as though I'd never been!
Let her bestow her hand on Karl Gustav,
The Swedish monarch. If so, I shall praise her.
I shall withdraw to my property on the Rhine,
Now building this – now that demolishing,
All bathed in sweat, to sow and reap, as though
For wife and child, yet for my sole enjoyment;
Once having harvested, I'll sow once more –
So chase my life, in circles, round and round,
Until at dusk, it weakens, sinks and dies.
ELECTRESS: So be it! Now, you'd best go back to prison!
That is the first condition of my favour.
HOMBURG: (*Stands up and turns towards NATALIA.*)
Poor girl in tears! The sun today has shone
Upon the early grave of all your hopes!
You chose myself as first in your affections
And by your manner, true as gold, I know
You'll never give your love to any other.
Poorest of men, what solace can I offer?
I would advise you, stay with cousin Thurn,
At Our Lady's convent on the Main. Or seek
In the hills a blond-haired boy like me;
Buy him for gold and silver, hold him tight
And teach the little fellow to say 'Mother'.
When he grows up – why then, instruct him how
To close the eyelids of a dying man.
That's all the happiness ahead of you!

NATALIA: (*Courageous and inspiring as she rises and places her hand in his.*)
Young hero, go! Return now to your cell
And on your way, look once again – serenely
This time – at the tomb, reserved for you.
It's neither darker nor a hair's breadth wider
Than that you faced a thousand times in battle!
Meanwhile, I – true to you till death –
Will risk a word for you in uncle's ear.
I may succeed in softening his heart
And yet release you from your misery!
(*Pause.*)

HOMBURG: (*Lost in contemplating her, presses his hands together as in prayer.*)
Had you, Princess, two wings upon your shoulders,
I swear that I'd mistake you for an angel!
God, did I hear aright? You'll speak for me?
Where did the quiver of your words lie hidden
Until today, dear child, that you dare seek
An audience with my lord on such a matter!
O light of hope that suddenly refreshes!

NATALIA: God grant me arrows which will find their mark!
But if the Elector cannot – I say, cannot –
Reverse the law's decree, so be it! You
Must bravely, to a brave man, then submit –
And one, so oft victorious in life –
Will prove alike victorious in death!

ELECTRESS: Away! The favourable moment's almost past!

HOMBURG: May all the saints protect you in your quest!
Farewell! Godspeed! Whatever else you do,
Grant me, I pray, a sign of your success!
(*Exeunt ALL.*)

End of Act Three.

ACT FOUR

Scene 1

The ELECTOR's study. The ELECTOR at a table, studying papers by the light of a candelabra. Enter NATALIA by centre door and kneels down some distance away from him.

NATALIA: My uncle Friedrich, Brandenburg's Elector!
ELECTOR: (*Pushes his papers aside.*)
    Natalia! (*Moves to raise her up.*)
NATALIA: Let me be!
ELECTOR: What is it, love?
NATALIA: Here, in the dust at your feet, as well befits,
    I beg your mercy for my cousin Homburg!
    My wish is not to save him for myself:
    My heart desires his, I confess to you,
    But I don't want to save him for myself –
    Let him espouse whatever wife he will –
    I only want him, uncle, to be there:
    Alive, unfettered, free and independent –
    Like some sweet flower that pleases me.
    That is my plea to you, high lord and friend,
    Which plea, I know, will not remain unheard.
ELECTOR: (*Lifts her up.*)
    My little daughter! What is that you say?
    You know of cousin Homburg's recent crime?
NATALIA: O uncle, dear!
ELECTOR: Then, is he innocent?
NATALIA: A youthful lapse, blue-eyed and fair,
    For which forgiveness ought to lift him up,
    Even before the child has lisped: 'I'm sorry!'
    You will not thrust him from you with your foot
    Rather embrace him for his mother's sake,
    Who bore him, saying: 'There now, do not weep!
    To me, you're precious as good faith itself!'
    Was it not ardour to enhance your fame
    That led him in the turmoil of engagement

To break the bounds of military law?
And having, youthfully, infringed the rules,
Did he not manfully defeat the serpent?
To crown the victor, then cut off his head,
Is surely not what history asks of you:
An act of such sublimity, dear uncle,
That one might almost label it 'inhuman'!
Yet God created none more mild than you!
ELECTOR: Sweet child! Were I a veritable tyrant,
Your touching words, I vow, could not have failed
To melt my heart, although my breast were bronze!
I put it to you, though: can I allow
Myself to overrule the court's decree?
And if so, what would be the consequence?
NATALIA: For whom? For you?
ELECTOR: For me? No! Why for me?
You know of nothing higher than myself?
You're unaware of that most sacred trust
Which, in the army, we call: Fatherland?
NATALIA: But what have you to fear for Fatherland?
It won't collapse in rubble, shattered by
A single act of mercy on your part!
What you, brought up in camp, disorder call –
To rip the judges' verdict into shreds –
To me, seems order of the highest kind:
Military law, I know, must be respected,
But so must also kindness and affection!
This Fatherland you have secured for us,
My noble uncle, stands – a mighty fortress –
Which many a fiercer tempest shall endure,
Than such a splendid victory unbidden!
The Fatherland will flourish in the future,
Extended, beautified by your descendants –
Adorned with spires – abundant, magical –
The joy of friends, the terror of all foes.
It needs no cold and desolate cement,
Compounded of a friend's blood, to outlast
The peaceful, glorious autumn of your days.

ELECTOR: Prince Homburg shares your view?

NATALIA: Prince Homburg?

ELECTOR: He thinks, it matters not to Fatherland
    Whether it's ruled by law or tyrant's whim?

NATALIA: Ah, that poor boy!

ELECTOR: Well?

NATALIA: Oh, my dearest uncle!
    By way of answer, I have only tears.

ELECTOR: (*Taken aback.*)
    Why, daughter? What on earth has happened?

NATALIA: (*Hesitant.*)
    He thinks of one thing only – being saved!
    The muskets on the shoulders of his guards
    Eye him so cruelly, that, surprised and dizzy,
    His every wish, except to live, is quenched.
    The kingdom could go up in fire and smoke,
    Before him; he'd not ask: 'What's happening?'
    Oh, uncle, what a hero's heart you've broken!
    (*Turns away, weeping.*)

ELECTOR: (*Utterly astounded.*)
    No, no, Natalia dear, that cannot be!
    Impossible! You say he begs for mercy?

NATALIA: If only you had never – never – damned him!

ELECTOR: You say he begs for mercy? God almighty!
    What happened, darling child, to make you weep?
    You spoke with him? Come, tell me all! You spoke?

NATALIA: (*Leaning against his chest.*)
    No time ago; 'twas in my aunt's apartments,
    Where he had crept in cloak and feathered hat,
    Taking advantage of the dusk to hide –
    Timid, distraught, in secret and unworthy.
    A most distressing, pitiable sight!
    I'd not have thought that one whom history dubs
    A hero could ever plumb such depths of misery!
    I am a woman and I shy away,
    If worm so much as creeps towards my heel:
    Yet so completely crushed, beyond control,
    So utterly confused and unheroic,

Not even I'd face death, were death a lion!
So much for human dignity and fame!
ELECTOR: (*Bewildered.*)
Then, sure as God is in his heaven, child,
Be of good heart! Take courage! He is free!
NATALIA: What did you say? He's free?
ELECTOR: I've pardoned him!
I'll have him sent the order right away.
NATALIA: Oh, dearest uncle! Is it true?
ELECTOR: You heard me!
NATALIA: He'll be forgiven? He won't have to die?
ELECTOR: Upon my oath! I swear it! How should I
Oppose the view of such a warrior?
As well you know, within my heart of hearts
I hold his feelings in extreme regard;
If he believes the sentence is unjust,
I'll overrule the findings: he is free!
(*Brings her a chair.*)
Sit down a moment please, will you, my dear?
(*Goes to the table, sits down and writes. Pause.*)
NATALIA: (*Aside.*)
O heart, why are you hammering like this?
ELECTOR: He's in the castle still?
NATALIA: Excuse me, no –
The Prince returned at once to custody.
ELECTOR: (*Finishes letter and seals it, then returns to
NATALIA.*)
Well, well! My child, my little niece was weeping!
And it was I, entrusted with her joy,
Who had to sadden those fair eyes of hers!
(*Puts his arm round her.*)
You'd like to take my note to him yourself?
NATALIA: To the town hall? How – ?
ELECTOR: Why not? Here, orderlies!
(*Enter ORDERLIES.*)
A carriage right away! Princess Natalia
Has business to transact with Prince von Homburg!
(*Exeunt ORDERLIES.*)

Thus, he can thank you for his life at once!
(*Embraces her.*)
My dearest child! You've quite forgiven me?

NATALIA: (*After a pause.*)
Uncle, what stirred your clemency so swiftly
I do not know and seek no explanation;
But I'm convinced – I feel it in my heart –
You'd not ignobly mock me in my grief.
Whatever you have written, I believe
Your letter spells salvation and I thank you!
(*Kisses his hand.*)

ELECTOR: Indeed it does, my daughter – just as surely
As that is what our cousin Homburg wishes.
(*Exit ELECTOR.*)

Scene 2

NATALIA's room. Enter NATALIA, followed by two LADIES-IN-WAITING and REUSS.

NATALIA: (*Hastily.*)
What is it, Count? Word from my regiment?
Urgent? Or can it wait until tomorrow?

REUSS: (*Handing her a letter.*)
A letter, ma'am. Direct from Colonel Kottwitz.

NATALIA: Quick, give it me! What's in it? (*Opens it.*)

REUSS: A petition.
Outspoken, as you'll see, but with respect,
Addressed to the Elector on behalf
Of our esteemed commander, Prince von Homburg.

NATALIA: (*Reading.*)
'A humble supplication to the Elector
From the Princess of Orange Regiment –' I see; (*Pause.*)
Whose hand wrote this petition, Captain Reuss?

REUSS: As the unsteady script might well suggest,
'Twas Colonel Kottwitz wrote the text himself.
His worthy name moreover heads the list.

NATALIA: What of the thirty signatures below?

REUSS: The names of all our officers, Your Highness,
In order of their rank and by formation.

NATALIA: And it's to me – to me, they've sent this plea?

REUSS: Inquiring of Your Highness, with respect,
    If you, as Colonel-in-Chief, would deign to fill
    The topmost space, left vacant, with your name.
    (*Pause.*)

NATALIA: From what I've heard, the Prince, my noble cousin,
    Is being pardoned at the Elector's wish;
    And therefore, no such step is now required.

REUSS: (*Delighted.*)
    What? Really?

NATALIA: Nonetheless, I'll not refuse
    To sign a document, which aptly timed,
    May weight the scale supporting his decision.
    The Elector may see fit to welcome it
    As helping him to justify the measure.
    I'll therefore, in accordance with your wish,
    In signing, place my person at your head.
    (*Prepares to sign.*)

REUSS: We're deeply grateful, ma'am, for your support!
    (*Pause.*)

NATALIA: (*Turning to him again.*)
    My regiment alone is represented;
    What of the Bomsdorf Cuirassiers and where,
    Count Reuss, are Götz's Anhalt-Pless Dragoons?

REUSS: It's not, as you might fear, their soldiers' hearts
    Less warmly beat for him than do our own!
    It's just unfortunate for our petition,
    The Colonel's quarters are away in Arnstein,
    Cut off from all the other regiments,
    Whose camps are situated round the town.
    Our plea could not be freely circulated,
    So could not gather strength from every source.

NATALIA: Is that the only reason names are few?
    Are you quite certain, Count, if you could speak
    To every officer gathered hereabouts,
    They'd all support this plea for clemency?

REUSS: Here in the town, my lady? To a man!
    The cavalry entire have pledged themselves
    By name. Indeed, as God above's my witness,

I do believe one could successfully
Open a list for every soldier in the army!

NATALIA: Then why not send out officers at once
To undertake a census in each camp?

REUSS: Beg pardon! That the Colonel wouldn't do;
He wished, he said, to take no step that might
Be misconstrued and dubbed an evil name!

NATALIA: A curious man! First bold, then hesitant!
By happy chance I now recall the Elector,
Hard-pressed with other work, commissioned me
To order Kottwitz, who is short of space,
To march this way. I'll just sit down and write it.
(*Sits down to write.*)

REUSS: By heaven, that's good news! Could anything
Be better-timed to further our petition?

NATALIA: (*Writing.*)
You must exploit it, Count, as best you can!
(*Finishes writing, seals letter and stands up.*)
Stay! Just a moment! Keep this in your wallet.
Don't go to Arnstein to deliver it
Until I give you more precise instructions.
(*Hands him the letter.*)
(*Enter an ORDERLY.*)

ORDERLY: The coach, my lady, as the Elector ordered,
Is harnessed ready for you in the courtyard.

NATALIA: Then let it in! I'm coming down at once!
(*A pause while she walks thoughtfully to the table, drawing on her gloves.*)
Would you accompany me, Count, to see the Prince
Von Homburg, whom I am about to visit?
There's room for you to travel in my carriage.

REUSS: My lady, I am honoured to assist...
(*Offers her his arm.*)

NATALIA: (*To her LADIES-IN-WAITING.*)
Follow me, ladies! Maybe I'll decide
Whether to send the letter when I see him!
(*Exeunt ALL.*)

Scene 3

*HOMBURG's prison. HOMBURG hangs his hat on the wall and
stretches himself nonchalantly on cushions strewn on the floor.*

HOMBURG: According to the dervish, life's a journey –
    Short at that! Head six feet up it starts
    And finishes, head six feet down below.
    I shall be laid to rest, it seems, midway.
    The head man bears today upon his shoulders,
    Tomorrow may hang quivering on his breast
    And lie the next day, severed, at his feet!
    It's true, they say the sun shines there as well
    On meadows even brighter than our own;
    I dare say…It's a pity, though, that eyes,
    Born to behold that glory, should decay.
    (*Enter NATALIA, led by REUSS. LADIES-IN-WAITING
    follow. A RUNNER with a torch precedes them.*)
RUNNER: Her Highness, Princess Natalia of Orange!
HOMBURG: (*Rising.*)
    Natalia!
RUNNER: She's here in person, sir!
NATALIA: (*Bowing to REUSS.*)
    Leave us alone a moment, if you would.
    (*Exeunt REUSS and RUNNER.*)
HOMBURG: Oh, dearest lady!
NATALIA: Oh, my dear, good cousin!
HOMBURG: (*Leading her forward.*)
    What's brought you here? What news of my appeal?
NATALIA: Good news! All's well. It's just as I predicted:
    You're pardoned – free! I've brought a letter with me
    As confirmation, in my uncle's own hand!
HOMBURG: It isn't possible! I must be dreaming!
NATALIA: Here, read the letter for yourself! You'll see!
HOMBURG: (*Reading.*)
    'Prince Friedrich, when I ordered your arrest,
    For launching your attack ahead of time,
    I thought my duty called for nothing less.
    Indeed, I counted on your own approval.

If you believe you've suffered an injustice,
Pray let me know in writing by return
And I will send you back your sword at once.'
(*NATALIA turns pale. A pause. HOMBURG looks at her
questioningly.*)
NATALIA: (*With an expression of sudden joy.*)
Well, there it is! A word or two will do!
My dear sweet friend! (*Squeezing his hand.*)
HOMBURG: My dearest lady!
NATALIA: Oh, what a blessed hour has struck for me!
Quickly, cousin, take the pen and write!
HOMBURG: Is that his signature?
NATALIA: Just 'F'. His mark!
O Bork! Rejoice with me! My uncle's grace
Is boundless as the ocean! Bring a chair!
His Highness must sit down at once and write!
HOMBURG: He says that if, in my opinion –
NATALIA: (*Interrupting.*)
                                        True!
Quick! Come on, sit down – and I'll dictate!
(*Pushes the chair towards him.*)
HOMBURG: I'd like to read his letter through again.
NATALIA: (*Snatching the letter from his hand.*)
What for? Did you not see the grave's wide open
Jaws, yawning to greet you in the cemetery?
For heaven's sake! It's urgent! Sit and write!
HOMBURG: (*Smiling.*)
Dear heart, you make it sound as though the grave
Were set to spring upon me like a panther!
(*Sits down and picks up pen.*)
NATALIA: (*Turns away and weeps.*)
Please write – unless you want to make me angry!
(*HOMBURG rings for a servant, who enters.*)
HOMBURG: Bring pen and paper, sealing-wax and seal!
(*A SERVANT collects these items and, after handing them
to HOMBURG, leaves the room. HOMBURG writes –
pauses, tears up the letter he has started and throws it
under the table.*)
A stupid opening! (*Takes another sheet of paper.*)

NATALIA: (*Picks up the letter.*)

                What did you say?

That's very good! I think it's excellent!

HOMBURG: (*Under his breath.*)

Sounds like some scoundrel! Certainly, no prince!

Let's see! I'll find a better turn of phrase.

(*Pause. He reaches for the ELECTOR's letter, which NATALIA is holding.*).

What exactly did his letter say?

NATALIA: (*Refusing to surrender it.*)

Why, nothing!

HOMBURG: Give it me!

NATALIA: You've read it!

HOMBURG: (*Snatches it.*)

                           Yes.

Just want to think how best to phrase my answer.

(*Opens and reads it.*)

NATALIA: (*Aside.*)

O God! I fear it's now all up with him!

HOMBURG: (*Perplexed.*)

Read that! A masterpiece, upon my soul!

Presumably, you overlooked that part?

NATALIA: No! Where?

HOMBURG: It's I myself, he says, who must decide!

NATALIA: Well, then!

HOMBURG: Most fair of him, indeed, most worthy!

As well befits a noble heart to speak!

NATALIA: His generosity is limitless!

It's your turn now to show him yours – so, write

What he desires! It's merely an excuse –

A pure formality, that's all that's needed:

As soon as he has your few words to hand,

The case is closed and done with!

HOMBURG: (*Lays the letter aside.*)

                  No, my dear!

I'd like to think it over till tomorrow.

NATALIA: I just don't understand you! What a change!

Why? What for?

HOMBURG: (*Leaps up from the chair, impassioned.*)
     Don't question me, I beg you!
 You haven't weighed the contents of that letter!
 I cannot write to him what he requires –
 That he has treated me unjustly! Should
 You force me to reply in present mood,
 God knows, I'll write: 'You've treated me correctly.'
 (*Sits down again, arms folded, and gazes at the letter.*)
NATALIA: (*Pale.*)
 You lunatic! You don't know what you're saying!
 (*Leans over him, deeply moved.*)
HOMBURG: (*Squeezing her hand.*)
 Just wait a moment! I believe –
NATALIA: Now what?
HOMBURG: I'll very soon know what I have to write.
NATALIA: (*Anguished.*)
 My Prince!
HOMBURG: (*Seizing pen.*)
    I'm listening –
NATALIA: Dear friend!
 I praise the impulse which has seized your heart
 But this I promise you: the regiment
 Is detailed which tomorrow, reconciled,
 Shall fire the last salute above your corpse!
 Noble you may be but, if you refuse
 To fight the sentence – help him countermand it
 By doing as he asks you in this letter –
 Then, I assure you – as the matter stands –
 He'll deal with you sublimely in the morning:
 And have you shot, as sentenced, without pity!
HOMBURG: (*Writing.*)
 No matter!
NATALIA: What?
HOMBURG: He'll do as he sees fit;
 I am concerned with acting as I should.
NATALIA: (*Frightened, moves closer.*)
 Cruel! Inhuman! Is that what you're writing?

HOMBURG: (*Finishing his letter.*)

    Homburg! Given at Fehrbellin, upon the twelfth –
    I am quite ready – Franz!
    (*Folds and seals letter.*)

NATALIA: Oh, God in heaven!

HOMBURG: (*Standing up.*)

    To the castle with this letter for my lord!
    (*Exit SERVANT.*)
    I would not have him, worthy as he is,
    Confronted by a man of lesser worth!
    I'm burdened by considerable guilt,
    As well I recognise – but if he can
    Forgive me only if I dispute that fact,
    Then I'm not interested in his pardon.

NATALIA: (*Kisses him.*)

    Receive my kiss! And were twelve leaden bullets
    To fell you here and now, I couldn't help
    But cry – in tears, though jubilant – 'I love you!'
    Still, since you are following your heart,
    I claim an equal right to follow mine.
    Count Reuss!
    (*The RUNNER opens door. Enter REUSS.*)

REUSS: Your Highness wishes?

NATALIA: Take your letter

    To Arnstein, please, for Colonel Kottwitz only!
    The regiment's to move: Elector's orders!
    I want them here by midnight at the latest!
    (*Exeunt ALL.*)

End of Act Four.

ACT FIVE

Scene 1

A hall in the castle. Enter the ELECTOR, half-undressed, from his adjoining study. He is followed by TRUCHSS, GOLZ and HOHENZOLLERN. PAGES with candelabra.

ELECTOR: Kottwitz, you say? Her Highness's dragoons?
    Here, in the city?
TRUCHSS: (*Opens a window.*)
                   Yes, my lord, they're here!
    The regiment's drawn up outside the castle.
ELECTOR: Can you explain this mystery, gentlemen?
    Who sent for them?
HOHENZOLLERN: I've no idea, Elector!
ELECTOR: The sector I allotted him was Arnstein!
    Quick! Somebody go down and bring him here!
GOLZ: He will appear before you, sir, at once!
ELECTOR: Where is he?
GOLZ: In the town hall, so I hear,
    Where all the officers of your general staff
    Are now foregathering in consultation.
ELECTOR: Why? What's the reason?
HOHENZOLLERN: That, I do not know.
TRUCHSS: My lord and my commander will permit
    The rest of us to join them for a moment?
ELECTOR: Where? At the town hall?
HOHENZOLLERN: To attend the meeting.
    We gave our word that we, too, would be there.
ELECTOR: (*After a short pause.*)
    You may dismiss!
GOLZ: Then, gentlemen, let's go!
    (*Exeunt TRUCHSS, GOLZ and HOHENZOLLERN.*)
ELECTOR: It's very strange! Were I the Dey of Tunis,
    I'd sound the alarm at such a suspect rally.
    I'd lay the silken thread upon my table,

Fast barricade the castle gates and all
My guns and howitzers position – loaded!
But since Hans Kottwitz, from Priegnitz, it is
Who beards me in his wilful, haughty way,
I'll deal with the affair in homely style:
By one of those three silver-gleaming locks
Adhering to his skull, I'll quietly lead him,
With his twelve squadrons, back to base in Arnstein!
Why rouse the sleeping city from its slumber?
(*After going to the window again for a moment, he returns to
the table and rings a bell. Two SERVANTS appear.*)
Go to the town hall and find out – discreetly –
What's happening there tonight!

1ST SERVANT: At once, my lord!

ELECTOR: (*To 2ND SERVANT.*)

Fetch me my clothes! I'll finish dressing here.
(*The 2ND SERVANT fetches his clothes. The ELECTOR gets
dressed and dons his regalia.*)
(*Enter DÖRFLING.*)

DÖRFLING: Rebellion, my lord!

ELECTOR: (*Still dressing.*)

                        Come, come, Field Marshal!
Well you know, I do not relish callers
Invading my apartments unannounced!
What do you want?

DÖRFLING: My lord, forgive me, but
A very grave affair has brought me here.
Colonel Kottwitz, moving without orders,
Is here in town; a hundred officers
Now massed about him in the Hall of Knights.
A document's being passed around among them,
Aimed at infringing your prerogative.

ELECTOR: I know all that! It's surely just a plea
For clemency in favour of Prince Homburg,
For whom the law's prescribed a firing-squad?

DÖRFLING: Indeed, that's it! You're absolutely right!

ELECTOR: Well, then! I'd have you know my heart is
                           with them!

DÖRFLING: It's said they planned today, the lunatics,
    To hand you their petition in the castle
    And should you then with unrelenting rigour
    Confirm the sentence, they – dare I report? –
    Would free him from captivity by force!
ELECTOR: Who told you that?
DÖRFLING: Who told me? Why, my lord,
    The lady Retzow – worthy of your trust –
    A cousin of my wife. She chanced to visit
    Her uncle, Drost von Retzow's house this evening,
    Where officers from the camp she overheard
    Discuss this brazen enterprise aloud.
ELECTOR: That tale I'd credit only from a man!
    I'd plant my boot before his door to save
    The Prince from would-be heroes of that ilk!
DÖRFLING: My lord, I urge you, if it's your intention
    To pardon Prince von Homburg in the end,
    Then do so, ere so dire a crime's committed!
    You know how every army loves its hero;
    Don't let this spark, that's now begun to glow,
    Become a hopeless, all-consuming blaze.
    Kottwitz does not yet know, nor his supporters,
    That I've already loyally warned you, sir.
    Send back the Prince's sword before they come!
    Send it, for well he earned it in the battle:
    Give history, sir, one noble exploit more –
    And one transgression less – to register!
ELECTOR: But first, I'll have to ask the Prince himself.
    As you're aware, it wasn't my caprice
    That ordered his arrest, nor can it free him.
    I'll see these gentlemen when they arrive.
DÖRFLING: (*Aside.*)
    Blast! His armour's proof against all arrows!
    (*Enter two ORDERLIES, one with a letter in his hand.*)
1ST ORDERLY: Colonels Kottwitz, Hennings, Truchss
                            and others
    Request an audience!
ELECTOR: (*To the 2ND ORDERLY, taking the letter from
    his hand.*)
            From Prince von Homburg?

2ND ORDERLY: Yes, my noble lord!

ELECTOR: Who gave it you?

2ND ORDERLY: The guard on duty at the gate below.
    He had it from the Prince's musketeer.
    (*The ELECTOR walks to the table and reads the letter.*
    Having done so, he turns and calls a PAGE.)

ELECTOR: Prittwitz! Go fetch the sentence for me, please.
    Also, the pass for Gustav Count von Horn,
    Ambassador of Sweden. Bring them here! (*Exit PAGE.*)
    (*To the 1ST ORDERLY.*)
    Bid Kottwitz and his officers come in!
    (*Enter KOTTWITZ, HENNINGS, SPARREN, TRUCHSS,*
    HOHENZOLLERN, REUSS, GOLZ, STRANZ, with other
    OFFICERS.)

KOTTWITZ: (*Bearing petition.*)
    Illustrious lord, permit me, if I may,
    To tender, on behalf of all the army,
    This document to you, in humble duty.

ELECTOR: Before I take it, Kottwitz, please explain:
    Who ordered you to come here, into town?

KOTTWITZ: With my dragoons?

ELECTOR: The regiment entire!
    I told you Arnstein was to be your base!

KOTTWITZ: My lord, I came here at your own command!

ELECTOR: Show me the order!

KOTTWITZ: Here it is, my lord!

ELECTOR: (*Reads it.*)
    'Natalia. Given this day at Fehrbellin
    In my most noble uncle Friedrich's name.'

KOTTWITZ: Oh, God! Don't tell me now, my lord,

                              the order
    Wasn't yours!

ELECTOR: No, no! I only meant,
    Who was it who delivered it to you?

KOTTWITZ: Count Reuss!

ELECTOR: (*After momentary pause.*)
             In fact, I welcome your arrival!
    For you and your twelve squadrons of dragoons

Will pay, tomorrow, final honours due
To Prince von Homburg, whom the court has sentenced.
KOTTWITZ: (*Shocked.*)
    Beg pardon, sir?
ELECTOR: (*Handing him back the order.*)
                      Your regiment is still
Outside the castle in the murk and mist?
KOTTWITZ: The murk, forgive me – ?
ELECTOR: Why not quarter them?
KOTTWITZ: I have, sir. Billets here in town for all
    Were requisitioned by your order, sir.
ELECTOR: (*Turning to the window.*)
    Why, bless my soul! A minute or two ago –
    You've lost no time in stabling the horses!
    So much the better! Welcome, yet again!
    What brings you here, though? Tell me, what's afoot?
KOTTWITZ: Sir, this petition from your loyal army.
ELECTOR: Show me!
KOTTWITZ: But sir, what you've just said, I fear,
    Has shattered all my most exalted hopes.
ELECTOR: Another's word could resurrect them all! (*He reads.*)
    'A plea for mercy at the highest level
    For our commander, woefully accused,
    The General Prince Friedrich Hessen-Homburg.'
    (*To the OFFICERS.*)
    A noble name, my friends – not undeserving
    Of your support in such impressive numbers!
    Who was it drafted this petition?
KOTTWITZ: I did.
ELECTOR: His Highness was informed of what you wrote?
KOTTWITZ: He'd no idea at all! By us alone,
    This plea was first conceived, then duly signed.
ELECTOR: Bear with me a moment, gentlemen!
    (*Walks to the table and studies the plea. Long pause.*)
    It's rather odd that you, an old campaigner,
    Defend the Prince's act. You justify
    His premature attack, despite my order?
KOTTWITZ: Yes, Elector and most noble lord! I do!
ELECTOR: That wasn't your opinion in the field!

KOTTWITZ: I hadn't weighed the implications, sir!
    The Prince is expert in the art of war –
    I should have followed him unquestioning.
    With the Swedes already wavering on the left
    And struggling to reinforce the right,
    Had Prince von Homburg waited for your order
    They'd have established outposts in the glens
    And you would not have gained your victory.
ELECTOR: That may well be your reading of the battle!
    But I'd sent Colonel Hennings, as you know,
    To start by capturing that Swedish bridgehead,
    Which was protecting General Wrangel's rear.
    Had you not disobeyed my orders,
    Then Hennings could have carried out his task,
    Have fired the bridges in two hours at most,
    And taken up position on the Rhyn;
    Then Wrangel's forces all – lock, stock and barrel –
    Had perished in their trenches or the swamp.
KOTTWITZ: To snatch at destiny's supreme award –
    The error of a prentice hand, not yours!
    Till now, you've always taken what fate offered.
    The brazen dragon which laid waste our marches
    Was put to flight, nursing a bloody head.
    Could one have hoped for more from one day's battle?
    What do you care, if, for a fortnight longer,
    Exhausted in the sand, he licks his wounds?
    Now that we've learned the art of beating him
    We're longing for another chance to practise.
    Let us meet Wrangel, boldly, face to face,
    Just one more time and that will finish him!
    We'll drive the Swedes for ever out to sea!
    Rome, wasn't built, my lord, in one short day!
ELECTOR: You'd be a fool to entertain such hopes,
    If anyone who likes, upon a whim,
    Can snatch the traces of my battle-wagon!
    Fortune, you think, will always be at hand,
    Rewarding disobedience with laurels?
    I want no victory which – a child of chance –
    Happens to come my way! I will uphold

The law, as mother of my crown, and breed
With her a dynasty of victories!
KOTTWITZ: My lord, the law, the highest – law supreme –
Which should inspire your generals, is not
Adherence to the letter of your will;
It is the Fatherland, it is the crown;
It's you, yourself – whose head supports the crown!
What matters it to you, my lord, what rules
Defeat the enemy, so long as he
Bows down before you with his flags and banners?
The rule that beats him is the best of all!
You'd turn this army – heart and soul devoted –
Into a tool, to match the lifeless sword
You wear suspended from your golden sash?
What wretched mind, bereft of all ideals,
Evolved that theory first? A policy
Short-sighted, niggardly it is that takes
One case in which emotion might do harm
As reason to suppress it in ten others,
Where nothing but emotion will avail!
Do I shed blood for you, my lord, in battle
For personal gain? For cash? For honours?
God forbid! Blood's worth far more than either!
No! It's my pleasure – of my own free will
And independent choice – to do so, for the sake
Of your transcending excellence, my lord,
And to the greater glory of your name!
That's the reward that purchases my heart!
Let's say, for his unbidden victory,
You now condemn the noble Prince to death;
If I, tomorrow, equally unbidden,
Stumble on victory 'twixt hill and dale,
While, like a shepherd, leading my dragoons,
By God, I'd be a scoundrel did I not
Repeat the Prince's deed with equal zest!
Were you to say, with rule-book in your hand,
'Kottwitz, your head is forfeit,' I'd reply:
'I know, my lord! You take it! Here it is!
That oath I swore of loyalty to the crown,

Commits me, hair and hide – my head included:
I'm giving you, in fact, what's yours already!'
ELECTOR: I cannot get the better of you, Kottwitz –
You're quite amazing! You're corrupting me
With all this crafty oratory of yours;
Being well disposed towards you, as you know,
I'll call an advocate to plead my case
And settle this dispute! (*He rings. A SERVANT enters.*)
                    The Prince von Homburg!
I want him brought here from the prison now!
(*Exit the SERVANT.*)
He'll teach you, Kottwitz, I can guarantee,
What's meant by discipline and obedience!
He's written me, at least, in different vein
From this sophistical discourse on freedom
With which you have regaled me, like a boy.
(*Returns to the table and begins reading.*)
KOTTWITZ: (*Astonished.*)
He's sent for whom?
HENNINGS: The Prince?
TRUCHSS: No, that can't be!
(*OFFICERS gather uneasily, talking among themselves.*)
ELECTOR: Who is the author of this second letter?
HOHENZOLLERN: I, my lord!
ELECTOR: (*Reading.*)
                    '...Proof that Elector Friedrich
The Prince's deed did much...'! In heaven's name!
Such impudence!
You dare attempt to shift the blame to me
For Homburg's reckless action in the field?
HOHENZOLLERN: To you, Elector! So says Hohenzollern!
ELECTOR: As God's my witness, this surpasses fiction!
One argues that the Prince is innocent;
The other one accuses *me* instead!
What proof have you to warrant such a charge?
HOHENZOLLERN: No doubt, my lord, you will recall
                                    the night
We came upon His Highness fast asleep

Under the plane trees in the palace garden –
Dreaming perhaps of victory on the morrow,
A crown of laurel clutching in his hand.
You, as though to test his inmost heart,
Removed the laurel, with a smile, and wound
Your golden neck-chain all about the wreath,
Then handed chain and laurel, intertwined,
To the Princess Natalia, your niece.
At which extraordinary sight, His Highness,
Blushing, rose – as though to seize so sweet
A prize bestowed by hand so dear to him.
But you withdrew the Princess hurriedly
And disappeared with her. The gate clanged shut.
Princess, chain and crown of laurel vanished;
His Highness – holding in his hand a glove
Which he had snatched, with no idea from whom –
Was left alone, asleep in midnight's lap.

ELECTOR: What sort of glove?

HOHENZOLLERN: Pray, let me finish, sir!
'Twas meant to be a joke, but soon I learned
How seriously the Prince had been affected.
For when I entered through the postern-gate
And found him in the garden – as by chance –
Aroused him and the Prince regained his senses,
Joy overwhelmed him at the recollection.
You can't imagine anything more touching!
The incident entire he sketched for me,
As though it were a dream, in finest detail.
He said he'd never dreamt a dream so real
And firmly, the conviction in him grew
That heaven had vouchsafed a sign to him:
All that which he had witnessed in his vision –
Princess, laurel-crown and golden chain –
God would accord him on the day of battle.

ELECTOR: Hm! Very odd! What of the glove?

HOHENZOLLERN: Indeed!
That item, giving substance to the dream,
At once destroyed and fortified his faith.
At first, wide-eyed, he stared at it amazed:

Not only its colour – white – but shape and style,
Confirmed a lady's glove. That night, however,
He'd spoken to no lady from whose hand
It could have come. His reverie disturbed
By my summons to attend the Marshal's briefing,
He just forgot what he could not explain,
And stuffed the glove, unthinking, in his tunic.

ELECTOR: What then?

HOHENZOLLERN: Why, thereupon, with pad and pencil,
Inside he went, respectfully alert,
To hear the Marshal give his battle-orders.
The Electress and her niece were there as well,
Both waiting to set out upon their journey.
But who could fail to notice how astonished
The Prince was, when Her Highness missed her glove.
Was it the glove he'd thrust into his tunic?
Repeatedly the Marshal called to him:
'Prince von Homburg!' He replied: 'Yes, Marshal?'
Trying vainly to collect his wits.
But still beset by wondrous visions, he
Would not have heeded had the heavens fallen!
(*Falls silent.*)

ELECTOR: Was it the Princess' glove?

HOHENZOLLERN: It was!
(*The ELECTOR is deep in thought. HOHENZOLLERN
continues.*)
He stood there like a statue, pencil poised,
Dead as a stone, yet seemingly alive:
All sensitivity, as if by magic,
Totally dispelled. Not till the morrow –
With shot and shell already thundering –
Did he come back to life and asked me then:
'What was it, friend, that Dörfling said last night
Regarding me when he was briefing us?'

DÖRFLING: My lord, I can corroborate his story!
As I recall, the Prince heard not a word
Of what I said. I've often seen him musing
But never so completely absent-minded,
So totally abstracted, as last night.

ELECTOR: In other words, if I have understood you,
  The case you've built against me comes to this:
  Had I, on this young dreamer in his state,
  Not played a dubious joke, he'd bear no guilt:
  His thoughts would not have wandered at the briefing,
  Nor had he disobeyed me in the field.
  Is that it? Well, come on! Speak up!
HOHENZOLLERN: My lord!
  I leave it to yourself to draw conclusions!
ELECTOR: Fool that you are, you stupid man! Had you
  Not called me down, yourself, into the garden,
  Then curiosity would not have made me
  Play that harmless joke upon the dreamer.
  Might I not therefore equally contend
  That *you* it was, who caused his dereliction?
  The Delphic wisdom of my officers!
HOHENZOLLERN: Enough, my lord! I'm certain, none
                                        the less,
  That you will pay due heed to what I've said!
  (*Enter an OFFICER.*)
OFFICER: Sir, the Prince will presently appear!
ELECTOR: Good! Let him enter!
OFFICER: In about two minutes!
  He stopped in passing by the churchyard, sir;
  He asked a watchman to unlock the gate.
ELECTOR: The churchyard?
OFFICER: Yes, my lord!
ELECTOR: Whatever for?
OFFICER: To tell the truth, I'm not quite sure, my lord;
  It seems he wished to look upon the vault
  Made ready to receive him by your order.
  (*The COLONELS gather together, talking among themselves.*)
ELECTOR: No matter! Bring him in, once he arrives!
  (*Returns to the table and looks at his papers.*)
TRUCHSS: The guard is leading in His Highness now.
  (*Enter HOMBURG and OFFICER with GUARDS.*)
ELECTOR: Young Prince, I must appeal to you for help!
  This plea, on your behalf, was brought to me

By Colonel Kottwitz, bearing – as you see –
The signatures of five score noblemen.
The army wants you freed, it would appear,
And disapproves your sentence by court martial.
Please read it for yourself and be informed!
(*Gives him the document.*)

HOMBURG: (*After glancing through it, turns and looks round
at the circle of OFFICERS.*)

Kottwitz, old friend, come – let me shake your hand!
You've done much more for me than I deserved
Of you, when we were in the field. But now,
Go quickly back to Arnstein, whence you came
And do not stir. I've thought the matter over.
I wish to die the death I've been awarded!
(*Hands back the petition.*)

KOTTWITZ: (*Nonplussed.*)

Oh no, my Prince! No! No! What words are these?

HOHENZOLLERN: He wants to die?

TRUCHSS: He must and shall not die!

(*Several OFFICERS pressing forward.*)

OFFICERS: My lord Elector! Our commander! Hear us!

HOMBURG: Quiet! I am inexorably resolved!

That sacred clause of military law,
Flouted by me, before the army's eyes,
Death, by my own free will, shall glorify!
What victory's important, noble friends –
Even the paltry one I might still wrest
From Wrangel – in comparison with such
A triumph over deadlier foes within us:
Ambition, arrogance and pride, which I
Shall gloriously defeat tomorrow? Then,
Let the foreigner who'd yoke us be struck down
And, on his native heath, the Brandenburger
Assert himself! This land is his alone –
These splendid plains for him alone created!

KOTTWITZ: My son! My dearest friend! How may I call you?

TRUCHSS: God of our Fathers!

KOTTWITZ: Let me kiss your hand!

(*The OFFICERS press about him.*)

HOMBURG: (*Turning to the ELECTOR.*)
    To you, my lord, who called me in the past
    A sweeter name – alas, now forfeited –
    I beg to kneel, sir, with profound emotion!
    Forgive me if, on that decisive day,
    I served your cause with over-hasty zeal:
    My death will now expunge my every fault.
    But grant my heart – serenely reconciled
    To your august decree – the consolation
    Of knowing that your own bears me no grudge
    And, in the hour of parting, as a sign,
    Accord me graciously one final wish!
ELECTOR: Speak, young hero! What do you desire?
    You have my word of honour, as a knight:
    Whatever it may be, it shall be granted!
HOMBURG: I beg of you, my lord, from Gustav Karl
    Do not buy peace with the Princess's hand,
    But from our camp, expel the mediator
    Who dared to make you such a vile proposal!
    Let chain-shot be your answer to the King!
ELECTOR: (*Kissing his forehead.*)
    It shall be as you say! This kiss, my son,
    Confirms the granting of your last request!
    Could ever I endure such sacrifice,
    Unless 'twere forced upon me by defeat?
    But every word that you have said betokens
    A future victory in which I'll crush him!
    She's Prince von Homburg's bride, is what I'll write;
    He died for his offence at Fehrbellin,
    And from his ghost, advancing with our banners,
    Strive, if you will, to win her in the field!
    (*Kisses him again and raises him.*)
HOMBURG: Your words have granted me new life, my lord!
    I now call every blessing down upon you,
    Which seraphim, about the throne of clouds,
    Rejoicing sprinkle on the heads of heroes!
    Go forth, my lord, to fight and overcome
    A world defiant! You deserve to win!

ELECTOR: Guard! Escort His Highness back to prison!
(NATALIA and the ELECTRESS appear at the door,
followed by LADIES-IN-WAITING.)
NATALIA: Please, mother! Who cares what is right or proper!
The most that I can do now is to love him!
My dear, unhappy friend!
HOMBURG: *(Leaving.)*
       Take me away!
TRUCHSS: Oh, no, my Prince!
(Several OFFICERS bar his path.)
HOMBURG: I said, lead me away!
HOHENZOLLERN: *(To the ELECTOR.)*
My lord! How can your heart – ?
HOMBURG: My tyrant friends,
You'd drag me off to die, still chained to you?
Let go of me! I've finished with the world!
(Exit HOMBURG with GUARDS.)
NATALIA: *(Laying her head on the ELECTRESS' breast.)*
O earth, receive me in your bosom, pray!
Why bear the light of day a moment longer?
DÖRFLING: O God! Why did it have to come to this?
(The ELECTOR is in serious private consultation with one
of the OFFICERS.)
KOTTWITZ: *(Coldly.)*
My lord, in view of what has taken place,
May we dismiss?
ELECTOR: No, you may not! Not yet!
I'll tell you, Colonel, when you're free to go!
(Looks him straight in the eye for a little while, then picks up
the papers, brought by the PAGE, and turns, holding them,
to DÖRFLING.)
Here is Count Horn of Sweden's travel pass!
Responding to the Prince, my cousin's plea,
Which I have pledged myself to implement:
Three days from now, let battle recommence!
(Pause. He glances at the death sentence.)
Judge for yourselves, you gentlemen! The Prince,
In this past year, through pride and negligence,
Has cost me two important victories –

And seriously jeopardised a third!
Now, bearing that experience in mind,
Are you prepared to trust him with the fourth?
KOTTWITZ/TRUCHSS: (*Talking across one another.*)
What, my most gracious lord! Revered commander!
ELECTOR: Well, answer me! Yes or no!
KOTTWITZ: By all that's holy!
You could be poised upon destruction's brink:
Unless you gave the order, he'd not stir
Or lift his sword to rescue you, unbidden!
ELECTOR: (*Tearing up the death sentence.*)
Then, follow me, my friends, into the garden!
(*Exeunt ALL.*)

Scene 2

HOMBURG, eyes blindfolded, is led by STRANZ through the wrought-iron garden gate, followed by OFFICERS and GUARDS. Drums and funeral music in the distance. ('Der gute Kamerad' by Kleist's contemporary, Ludwig Uhland, might be appropriate.)

HOMBURG: Now you are mine, O immortality!
You pierce this blindfold, wrapped about my eyes,
With radiance equal to a thousand suns!
I feel wings sprout upon my either shoulder;
My spirit hovers in ethereal space
And, as a ship, propelled by breath of wind,
Watches the bustling harbour sink behind it,
So all of life behind me fades away:
Now I can just distinguish shape and colour,
Now all below me's blanketed in mist.
(*HOMBURG sits down on the bench, erected in the centre of the space about the oak tree. STRANZ walks away from him and looks up towards the ramp leading down from the castle.*)
How sweet the scent of this nocturnal violet!
Can you smell it?
(*STRANZ comes back to him.*)
STRANZ: I see carnations and some gilly-flowers.
HOMBURG: Gilly-flowers? From where?

STRANZ: I don't quite know.

It seems some girl or other planted them.

Shall I pluck you a carnation?

HOMBURG: My dear fellow!

When I get home, I'll put it into water.

(*Enter the ELECTOR carrying a laurel wreath wound about with his golden chain – the ELECTRESS, NATALIA, DÖRFLING, KOTTWITZ, HOHENZOLLERN, GOLZ and so on. LADIES-IN-WAITING, OFFICERS and torches appear on the castle ramp. HOHENZOLLERN steps to the railing with a cloth and signals to STRANZ, whereupon the latter leaves HOMBURG and has a word with the GUARDS.*)

HOMBURG: What is that spreading gleam of light I sense?

STRANZ: (*Returning to him.*)

Would you be good enough to rise, Your Highness?

HOMBURG: What is it?

STRANZ: Nothing to alarm you, sir!

I wish to take the blindfold from your eyes.

HOMBURG: The moment's come to end my torment?

STRANZ: Yes...

Long life and blessings, Prince! You have deserved them!

(*The ELECTOR hands the wreath, with the chain hanging from it, to NATALIA and leads her down the ramp, followed by LORDS and LADIES. Surrounded by torches, NATALIA walks towards HOMBURG who rises in astonishment. She places the crown on his head, hangs the chain round his neck and presses his hand to her heart.*

HOMBURG falls unconscious.)

NATALIA: Oh, God! The joy – the shock of it will kill him!

HOHENZOLLERN: (*Lifting him.*)

Quick! Help!

ELECTOR: Let the thunder of the guns revive him!

(*Sound of gunfire. A march being played. The castle is bathed in light.*)

KOTTWITZ: Long live the Prince von Homburg!

OFFICERS: Long life to him!

ALL: Victor in the battle of Fehrbellin!

(*Momentary silence. HOMBURG is recovering from his shock.*)

HOMBURG: Tell me – is this a dream?
KOTTWITZ: A dream – what else?
OFFICERS: Into the field!
TRUCHSS: To battle!
DÖRFLING: Victory!
ALL: And death to all the foes of Brandenburg!

The End.

THE BROKEN PITCHER

(Der zerbrochene Krug)

a comedy

Characters

WALTER
district judge

ADAM
village magistrate

LICHT
clerk of the court

MISTRESS MARTHA RULL

EVE
her daughter

VEIT TÜMPEL
a farmer

RUPERT
his son

MISTRESS BRIDGET
sister of Veit

A SERVANT

BEADLE

LISA/GRETA
two maids

This translation, adapted for radio by the translator, was first broadcast by the BBC World Service in March 1998 with the following cast:

WALTER, Brett Usher

ADAM, Nigel Lambert

LICHT, Jonathan Tafler

MISTRESS MARTHA, Pat Keen

EVE, Julia Ford

VEIT TÜMPEL, Christopher Wright

RUPERT, Robert Harper

MISTRESS BRIDGET, Rachel Atkins

SERVANT, Christopher Wright

LISA, Allison Pettitt

GRETA, Sarah Rice

Director, Andy Jordan

Scene 1

A courtroom in the Dutch village of Huisum.

The village magistrate ADAM sits, bandaging his leg.

Enter LICHT, his clerk.

LICHT: For heaven's sake, what's happened, Master Adam?
    Done something to your leg? You look like death!
ADAM: Two feet are all you need to take a tumble!
    This floor's quite smooth. Look, not a bump in sight!
    And yet I stumbled; every one of us
    Carries his blasted stumbling-block around.
LICHT: What is that you say, friend? Each one carries –
ADAM: Inside himself!
LICHT: A likely tale!
ADAM: I'm sorry?
LICHT: True, you're descended from a lusty forebear,
    Whose fall, before the world had scarce begun,
    Secured old father Adam lasting fame.
    You cannot mean –
ADAM: Well?
LICHT: You, too?
ADAM: As if I...!
    You heard me, didn't you? I tripped and fell!
LICHT: Literally – measured your length?
ADAM: Yes – literally!
    Perhaps I didn't make the picture clear.
LICHT: And when, pray, did this accident occur?
ADAM: Just now, as I was getting out of bed.
    I'd scarce begun to sing my morning hymn,
    When I was pitchforked – smack, into the day!
    No time to even start the daily round
    Before the Lord God goes and twists my foot.
LICHT: The left one that would be, no doubt?
ADAM: The left?
LICHT: The one you're bandaging?
ADAM: Of course!
LICHT: Praise be!
    It found it hard to tread the path of sin?

ADAM: My foot? Hard? Why?
LICHT: Your club-foot?
ADAM: Club-foot? No!
    One foot is just as cloddish as the other!
LICHT: Beg pardon! But you do your right foot wrong!
    The right one's built less – weightily…and so
    Can tread more safely on thin ice!
ADAM: That's poppycock!
    Where one dares go, the other swiftly follows!
LICHT: But how is it your face was 'twisted', too?
ADAM: My face?
LICHT: Don't ask me to believe you didn't know!
ADAM: I cannot tell a lie! How does it look?
LICHT: How does it look?
ADAM: Yes, friend.
LICHT: It looks appalling!
ADAM: Be more precise!
LICHT: As though you had been flayed!
    A fearsome sight! The chunk that's missing from
    Your cheek's so big, I'd need a scales to weigh it.
ADAM: Can't be true!
LICHT: (*Fetching a mirror.*)
                    Here, look! See for yourself!
    A sheep, chased through a thorn hedge by the hounds
    Would leave less wool behind than you've lost flesh –
    The Lord alone knows where and how you did it.
ADAM: Hm! True enough! It's not a pretty sight…
    My nose has suffered, too.
LICHT: Your eye, as well!
ADAM: No, surely not my eye.
LICHT: Yes, can't you see?
    A glancing blow – all bruised and bloodshot – looks
    As though some frenzied foreman swung a punch.
ADAM: That's just my cheekbone – really nothing much;
    To tell the truth, I hadn't even noticed.
LICHT: You wouldn't, would you? – in the heat of battle.
ADAM: Battle is right! As I recall, I fought
    With that damned ornamental goat,
    Perched on the corner of the stove.

Losing my balance, like a drowning man,
I clutched the air around me and so grabbed
A pair of soaking trousers which I'd hung
To dry upon the clothes-horse overnight:
Laid hold of them, you see, thinking the while
The foolish thing I'd done. The waistband split
And waistband, trousers and myself, all three
Plunged headlong, so my forehead struck the stove
Just where the muzzle of the goat sticks out.

LICHT: (*Laughing.*)
    I see!

ADAM: God damn it!

LICHT: First Adam you must be
    To fall not in, but jumping *out* of bed!

ADAM: Enough! I meant to ask what news you've brought?

LICHT: You may well ask! There's news enough for once!
    I all but quite forgot to tell you –

ADAM: What?

LICHT: Prepare to greet an unexpected guest
    From Utrecht.

ADAM: Well?

LICHT: The District Judge is coming.

ADAM: Who?

LICHT: Judge Walter's on his way now from Utrecht!
    He's making an inspection tour of courts
    And he'll be here to look at ours today.

ADAM: Today? You can't be serious!

LICHT: I am!
    He was in Holla village yesterday,
    Where he has duly carried out his mission.
    A peasant saw his horses ready harnessed,
    About to leave for Huisum right away.

ADAM: Today! That Judge from Utrecht coming here?
    A decent man, who knows what's good for him –
    Who hates these farcical inspections –
    Come all the way to Huisum just to plague us?

LICHT: He's come as far as Holla, so we're for it!
    You'd best watch out!

ADAM: What nonsense!

LICHT: It's a fact!

ADAM: Please! No more fairy tales! I mean it!

LICHT: The peasant saw him with his own two eyes!

ADAM: *Who* knows what some blear-eyed peasant saw?
 Those oafs can't tell the difference between
 A man's face and a bald head from the rear!
 Stick a three-cornered hat atop my cane,
 A cape above and riding boots below –
 They'd say it's anyone you care to name!

LICHT: Have it your own way! Go ahead and doubt
 Until the Judge walks in!

ADAM: Walks in? The Judge?
 Without a word of warning in advance?

LICHT: You're wrong, you know! It's not as though the last
 Judge – Juniper by name – were still about!
 It's now Judge Walter who inspects the courts.

ADAM: I don't care if it is! Just let me be.
 The man has surely sworn his oath of office
 So must observe, no less than we ourselves,
 The rules and edicts currently in force.

LICHT: Let me assure you that the Judge arrived
 Out of the blue in Holla yesterday,
 Inspected all the records and the funds,
 And then suspended magistrate and clerk,
 For unknown reasons, *ab officio.*

ADAM: The deuce he did! That peasant told you, did he?

LICHT: And more besides –

ADAM: Such as?

LICHT: You want to know?
 Today, at dawn, they went to fetch the justice
 Who'd been suspended under house arrest.
 Instead, they found his body in a barn,
 Strung from a beam and dangling aloft.

ADAM: What's that?

LICHT: By chance, assistance was at hand.
 They cut him down, massaged and watered him –
 Which brought him back to life, but only just.

ADAM: They brought him back?
LICHT: And now he's locked
   Inside his house securely, sworn and sealed;
   But he might just as well be dead already –
   He's lost his job as village magistrate.
ADAM: Ye gods! A slovenly rogue, I must admit,
   But still, at heart, a decent sort of chap.
   Easy enough to get along with...though,
   He certainly let things slide and no mistake!
   No wonder, if Judge Walter went to Holla,
   The poor wretch couldn't help but come unstuck!
LICHT: If he's the only one, the peasant said,
   It's just that Walter hasn't yet been here.
   But he'll arrive by midday without fail.
ADAM: Midday! If so, let friendship prove its worth!
   You know how two can function hand in glove?
   I know you'd like to be a magistrate –
   And you deserve it, no one more deserving!
   But not today: the time is not yet ripe.
   Just let that chalice pass you by for now!
LICHT: A magistrate? Me? What do you take me for?
ADAM: A connoisseur of highflown oratory,
   You've studied Cicero from end to end,
   Outshone them all, at school in Amsterdam.
   But hold ambition well in check today!
   You'll have no end of opportunities
   To demonstrate your prowess later on.
LICHT: Aren't we good friends? No need to talk like that!
ADAM: The great Demosthenes, himself, knew when
   To hold his tongue. You follow his example!
   I may not be the King of Macedonia
   But I too can be grateful in my way.
LICHT: No call to hint at jealousy, I tell you!
   When have I ever – ?
ADAM: Look, I too observe
   The noble Greek's example. Could I not,
   If so disposed, hold forth at length about
   Embezzled funds and interest pocketed?
   But who would want to spout such dreary stuff?

LICHT: Indeed!

ADAM: In that respect, I'm free from blame.
 The rest was just a bit of fun, that's all –
 A bedroom farce that shuns the light of day.

LICHT: I understand.

ADAM: No reason why a judge –
 Unless, of course, he's on the bench in court –
 Should always act as solemn as an owl.

LICHT: I quite agree!

ADAM: So come with me, my friend;
 The registry's a sight! We must clear up
 Those heaps of documents all strewn about –
 Like rubble from the ruined tower of Babel.

Scene 2

Enter a SERVANT and presently two maids, LISA and GRETA.

SERVANT: Good day, your honour! Greetings from
          Judge Walter!
 His lordship will be with you right away.

ADAM: God help us! Does that mean that he's already
 Done with Holla?

SERVANT: He's in Huisum now.

ADAM: Hi! Lisa! Greta!

LICHT: Steady, hold! Keep calm.

ADAM: What shall we do?

LICHT: Best send the Judge your thanks.

SERVANT: Tomorrow, we move on to Hussahe.

ADAM: What to do and what to leave?
 (*He makes a grab for his clothes.*
 Enter LISA.)

LISA: Here, sir!
 (*ADAM in confusion slips his arms into the trouser-legs.*)

LICHT: You're putting on your trousers? Are you mad?
 (*Enter GRETA.*)

GRETA: I'm here, your honour!

LICHT: Wear your robe, that's all.

ADAM: (*Looking round.*)
    Who? The Judge is here?
LICHT: No, that's the maid.
ADAM: My bands, cape, stock!
LISA: Your waistcoat first!
ADAM: What? Then, get my robe off, quick!
LICHT: (*To the SERVANT.*)
                           The Judge
    Will be most welcome here. Please tell him we'll
    Be ready to receive him in a moment.
ADAM: The deuce we will! You tell him Justice Adam
    Asks to be excused.
LICHT: Excused?
ADAM: Excused!
    Judge on his way, is he?
SERVANT: Still at the inn;
    He's waiting for the blacksmith to arrive.
    His coach broke down.
ADAM: Good! Give him my respects!
    The smith won't rush. Just tell the Judge I'm sorry:
    My neck and legs have practically been broken.
    See for yourself the awful state I'm in!
    The slightest shock affects me like a purge!
    Say that I'm ill!
LICHT: Have you quite lost your wits?
    His lordship's said to be a charming man.
    You want to –
ADAM: Blast it!
LICHT: What?
ADAM: The devil take me!
    I don't feel well – as though I'd drunk a powder!
LICHT: Keep on like that, you'll drive the man away!
ADAM: Greta – make haste, you idle bone-bag! Lisa!
LISA/GRETA: We're here! What's wrong?
ADAM: Be off with you, I say!
    Cheese, ham, butter, sausages and bottles –
    Run, fetch them from the record-office – quick!
    Not Greta! Lisa! You there, monkey-face!
    Stable-maid to record office, fly!

(*Exit LISA.*)

GRETA: Then tell us proper, so we'll understand!

ADAM: Shut up, you hussy! Go and fetch my wig!
   It's in the bookcase! Get a move on! Run!
   (*Exit GRETA.*)

LICHT: (*To the SERVANT.*)
   I trust his lordship suffered no mishap
   As he was coming here today from Holla?

SERVANT: Indeed, he did! Our carriage overturned.

ADAM: Plague on this foot! It's raw! Can't get my boots on!

LICHT: Heavens above! You say you overturned?
   But nothing worse –

SERVANT: Well, nothing serious:
   It's true, his lordship slightly sprained his hand.
   The axle broke.

ADAM: (*Aside.*)
                Wish it had been his neck!

LICHT: He sprained his hand! And did the blacksmith come?

SERVANT: Yes, for the axle.

LICHT: What?

ADAM: You mean, the doctor.

LICHT: What?

SERVANT: For the axle?

ADAM: No, you fool, the hand!

SERVANT: Good day, gentlemen! (*Aside.*) They're raving mad!
   (*Exit SERVANT.*)

LICHT: I meant the smith.

ADAM: You give yourself away.

LICHT: How so?

ADAM: You get embarrassed.

LICHT: How do I?
   (*Enter LISA.*)

ADAM: What's that you've got?

LISA: It's Braunschweig sausage, sir.

ADAM: Those are the documents for wards of court!

LICHT: *Me* embarrassed?

ADAM: Put those back at once!

LISA: The sausages?

ADAM: No, no! The wrapping paper!

LICHT: A slight misunderstanding!
(*Enter GRETA.*)
GRETA: Sorry, sir,
I couldn't find no wig, sir, in the bookcase.
ADAM: Why's that?
GRETA: Because you...
ADAM: Well?
GRETA: Last night, you came
Home at eleven...
ADAM: Yes?
GRETA: If you recall,
You didn't have no wig on...
ADAM: Didn't I?
GRETA: It's a fact. Young Lisa'll bear me out.
Your spare wig's still away, sir, being repaired.
ADAM: You say I –
LISA: Cross my heart, sir, Master Adam!
You were bald when you came home last night.
Beg pardon, sir, don't you remember saying
As how I was to wash your bleeding head?
ADAM: (*To LICHT.*)
The shameless wretch!
LISA: I swear it! Cross me heart!
ADAM: Be quiet, I say! All lies, so help me God!
LICHT: You've had the wound since yesterday?
ADAM: No, no! Today!
The wound today, the wig was yesterday.
I had it on my head, fresh powdered white,
And took it off when I came home, I swear,
Together with my hat – by oversight.
What she may think she washed, I've no idea!
Now, go to hell since that's where you belong –
Back to the registry.
(*Exit LISA.*)
                    You, Greta, go
And tell the sexton he must lend me his:
Tell him the cat gave birth in mine this morning;
It's underneath my bed, completely ruined.

LICHT: The cat? What's this? Are you –
ADAM: It's true, I swear!
   Five kittens, black-and-tan, and one that's white.
   I'll have to drown the black ones in the river.
   It can't be helped. You wouldn't care to take one?
LICHT: In the wig, you say?
ADAM: Good God, man – yes!
   I'd hung it on a chair beside my bed
   The way I do, retiring for the night.
   I must have knocked it in the dark. It fell –
LICHT: The cat then caught it in its jaws –
ADAM: Quite so!
LICHT: Dragged it under the bed and then gave birth.
ADAM: In its jaws? Why, no!
LICHT: How...?
ADAM: Damn the cat!
LICHT: It must have...Or did you – ?
ADAM: Its jaws? I think...
   I kicked it out this morning when I woke
   And saw the mess.
LICHT: I see.
ADAM: The filthy creatures!
   Couple and drop their young just anywhere.
GRETA: (*Giggling.*)
   Shall I be going?
ADAM: Yes, and my respects
   To Mistress Blackfrock – er, the sexton's wife –
   I'll send her back the wig in good condition
   Later today – you needn't talk to *him.*
   Is that quite clear?
GRETA: I'll fetch it right away.
   (*Exit GRETA.*)

Scene 3

ADAM: I've got a feeling that the day bodes ill.
LICHT: Why?
ADAM: Nothing's going right. I'm all at sea!
   Aren't we in court today?

LICHT: We are indeed.
    The plaintiffs are already queueing up.
ADAM: I had a dream in which a plaintiff seized me,
    And dragged me into court before the bench,
    Where I was also sitting as the judge;
    Myself I charged with being a knave and villain,
    Whom I then sentenced to be clapped in irons.
LICHT: Sentenced yourself?
ADAM: As I'm an honest man!
    Then the two 'me's' became as one and fled
    To shelter for the night among the pines.
LICHT: Do you suppose the dream – ?
ADAM: To hell with it!
    If not the dream, then some malicious sprite
    Is hard at work to thwart my every move!
LICHT: A childish fear! But best make sure that, while
    Judge Walter's present, justice you dispense
    To plaintiff and accused as law prescribes,
    Lest, in some other way, that dream of yours
    About the judge being judged, should come to pass.

Scene 4

Enter JUDGE WALTER.

WALTER: Good day, Judge Adam!
ADAM: Sir, I bid you welcome!
    Welcome, your lordship, welcome here in Huisum!
    Who, as God is just, would have expected –
    Out of the blue – a visit so auspicious?
    As late as eight o'clock, no dream of mine
    Dared hint at such good fortune in the offing!
WALTER: I know it's rather sudden but I must,
    Throughout this journey on our states' behalf,
    Be satisfied if my successive hosts
    Can bid me, as I leave, a warm farewell.
    As for my welcome, I can only say –
    Now that I'm here – I come with good intentions.
    The High Court in Utrecht's concerned to see

The standards of our rural justice raised.
These, it would seem, leave much to be desired
And all shortcomings will be sternly dealt with.
However, on this tour, my brief is mild:
I've simply come to see and not to punish.
If things, I find, are not quite all they should be,
I'll be content if they are bearable.

ADAM: An outlook so enlightened merits praise!
Here and there, your lordship will, no doubt,
Find righteous cause to blame some old tradition –
Though dating back as far as Charles the Fifth:
No end of ancient customs spring to mind.
The world grows wiser, as our proverb says –
And nowadays, everyone reads Puffendorff.
However, Huisum's but a tiny spot on earth,
Entitled only to its share – no more, nor less –
Of universal wisdom in the making.
Kindly illuminate our justice here in Huisum
And be assured, your lordship will no sooner
Have turned your back on us than Huisum's court
Will function to your fullest satisfaction.
But it would be a wonder were your lordship
To find things to your liking here and now:
Since we're still in the dark about your wishes.

WALTER: It's true, rules lack or rather, they're too many.
We'll doubtless have to sift them carefully.

ADAM: Big sieve we'll need! There's lots and lots of chaff!

WALTER: Is that your clerk there?

LICHT: I am Licht, the clerk,
And at your lordship's most respected service.
Nine years in office here, come Easter next.

ADAM: (*Brings a chair.*)
Be seated!

WALTER: Sooner stand!

ADAM: You've come from Holla?

WALTER: Two short miles away. How did you hear?

ADAM: How? Your lordship's servant –

LICHT: 'Twas a peasant
Just arrived from Holla told me so.

WALTER: A peasant?

ADAM: So it was.

WALTER: Well, yes – it's true,
   A painful incident occurred at Holla
   Which robbed me of that equitable temper
   That should sustain us on official duty.
   You've heard about what happened, I suppose?

ADAM: Can it be true, sir, that the magistrate,
   Sent to his quarters under house arrest,
   Surrendered to despair – the sorry fool –
   And hanged himself?

WALTER: Thus making matters worse.
   What first seemed due to chaos and confusion,
   Now looks more like embezzlement and fraud,
   Against which, as you know, the law's unsparing.
   How many funds have you?

ADAM: We've five in all.

WALTER: How – five? I'm misinformed. The chests are full?
   They told me there were only four –

ADAM: Beg pardon!
   There's the Rhine Flood Contribution Fund.

WALTER: A chest, you say, for Rhine Flood contributions?
   The Rhine is not in flood just now, so why
   Should contributions still be coming in? (*Pause.*)
   Isn't your court supposed to sit today?

ADAM: Is it...?

WALTER: Eh?

LICHT: Yes, first time this week.

WALTER: That crowd of people, then, I saw outside
   Waiting in your meadow, are they –

ADAM: They'd be –

LICHT: Plaintiffs gathered to address the court.

WALTER: Good! I'm glad to hear it. In that case,
   Be kind enough to let them now appear.
   I shall observe the conduct of the court
   And see how things are managed here in Huisum.
   We'll check the records and the cash in hand,
   After the present matter's been resolved.

ADAM: As you wish, your grace! Hi, Beadle! Beadle!

Scene 5

Enter GRETA.

GRETA: The sexton's wife salutes you, Justice Adam!
  Much as she'd like to lend the wig –
ADAM: She can't?
GRETA: She's sorry, but today is morning-sermon,
  So Sexton's wearing it himself; his other's
  Unusable, she says, and had to go
  To the wig-maker today to be repaired.
ADAM: Confound it!
GRETA: But as soon as Sexton's home,
  She says she'll send you his without delay.
ADAM: I do apologise, my lord –
WALTER: What's wrong?
ADAM: By sheer mischance – a cursed stroke of fate
  Has robbed me of two wigs, and now a third,
  Which I had hoped to borrow, can't be had!
  So I must sit bare-headed on the bench.
WALTER: Bare-headed!
ADAM: Yes, by heaven, much as I,
  Bereft of wig's support, cannot but fear
  For my judicial bearing and decorum.
  I'll have to try once more. There is a farm
  Whose tenant could perhaps...
WALTER: A farm, you say?
  Surely, there must be someone in the village?
ADAM: Not a soul!
WALTER: Perhaps the preacher could –
ADAM: The preacher?
WALTER: Or the school-master, perhaps?
ADAM: Got rid of both, your grace, on tithe-day last,
  For which I was in part responsible,
  So I cannot rely on help from either.
WALTER: Well, Justice Adam? What about your court?
  You'll sit here waiting for your hair to grow?
ADAM: I'd sooner try the farm, with your permission.
WALTER: How far away is it?

ADAM: A little matter
    Of half an hour, I'd say –
WALTER: What! Half an hour!
    Your session is already overdue!
    Get on! I want to be in Hussahe today!
ADAM: Why yes! We must get on –
WALTER: Powder your pate!
    How the devil did you lose those wigs?
    Do everything you can! I'm in a hurry!
ADAM: Disaster!
    (*Enter the BEADLE.*)
BEADLE: Beadle here!
ADAM: Will you partake
    Meanwhile of breakfast – Braunschweig sausage and
    A little glass of Danziger?
WALTER: No, thanks!
ADAM: No trouble!
WALTER: Thank you, no! We've breakfasted.
    Go ahead and use the time. I need a moment
    To make a few notes in my little book…
ADAM: Just as you wish, my lord! Come, Greta, come!
WALTER: You've hurt yourself quite badly, Justice Adam;
    Did you fall down?
ADAM: I took a mortal toss
    This morning early, getting out of bed –
    Entered the room as though it were my grave!
WALTER: I'm sorry. It will not, I trust, have further
    Consequences?
ADAM: That I doubt, my lord.
    Nor will it now delay my present duty.
    Will you excuse me?
WALTER: Go! Go!
ADAM: (*To BEADLE.*)
                   Call the plaintiffs!
    (*Exeunt ADAM, GRETA and BEADLE.*)

Scene 6

Enter MISTRESS MARTHA, EVE, VEIT and RUPERT TÜMPEL.
In the background, WALTER and LICHT.

MARTHA: You pitcher-vandals! Riff-raff, all of you!
    I'll make you pay!
VEIT: Mistress Martha, calm yourself!
    The case will be decided here in court.
MARTHA: Decided! Listen to him! Master Know-all!
    My pitcher's smashed! What more's to be decided?
    The pitcher's done for! Who can now undo it?
    Whatever they decide, my jug stays smashed –
    Decidedly! If that's the court's decision,
    I wouldn't give a pot-shard for the hearing!
VEIT: If you can prove your case in law, I swear
    That I'll replace it.
MARTHA: He'll replace my pitcher!
    If I can prove my case, then he'll replace it!
    Let him replace it, let him just but try –
    Replace it! Put it back upon the shelf!
    Replace, my foot! A limbless pitcher that
    Can't lie, or sit or stand! Replace, indeed!
VEIT: The woman's raving mad! Who could do more?
    If one of us, in fact, *did* break her pitcher,
    The damage will be paid for.
MARTHA: Damage paid for!
    My billy-goat, so help me, talks more sense!
    Do you suppose that justice is a potter?
    Even if all our ministers of state
    Conveyed these bits and pieces to the kiln,
    What could they do to resurrect my pitcher?
    Just compensate me for it? Compensate!
RUPERT: Leave her, father! Come with me! The dragon!
    It's not the broken pitcher that torments her:
    The match that she was planning's sprung a leak;
    And here, she hopes to patch it up by force!
    But I've made up my mind; I'll not be swayed.
    I'm damned if I'll agree to wed a trollop!

MARTHA: You fickle lout! What, me! Patch up the wedding?
    A wedding not worth patch-thread, from the start –
    Not even worth a single pitcher-shard!
    Why, if that wedding faced me still, aglitter –
    As yesterday my pitcher on its shelf –
    I'd pick it up with both my hands and smash it,
    With a resounding crash – upon his head!
    As if I'd try to patch the shards up here!
    Patch them, indeed!
EVE: Rupert!
RUPERT: Clear off!
EVE: Dear Rupert!
RUPERT: Out of my sight!
EVE: But dearest, I beseech you!
RUPERT: You slatternly – I'd sooner not say what.
EVE: Allow me just one word in private –
RUPERT: No!
EVE: But Rupert, now you're going to join the army,
    Who knows, once you have learnt to fire a musket,
    If I shall see you in this world again?
    You're going off to war, just think of that:
    You'd leave me with your heart so full of hate?
RUPERT: Hate? God forbid! Indeed, I don't want that.
    God grant you what prosperity he can spare!
    But were I to return from war unhurt,
    With body bulletproof as bronze, and live
    In Huisum till I'm eighty years of age,
    Still, with my dying breath, I'd call you 'slattern!'
    As you, yourself, will testify in court.
MARTHA: (*To EVE.*)
    Leave him! What did I tell you? Why allow him
    To go on insulting you? That Corporal's
    The man for you – the worthy Pegleg who
    Used his stick on soldiers – not that lout
    Whose own backside's about to feel the rod!
    Were you betrothed, wed, baby christened – all today,
    I wouldn't care were this my burial day –
    If I could first deflate that cockerel's comb,
    Swollen with pride at having smashed my pitcher!

EVE: Mother! Forget the pitcher! Let me try
 To find a craftsman skilled enough in town
 To fit the shards together to your liking.
 Or if I can't, then take my savings-box
 And go and buy yourself a brand new pitcher.
 For sake of just one broken earthern pot –
 Were it so old that Herod could have used it –
 Who'd think of making all this fuss and mischief?
MARTHA: You don't know what you're saying, Eve! Will you
 Next Sunday wear a bridle into church
 And there, remorsefully, do public penance?
 Your good name was invested in that pot
 And perished with it in the world's esteem,
 If not in God's eyes, or in yours and mine.
 Let judge and beadle be my journeymen –
 Their tools: the stocks, the lash – so sorely needed –
 The stake, at which these rabble should be burned,
 The only way to cauterise our honour –
 And, to this pitcher here, restore its glaze!

Scene 7

Enter ADAM in robes but without wig.

ADAM: (*Aside.*)
 It's little Eve, together with that Rupert –
 The beefy lout – and all the gang! Dear Lord,
 They cannot mean to make me try myself!
EVE: Mother dear, come home with me, I beg you!
 Let's both escape from this ill-fated room!
ADAM: Well, friend, what problem's brought them
          here today?
LICHT: How would I know! Some stupid trifling dispute!
 A pitcher has been broken, so I hear.
ADAM: A pitcher? Bless my soul! Who broke it, pray?
LICHT: Who broke it?
ADAM: Yes, dear friend. I'd like to know.
LICHT: Sit down, for heaven's sake, and you'll find out!

ADAM: (*Quietly.*)
   Eve, my dear!
EVE: (*Quietly.*)
        Be off!
ADAM: A word!
EVE: Not one!
ADAM: What's wrong?
EVE: I said: 'You've got to go!'
ADAM: But Eve, my dear! What's that supposed to mean?
EVE: You've got to go at once, I said. Leave me alone!
ADAM: (*To LICHT.*)
   Listen, my friend – I swear I can't go on!
   My damaged shin is playing merry hell!
   You hear the case! I'm going back to bed!
LICHT: To bed? You want me to – you must be mad!
ADAM: Damn and blast! I simply must hand over!
LICHT: Sheer lunacy! You've only just got up!
   Well, if you want, I can…You'd better ask him;
   His lordship may consent…But what's the trouble?
ADAM: (*To EVE again.*)
   Eve, my dear, I beg – by all that's holy –
   Tell me, what is it?
EVE: You'll hear soon enough.
ADAM: Is it that pitcher there your mother's holding,
   Of which I've –
EVE: Yes, it's just that broken pitcher.
ADAM: Nothing more?
EVE: No, nothing.
ADAM: You're quite sure?
EVE: Go, I said, just leave me here in peace!
ADAM: You watch that tongue of yours! I'm warning you!
EVE: You shameless wretch!
ADAM: This deposition bears
   The name, spelt out in Gothic, Rupert Tümpel.
   I've got it all here ready in my pocket.
   There, listen to it rustle! You can fetch it
   A year from now, if need be – that's a promise –
   And have your widow's weeds and bodice made,

When you get news that Rupert, in Batavia,
Has perished of – I know not what disease –
Yellow or scarlet fever – laziness?

WALTER: No private chat with either side, Judge Adam,
Before the case. Sit down and question them.

ADAM: What's he say? What did your grace command?

WALTER: What did I command? I told you clearly
Not to conduct equivocal discussion
With either side before the court's in session!
This is the place to exercise your office:
A public hearing is what I expect.

ADAM: (*Aside.*)
Damn! I can't make up my mind to face it!
I did hear something crash as I was leaving!

LICHT: (*Shaking ADAM.*)
Justice Adam, are you – ?

ADAM: No – I swear!
I hung it up most carefully,
I'm not that clumsy –

LICHT: What?

ADAM: What's that?

LICHT: I asked –

ADAM: You asked me –

LICHT: Whether you are deaf, I asked.
Did you not hear his lordship calling you?

ADAM: I thought I heard – who called?

LICHT: His lordship did.

ADAM: (*Aside.*)
Damn my eyes! We've got two cases here;
More than enough! What cannot bend must break.
At once! Now! Right away! What does your grace
Command? Should we begin proceedings now?

WALTER: You're strangely absent-minded. What's
                              the trouble?

ADAM: My lord, forgive me, but a guinea fowl,
Sold me by someone home from India,
Has caught the pip and needs to be force-fed.
Being such a fool in matters of this kind,

I just asked this young person for advice.
My hens, you know, are dear to me as children.
WALTER: Sit down, then call the plaintiff. Hear the plea –
And you, Clerk of the Court, record what's said!
ADAM: Is it your lordship's wish to have proceedings
Conducted formally or else as we
In Huisum normally conduct a hearing?
WALTER: In keeping with judicial regulations
As they're observed in Huisum – nothing more.
ADAM: That's fine. I know exactly what's required.
Ready, Clerk of the Court?
LICHT: I'm at your service!
ADAM: So, we may start! Let justice take its course!
Step forward, plaintiff.
MARTHA: Here I am, your honour.
ADAM: Who are you?
MARTHA: Who?
ADAM: You!
MARTHA: Who I –
ADAM: Who are you?!
Your name, address, your job et cetera.
MARTHA: Your honour must be joking?
ADAM: That, I'm not!
I'm representing justice, Mistress Martha,
And justice wants to know just who you are.
LICHT: (*Sotto voce.*)
Don't ask such questions...
MARTHA: Do you not
Peep in the window at me every Sunday,
When going to the farm?
WALTER: You know this woman?
ADAM: She lives close by, my lord. Just round the corner –
That's if you take the footpath through the hedge;
Caretaker's widow, she's a midwife now –
Otherwise, honest and of good repute.
WALTER: Judge Adam, if you know all that about her,
Clearly, such questions are superfluous.
Just let her name be entered in the record
And put beside it: 'Known to the court.'

ADAM: Of course. You do not like formalities...
  Just write down what his lordship has instructed.
WALTER: And now, inquire the subject of complaint.
ADAM: Should I –
WALTER: Yes, find out what it's all about!
ADAM: That's also known to be a pitcher –
WALTER: 'Also'?
ADAM: A pitcher. Just a pitcher. Write that down
  And put beside it: 'Known to the court.'
LICHT: Relying on my casual assumption,
  Mightn't your honour –
ADAM: Since I've told you, write it!
  A pitcher, Mistress Martha, is it not?
MARTHA: This pitcher here –
ADAM: You see!
MARTHA: It's smashed to bits!
ADAM: Pedantic quibbling!
LICHT: Your honour, please!
ADAM: Who broke it, then? No doubt that good-for-nothing?
MARTHA: Yes, him – that rascal over there!
ADAM: (*Aside.*)
                    That's all I need.
RUPERT: Your honour, that's not true!
ADAM: (*Aside.*)
                    Brace up, old Adam!
RUPERT: She's lying in her teeth –
ADAM: Be quiet, you oaf!
  You'll find yourself in irons soon enough!
  Put down 'a pitcher', Clerk, the way I told you
  Together with the name of him who smashed it.
  It won't take long to clear this matter up!
WALTER: Judge Adam, your procedure's much too violent!
ADAM: How so?
LICHT: Shouldn't you formally –
ADAM: Why, no!
  Your lordship doesn't like formality.
WALTER: If you, as village magistrate, don't know
  How evidence is gathered for a trial,
  Then this is not the time or place to teach you.

If that's your sole idea of justice, then
    You'd best resign. Your clerk, perhaps, knows better.
ADAM: Forgive me, but your lordship ordered me
    To act as we in Huisum do. I did.
WALTER: Would I –
ADAM: My word of honour!
WALTER: What I said
    Was: render justice as the laws prescribe;
    And, here in Huisum, I assumed the laws
    Were those in force elsewhere throughout the land.
ADAM: Then I must humbly beg your lordship's pardon!
    If you'll allow, we've statutes here in Huisum
    Peculiar to ourselves. Not written, true,
    But handed down to us by sound tradition.
    From this long-hallowed usage, I dare hope,
    I've not departed by one jot or tittle.
    But in this other mode of which you speak,
    Observed elsewhere, I'm also quite at home.
    You ask for proof? By all means! Just command!
    One way or t'other, I'll see justice done!
WALTER: You make a poor impression, Justice Adam.
    But never mind! Begin the case again.
ADAM: Of course, my lord! You shall be satisfied.
    Mistress Martha Rull, present your plea!
MARTHA: My plea, as you're aware, concerns this pitcher.
    But first, before I give the court the details
    Of what befell my pitcher, let me tell you
    What it was like before.
ADAM: You're free to speak.
MARTHA: You see this pitcher, here, your honours? Look!
    You see my pitcher?
ADAM: Oh yes, we can see it!
MARTHA: Oh no, you can't! All you can see are shards:
    The loveliest of pitchers smashed to bits!
    Here in this hole, where nothing's to be seen,
    The provinces of all the Netherlands
    Were being surrendered to the King of Spain.
    Here, in full robes, stood Emperor Charles the Fifth –

Of whom you now see nothing but his legs.
Here knelt King Philip to receive the crown:
He's now inside the pot, all but his bottom –
And even that received a blow as well.
There, deeply moved, his aunts dried one another's
Tears – the Queens of France and Hungary;
Now only one queen's hand still holds a hanky,
Whose owner might be weeping for herself.
Among the courtiers, Philibert still rests
Upon his sword; the Emperor caught the brunt,
Yet now, he, too, is bound to fall, along
With that scoundrel, Maximilian!
The swords below have also been struck off.
Here, in the middle in his holy hat,
The Archbishop of Arras could be seen;
The Devil did for him – yes, good and proper!
Only his shadow left, across the pavement.
And in the background, there were bodyguards,
With halberds, tightly packed, and pikes as well.
Here, houses on the market square of Brussels –
With, here, a burgher, peering from his window –
Though goodness knows what's left for him to see!
ADAM: Spare us the shattered treaty, Mistress Martha,
Unless essential to the case in hand.
The hole concerns us, not the provinces
Being handed over on its former surface.
MARTHA: Beg pardon! But the beauty of the pitcher
Is relevant. 'Twas seized by Childerich,
The tinker, when the Prince of Orange
With his Sea-Beggars, took the town of Briel.
A Spaniard had just raised it, full of wine,
And set it to his lips when Childerich
Attacked him from behind, the pitcher grasped,
And, having drained it, went upon his way.
ADAM: Sea-Beggar worth his salt!
MARTHA: Grave-digger Feargod –
No great drinker – then inherited
The jug, used it but thrice, the sobersides,

And took great care to mix his wine with water.
First time he drank – already in his sixties –
Was when he wed a young wife. Three years later,
He drank again, when he became a father;
Then, when she'd borne him fifteen children more,
He took his third drink as the lady died.

ADAM: Is that a fact? What happened next?

MARTHA: Zachaeus,
Tailor of Tirlemont, obtained the pitcher;
'Twas he himself told my late husband what
I've now the honour to inform the court.
It happened when the French were pillaging:
He threw this pitcher with his goods and chattels
Clean through the window, then he jumped himself,
Breaking his neck, the clumsy idiot.
The earthern pitcher, though – this pot of clay –
Fell on its feet and somehow stayed intact.

ADAM: Get to the point, the point, good Mistress Martha!

MARTHA: Next, in the holocaust of 'sixty-six,
My husband had it – heaven rest his soul!

ADAM: For God's sake, woman! Is there more to come?

MARTHA: If I am not to have my say, Judge Adam,
No point my being here; I'll go at once
And find a court prepared to hear me out.

WALTER: Speak freely by all means, but not of things
Completely unrelated to your case.
How much the pitcher meant to you, we know:
Enough, that is, for us to reach a judgement.

MARTHA: How much you need to know to reach a judgement,
I've no idea and I shall not inquire.
What I know *is*: if I'm to lay a charge,
I must be free to tell you what about.

WALTER: Well, then – to round things off – what next befell
The pitcher in the fire of 'sixty-six?
That's what we want to hear – the pitcher's fate!
What was it happened to the jug?

MARTHA: What happened?
Why, nothing happened to the jug, your lordships!
Nothing, in *anno domini* 'sixty-six.

The jug survived the fire, amid the flames,
And I retrieved it, perfect, from the ashes.
Beautifully glazed it was, the morning after –
Bright as the day it left the potter's kiln.

WALTER: Very well, then. Now we know the jug –
What happened to it and what didn't happen.
What else is there?

MARTHA: Now, see my pitcher's state!
In bits, yet still worth more than one undamaged –
Fit for the fairest lips; 'twould not have shamed
Those of the highest lady in the land.
This pitcher, I inform your honours both,
Was shattered by that ruffian over there!

ADAM: Who by?

MARTHA: By him! That Rupert!

RUPERT: It's a lie,
Your honour!

ADAM: Be silent, you! Until you're asked a question!
Your turn to speak will come today as well.
You've made a note of that, I hope?

LICHT: I have!

ADAM: Then tell us how it happened, Mistress Martha.

MARTHA: 'Twas yesterday, eleven o'clock –

ADAM: What time?

MARTHA: Eleven!

ADAM: Morning?

MARTHA: No, beg pardon, evening!
Just as I made to douse my bedside lamp,
I got a fright. I heard men's voices raised
In sudden angry tumult in the room
My daughter sleeps in, far away from mine.
I thought the house was being broken into.
Down the stairs I raced, only to find
Her chamber door forced open and my ears,
Assaulted by a torrent of abuse!
Then, as I shed light upon the threshold,
What do I see, your honours, what indeed?
My shattered pitcher lying on the floor –

The shards in every corner of the room;
Wringing her hands, my daughter – and that lout,
Stood in the middle, raging like a demon!

ADAM: Great heaven!

MARTHA: What?

ADAM: So, Mistress Martha?

MARTHA: Yes!

Completely overcome by righteous fury,
I felt as though I'd grown ten extra arms –
Each one as fierce and strong as any vulture.
I tackled him at once, demanding what
He meant by breaking in so late at night
And smashing all my pitchers in his rage.
The scoundrel's answer you would never guess,
The shameless rogue! That villain over there!
I'll have him broken on the wheel, I will,
Or never more sleep soundly in my bed!
He said that someone else had knocked it off
The shelf! I ask your honours – someone else! –
Who'd managed to escape ahead of him;
And then he called my daughter filthy names.

ADAM: Sheer poppycock! What then?

MARTHA: Well, at his words,
I gave my girl a searching look. She stood
There, like a corpse, and I said: 'Eve!'
While she sat down. I asked: 'Was there another?'
'Mary and Joseph!' she exclaimed, 'What next!
How could you think that, mother?' 'Tell me, then –
Who was it?' I demanded. 'Who but he?
Who else could it possibly have been?'
And then she swore, indeed, that it was he!

EVE: What did I swear to you? What did I swear?
I never swore a thing!

MARTHA: Eve!

EVE: No! You're lying!

RUPERT: You heard her?

ADAM: Damn your insolence! Shut up!
Or must I stop your blether with my fist?
We'll hear you later on. Not now!

MARTHA: You say you didn't –

EVE: No, you made that up!
    It grieves me deeply, mother – that it does –
    To be obliged to say so publicly:
    The fact is, I swore nothing! Not a thing!

ADAM: Stop squabbling, children!

LICHT: This is all most odd!

MARTHA: But did you not assure me, Eve, 'twas so –
    Appealing both to Joseph and to Mary?

ADAM: Come, Mistress Martha, what are you playing at?
    You're frightening the poor child half to death!
    Let the girl think it over and recall
    Precisely what it was that came to pass;
    Exactly what transpired, I say – and what –
    Should she speak out of turn – may yet transpire!
    Tell us today what happened yesterday,
    No matter what she swore or didn't swear,
    And please leave Joseph and Mary out of this.

WALTER: No, Justice Adam, no! Whoever heard
    Of giving such equivocal instruction!

MARTHA: If she can look me in the face and calmly say,
    The shameless hussy, that it wasn't him –
    Not Rupert, but another – for my part,
    She can go...well, I'd sooner not say what!
    But this I can assure you, Justice Adam –
    Even if I am not to say she swore –
    She *said* it yesterday! That much, I swear –
    And I appeal to Joseph and to Mary.

ADAM: I think the girl has something else –

WALTER: Judge Adam!

ADAM: Yes, your grace? (*To EVE.*) Is that not so, dear child?

MARTHA: Out with it, wench! Wasn't that what you said?
    Wasn't that what you told me yesterday?

EVE: Who denies I said it?

ADAM: You, yourself!

RUPERT: The trollop!

ADAM: Write that down!

VEIT: Fie! Shame on her!

WALTER: In view of your behaviour, Justice Adam,
    I don't know what to think! If you yourself
    Had smashed the pitcher, you could hardly have
    Done more to shift the blame to that young man.
    Clerk, you'll record, I trust, only the girl's
    Admission of her statement! Not the fact.
    Is she supposed to testify again?
ADAM: Bless me, if not – then I can only say
    One's easily mistaken in these matters!
    Whom should I then be calling? The accused?
    I'm always glad to learn a useful lesson!
WALTER: Impartiality! Yes! The accused!
    Question him and get it over with!
    This is the last case you will ever try!
ADAM: The last? Yes, the accused, of course!
    What can I have been thinking of, your grace?
    Confound that guinea fowl and blast its pip!
    Why couldn't the bird have croaked in India?
    That paste-ball's like a millstone on my mind!
WALTER: What's like a millstone?
ADAM: It's this ball of paste,
    Begging your pardon, I must give the fowl;
    Unless that carrion's made to take its pill,
    Upon my word, I don't know what will happen.
WALTER: For pity's sake! Get on and do your duty!
ADAM: Step forward, the accused!
RUPERT: I'm here, your honour!
    Rupert of Huisum, son of Veit the builder.
ADAM: Accused, you've heard the charge that
                             Mistress Martha
    Has laid against you here in court today?
RUPERT: Yes, your honour, that I did!
ADAM: You venture
    To dispute the accusation, eh?
    Will you confess, or like some godless creature,
    Face the court and still deny your guilt?
RUPERT: You ask, your honour, whether I deny it?
    With your permission, I would like to say
    That not a single word she spoke was true.

ADAM: Indeed? You think that you can prove it, do you?

RUPERT: Oh, yes!

ADAM: Good Mistress Martha, patience, please!
    Don't get excited. We'll see, by and by!

WALTER: What's Mistress Martha got to do with you?

ADAM: With me, your lordship? Shouldn't I, as a Christian –

WALTER: Report the words of the accused in answer!
    Clerk of the Court, can you conduct a hearing?

ADAM: What an idea!

LICHT: Can I? Well – if your grace –

WALTER: What's he gaping at? What's his reply?
    Why is the ass behaving like an ox?
    What have you to say?

RUPERT: What should I say?

WALTER: Tell us – in your *own* words – what took place.

RUPERT: I would, if he would only let me speak!

WALTER: He's right, Judge Adam, this is past enduring.

RUPERT: Round ten o'clock at night, it must have been –
    Though, for a night in January, 'twas warm
    As May – when I said to my father: 'Father,
    I think I'll go and have a word with Eve.'
    For you should know, I meant to marry her.
    Young Eve's a strapping wench. At harvest time,
    I'd seen the way she worked, you'd not believe:
    She tossed the hay as though 'twere second nature.
    So I said: 'Will you?' and at first, she said:
    'Don't talk so silly!' Then she says: 'Why, yes!'

ADAM: Stick to the point! No need for 'talk so silly'!
    You asked her if she would and she said 'yes'.

RUPERT: Without a word of lie!

WALTER: Go on!

RUPERT: So then,
    I asked my father, had he heard me? Could I go?
    We talked a little longer at the window
    And he said: 'Run along! You're staying out?'
    'Why yes,' says I, 'I promised I would go.'
    'Then go,' says he. 'Be back here by eleven!'

ADAM: You cackle on and on – it's never-ending!
    Is there much more?

RUPERT: I said to myself, I said:
'That's good enough.' So I put on my cap
And off I went. I meant to cross the ford,
But, river being in flood, walked through the village.
Says I to myself: 'That's damn bad luck because
The garden gate at Martha's will be shut.
Eve only leaves it open until ten.
If I'm not there by ten, means I can't come.'
ADAM: Nice goings-on, I must say!
WALTER: Yes, what then?
RUPERT: Well, as I was approaching through the lime trees
Near Martha's place – they make a vault above,
As dark as our cathedral in Utrecht –
I heard the squeak of hinges in the distance.
'Look sharp, Eve's still about,' I told myself,
And sent my eyes to see from whence my ears
Had brought me such a welcome piece of news.
But back they came with nothing and I cursed
Their blindness and dispatched them yet again
To take a closer look, then called them worthless
Slanderers, alarmists and tale-bearers –
And sent them off a third time, thinking that
They, having done their duty, would resent
Being torn a third time from their sockets
In order to perform another errand:
Yes, it was Eve; I knew her by her kerchief –
And someone else was with her –
ADAM: Someone else? And who might that be, know-all?
RUPERT: Who? You ask me that, your honour?
ADAM: Well?
No names, no pack-drill, as the saying goes.
WALTER: Get on with it! Proceed with your account!
Why interrupt his story, Justice Adam?
RUPERT: I couldn't swear the truth of it on oath:
Pitch-black it was; by night all cats are grey...
But you should know, I think, the village cobbler –
Lebrecht, not long out of uniform –
Has had his eye on this same Eve of mine.

I told her, autumn last: 'Just you watch out:
I've seen that villain hanging round your house.
You tell him you've got other fish to fry,
Or, sure as eggs, I'll throw him out myself!'
She said: 'You're teasing me! You tell him straight:
That's neither here nor there, nor fish nor fowl!'
So I went round and knocked the rascal down.
ADAM: You did? He's called Lebrecht?
RUPERT: He is.
ADAM: That's good!
Now that we have a name, we shan't be long!
You've put it in the record, have you, Clerk?
LICHT: I have, your honour! All the rest as well.
ADAM: Then, Rupert, you may carry on!
RUPERT: Since I
Had come upon the couple at eleven –
While I had always used to leave by ten –
I saw the way things were! Says I: 'My lad,
Rupert, hold hard, you're only just in time:
You haven't grown a pair of antlers yet!
Best feel your forehead, though, to make quite sure
There's nothing horn-like just about to sprout!'
So I stole softly through the garden gate
And hid myself behind a clump of yew,
Where I could hear them whispering and joking –
A scuffling, sir, a bit of slap an' tickle;
My word, I thought I'd –
EVE: You're a wicked man!
How could you act so shamefully?
MARTHA: You villain!
Wait till I get you on your own, I'll show you
What I'm made of! Little do you know
Where I've got muscles! But you'll soon find out!
RUPERT: A quarter of an hour or so it lasted:
'What's this?' I thought. 'Could be their wedding-day!'
I hadn't thought it through, when – whoosh! Indoors
They rushed – not waiting for the pastor.
EVE: Mother, I'll tell the truth, whatever happens!

ADAM: You, miss, hold your tongue! Take my advice!
    Or lightning strike you, babbling out of turn!
    Just wait until I call on you to speak.
WALTER: All this sounds most peculiar!
RUPERT: Then, your honour,
    I was dumbfounded by a rush of blood.
    I fought for breath; my waistcoat-button burst!
    I ripped the garment off – to get some air!
    Then I went pounding after them, like thunder,
    And, finding that the trollop's room was locked,
    I charged the door and broke it down by force!
ADAM: You hooligan!
RUPERT: Then, as the door collapsed,
    The pitcher, on its shelf, crashed to the floor,
    And – licketysplit – a man leapt out the window!
    I can see his coat-tails flapping now.
ADAM: Lebrecht, was it?
RUPERT: Who but he, your honour?
    The girl stood up; I elbowed her aside
    And hurried to the window, there to find
    The man still hanging from the trellis which
    Supports the vine that reaches to the roof.
    Clutching the door-latch still – the one I seized
    When I burst in – I hit him with it, sir:
    A pound of iron, smack across his pate,
    As luck would have it, just within my reach!
ADAM: A latch, was it?
RUPERT: What?
ADAM: Was it –
RUPERT: Yes, the door-latch.
ADAM: That's why –
RUPERT: I s'pose you thought it was a sword?
ADAM: A sword? Why should I think –
RUPERT: A sword!
LICHT: Come, now!
    It's easy to mishear a word. A latch
    Is not so very different from a sword.
ADAM: I thought –
RUPERT: God's teeth! You thought it was the handle?

ADAM: The handle!

RUPERT: No, your honour, that it wasn't.
   It was the latch's other end, for sure!

LICHT: Ah! I see!

ADAM: The latch's other end!

RUPERT: I must admit, there was a chunk of lead,
   Fixed to the latch's handle, like a sword hilt.

ADAM: Yes, like a hilt –

LICHT: Good – like a sword hilt, then.
   It must have been some kind of fiendish weapon:
   I thought as much, your honour, all along.

WALTER: Come, gentlemen – the point! Must I remind you?

ADAM: All that's of no importance, Clerk!

                        (*To RUPERT.*) Go on!

RUPERT: He fell and I was just about to turn,
   When I could see him moving in the dark.
   'You're still alive,' I thought, so up I climbed
   On to the windowsill to finish him,
   But, just as I was ready, set to jump,
   I got a shower of sand-grains in the face –
   And him below, night, world and windowsill
   On which – so help me – I was balancing,
   The whole damn lot just vanished, out of sight –
   Like when a hailstorm hits you in the eyes.

ADAM: Good gracious! Who did that?

RUPERT: Who? Why, 'twas Lebrecht.

ADAM: The knave!

RUPERT: A knave, indeed! If he it was...

ADAM: Who else?

RUPERT: 'Twas like being blasted off a mountain-
   Ledge, by swirling sleet, as down I crashed
   Into the room, from windowsill to floor!
   I thought I couldn't help but split the boards!
   Yet neither neck nor shoulders did I break,
   Or even hips – nor anything at all!
   The villain, though, escaped me while I sat
   And tried to rub the sand-grains from my eyes.
   Eve came across and shouted: 'God preserve us!'

And: 'Rupert, what's the matter?' I let fly.
As well I couldn't see what I was kicking!
ADAM: No doubt the sand to blame?
RUPERT: Yes sir, the sand.
ADAM: By God! His aim was good!
RUPERT: Then, fighting mad,
I stood up, but I thought, why shame my fists?
So I abused her, called her 'filthy slut!'
And reckoned that would serve her well enough.
But I could hardly speak for tears, your honour.
Then in comes Mistress Martha, lifts her lamp,
And there's Eve, shuddering fit to break your heart –
She, who always looked so brave and handsome;
'Blindness,' I told myself, 'can be a mercy' –
I'd happily have given both my eyes
For anyone to play a game of marbles.
EVE: Oh, what a scurvy rascal!
ADAM: Silence, you!
RUPERT: The rest you know, sir.
ADAM: What do you mean, the rest?
RUPERT: Well, in came Mistress Martha, breathing fire,
Then neighbour Ralf and neighbour Hinz, as well;
Aunt Suzy and Aunt Lisa came in, too –
Grooms and maids and dogs and cats arrived:
A right old circus! Mistress Martha asked
Her daughter who it was had smashed the pitcher.
And she said, as you've heard, that it was me.
Nor was she altogether wrong at that:
I smashed the jug *she* carried to the well –
The cobbler's got a broken head to prove it.
ADAM: Mistress Martha, what have you to say?
You may speak!
MARTHA: About that speech of his,
I'd say, your grace, it sneaked in like a ferret
To strangle truth, as though a clucking hen!
Right-minded folk should all pick up their cudgels
And beat to death this vermin in the night!
ADAM: You'll have to furnish us with proof, you know.

MARTHA: I'll gladly do so. Here's my witness: speak!
ADAM: Your daughter, Mistress Martha? No!
WALTER: Why not?
ADAM: She can't bear witness, for the lawbook says –
    Titulo quarto, your grace – or is it *quinto*? –
    In cases where a pitcher or the like
    Has been destroyed by some young jackanapes,
    No daughter may bear witness for her mother.
WALTER: In your mind, Justice Adam, fact and fiction
    Are mixed as thoroughly as baker's dough!
    You serve me some of each with every slice.
    She isn't bearing witness – merely stating.
    If and for whom she will or can bear witness
    Depends upon the statement she will make.
ADAM: She's stating…Good! I see: *Titulo sexto.*
    Whatever she states, though, cannot be believed.
WALTER: Step forward, daughter!
ADAM: Lisa, hey there! Sorry –
    My tongue feels very dry – or, Greta! Please!

Scene 8

Enter GRETA.

ADAM: A glass of water!
GRETA: Right away!
ADAM: Your lordship?
WALTER: No, thanks!
ADAM: A drop of wine? German or French?
    (*WALTER bows but declines; GRETA brings water and then
    exits.*)

Scene 9

ADAM: If I may venture to observe, your grace,
    A reconciliation might be tried.
WALTER: Reconciliation? What d'you mean?
    With reasonable people – yes, perhaps.
    But what you'd base it on in such a case,
    Where matters are completely unresolved,

I'd be intrigued to hear from you, Judge Adam.
Kindly explain how you would set about it?
Have you already reached your verdict?

ADAM: Well,
Were I – since law has left me in the lurch –
To seek assistance from philosophy,
Then I'd say Lebrecht –

WALTER: Who?

ADAM: If not, then Rupert –

WALTER: Who?

ADAM: Or Lebrecht – was the one who smashed it.

WALTER: Which of them was it, then – Rupert or Lebrecht?
I see you're groping blindly like a hand
Searching for something in a sack of peas.

ADAM: Beg pardon?

WALTER: That's enough!

ADAM: It's as you will!
I'd personally be more than satisfied
If it turned out that they were both to blame.

WALTER: You'll learn the truth; keep asking –

ADAM: That I will.
But I'll be damned, if ever it comes out!
You've got the record ready, have you, Clerk?

LICHT: Complete.

ADAM: That's good.

LICHT: I'll start a fresh page now:
Can't wait to see what it will have to show.

ADAM: A fresh page? Excellent.

WALTER: (*To EVE.*)
                          Come, child. Speak up!

ADAM: Speak, young lady, speak! Come, little Eve,
Tell God, my dear child, I implore you, tell
God and the world a particle of truth!
Imagine you're before God's judgement seat.
You must take care not to confuse your judge
With false disclaimers and with idle blether
Unrelated to the case. Now, you're no fool.
A judge remains a judge, as well you know:

Today, *one* needs him; next day, it's another!
If you say 'twas Lebrecht – well and good!
Or, if you say 'twas Rupert – also good!
One way or t'other, I'm no simpleton,
And all will be resolved as you would wish.
But, just start prattling about another –
A third man or the like, start naming names,
Then, you watch out, my child! I'll say no more.
No one in Huisum would believe you, Eve –
Nor anyone in all the Netherlands.
Blank walls, as you're aware, can't testify.
Besides, he would defend himself with ease.
As for your Rupert, there, a pox on him!

WALTER: If you would just give over making speeches!
Such balderdash, with neither rhyme nor reason!

ADAM: Your lordship doesn't follow me?

WALTER: Get on with it!
You've been pontificating far too long!

ADAM: I grant you I've not studied much, your grace.
If men from Utrecht cannot understand me,
That's not to say that local folk cannot;
I'll bet *she* knows exactly what I mean.

MARTHA: What's the matter, girl? Come – out with it!

EVE: My dearest mother!

MARTHA: You – ! I'm warning you!

RUPERT: Clear speaking's not so easy, Mistress Martha,
When someone's got her conscience in her mouth!

ADAM: You hold your tongue, you cheeky rogue!

MARTHA: Who was it?

EVE: Jesus!

MARTHA: That blockhead! That disgraceful lout!
Treating the girl as though she were a whore!
Jesus, was it?

ADAM: Mistress Martha – reason!
What a thing to say! Just let her be!
Scaring the child with words like whore and blockhead
Will get us nowhere. She'll recall, you'll see.

RUPERT: Recall is right!

ADAM: I said shut up, you bumpkin!

RUPERT: The cobbler, doubtless, she will call to mind!
ADAM: That demon! Where's the beadle! Hey, Hanfriede!
RUPERT: Don't want to speak, sir, but I'd let it rest;
    It won't be long before she names the man.
MARTHA: Listen! Don't try to make a fool of me!
    I've lived my nine-and-forty years with honour
    And hope to be alive when I am fifty.
    My birthday is the third of February.
    Today's the first. So hurry up! Who was it?
ADAM: I'm with you, Mistress Martha Rull! Well said!
MARTHA: Dad said when he was dying: 'Listen, Martha!
    Make sure you find the girl a decent husband;
    And should she ever prove to be a strumpet,
    You give the grave-digger a tip, d'ye hear?
    So's I can rest again upon my back –
    For you can bet your life, I shall have turned.'
ADAM: Well, that makes sense!
MARTHA: Now, Eve, if you still honour
    Father and Mother, as the fourth commandment
    Bids you, tell us whether it was the cobbler
    Or someone else. Your bridegroom it was not.
RUPERT: I'm sorry for her. Please forget the pitcher!
    I'll take it to Utrecht myself. A jug like that –
    Indeed, I wish it *had* been me who smashed it!
EVE: You miserable coward! Shame on you
    For not admitting that you broke the pitcher!
    And, Rupert, shame again for lacking faith
    In my fidelity and good behaviour!
    Did I not give my hand and answer 'yes',
    The day you asked if I would marry you?
    You think yourself less worthy than the cobbler?
    Even if you had spied me through the keyhole,
    Drinking with Lebrecht from that very pitcher,
    You should have thought: 'My Eve's a decent girl;
    The explanation's bound to do her credit,
    If not in this life, surely in the next:
    The day will come when we shall rise again!'
RUPERT: By heaven, that's too long for me to wait.
    All I can say is – seeing is believing!

EVE: Let us suppose, in fact, that it was Lebrecht:
    Given that I'd have sooner died for ever
    Than not have trusted you above all others –
    Why, then, in front of neighbours, groom and maids –
    Assuming I had reason to conceal it,
    Why, Rupert, why – counting on your support –
    Should I then not have said that it was you?
    Why should I not? Why should I not have said it?
RUPERT: By all means say it, girl; I won't object –
    To save you being paraded in disgrace.
EVE: You're horrible! What an ungrateful wretch!
    'Twould serve you right, were I to say the word
    That would spare *me* the torment of the bridle –
    But bring about your final ruination.
WALTER: Well – what word is that? Don't hold us up!
    The fact is, then, it wasn't Rupert?
EVE: No, your grace, since he himself agrees
    And I concealed it only for his sake:
    No! Rupert did not smash my mother's pitcher:
    What he himself denies, you may believe.
MARTHA: Eve! Not Rupert!?
EVE: No, not Rupert, mother!
    And if I said so yesterday, I lied!
MARTHA: I'll beat you black and blue, my girl!
    (*MARTHA lays down the pitcher.*)
EVE: Do what you will!
WALTER: (*Threateningly.*)
                Now, Mistress Martha!
ADAM: Beadle!
    Throw her out of court, the scheming hag!
    Why *must* it have been Rupert broke the pitcher?
    Was she there, watching them, by candlelight?
    It seems to me the girl herself must know:
    But if it wasn't Lebrecht, I'll be damned!
MARTHA: Then was it Lebrecht? Was it Lebrecht, Eve?
ADAM: Speak up, Eve dearest! Lebrecht, was it not?
EVE: You shameless villain! You – you scurvy knave!
    How can you say that it was Lebrecht?

WALTER: Miss!
    How dare you use such language? That's no way
    To treat a magistrate with due respect!
EVE: Respect, indeed! The magistrate, himself,
    Should face the court – a miserable sinner!
    Only too well he knows the one to blame!
    (*Turning to ADAM.*)
    Did you not yesterday send Lebrecht off
    To Utrecht, armed with a certificate,
    To show the board recruiting for the army?
    How can you dare to say that it was Lebrecht,
    Knowing that Lebrecht wasn't even here?
ADAM: Who else could it have been, for heaven's sake?
    Not Rupert, and not Lebrecht? Watch your step!
RUPERT: Allow me to inform you, Justice Adam,
    In this respect, the maid may not be lying.
    I myself met Lebrecht yestermorn,
    Bound for Utrecht, he was, round eight o'clock.
    Unless he cadged a lift in someone's cart –
    Bow-legged as he is – the fellow couldn't
    Have been back home by ten o'clock at night.
    So it may well have been some other man.
ADAM: Bow-legged? Rubbish! Blockhead! Let me tell you,
    He rides old shanks's mare as well as any!
    May I be legless, if a fair-sized sheepdog
    Wouldn't have to trot to match his pace!
WALTER: Tell us the rest.
ADAM: Begging your grace's pardon,
    I don't think she can help your lordship further.
WALTER: Not help? Not help me further? Pray, why not?
ADAM: A silly child – you've seen – good girl, but silly,
    Still very young, not yet confirmed, turns scarlet
    At sight of an approaching beard. Her kind
    May suffer untold horrors in the dark;
    Come daylight, they'll deny it to a judge.
WALTER: You're most considerate, aren't you, Justice Adam?
    So mild in all pertaining to this maid…
ADAM: To tell the truth, your lordship, it's like this:
    Her father was a special friend of mine.

And if your grace feels bountiful today,
May we not do what simple duty bids us,
And let his daughter leave the court at once?
WALTER: I'm conscious of a great desire, Judge Adam,
To plumb this strange occurrence to its depths.
Be brave, my child! Who was it broke the pitcher?
No one you stand before in court today
Would grudge forgiveness for a single lapse.
EVE: Why then, my dear, esteemed and gracious sir,
Allow me to recount what happened next.
But please don't take my reticence amiss.
It is the heaven's wondrous ordinance
That keeps me still from telling all I know.
I will confirm, by oath if you so wish,
Before the holy altar, sir, that Rupert
Was not the one who struck my mother's jug.
However, yesterday's occurrence – that apart –
Was my affair and mother can't demand
The cloth entire, for sake of just one thread,
Which – hers, and hers alone – runs through the weave.
I cannot here disclose who broke the jug;
For that would mean revealing secrets not
My own and unconnected with the pitcher.
Sooner or later I shall tell her all,
But this tribunal, sir, is not the place
Where she has any right to question me.
ADAM: No right whatever! On my word of honour!
She knows the limits of our competence.
Were she to swear an oath before this court,
Her mother's case would then collapse at once:
And there'd be nothing left to talk about.
WALTER: Mistress Martha, what say you to that?
MARTHA: If I can make no adequate response,
I ask you to believe me, noble sir:
The shock's completely paralysed my tongue.
There have been instances of souls depraved
Who, seeking to retain the world's esteem,
Have ventured perjury before a judge;

But who, sir, ever heard of anyone
Forswear herself upon the holy altar
In order to be pilloried and whipped?
If there were grounds for thinking anyone,
Save Rupert, could have slipped into her room –
If that were even possible, your grace –
Believe me, I would tarry here no longer.
I'd turn her out at once, sir, bag and baggage!
Be off, my child! I'd say, the world is vast;
There, you can live rent-free and your long hair
Will do to hang yourself when wisdom dawns.

WALTER: Hush, Mistress Martha, hush!

MARTHA: However, since
I can prove nothing here without her help –
Which service she's refused me – and convinced
That Rupert and no other smashed my pitcher,
This wish to swear my case away by oath
Has roused in me another dark suspicion:
Last night may have a second crime to hide,
Besides the desecration of my pitcher.
You should know, your grace, that Rupert there
Has been called up and in a few more days
Will swear his oath of loyalty in Utrecht.
Young men, thus summoned, frequently desert.
Assuming that last night he might have said:
'What do you think, Eve? Come, the world's before us.
You've got the keys to all the chests and boxes,'
She would doubtless have resisted him.
And so, since then it was that I disturbed them,
There could have come to pass what you've been told:
He, acting in revenge; she, still for love.

RUPERT: You carrion crow! How dare you say such things?
The keys to chests!

WALTER: Be quiet!

EVE: Him desert!

WALTER: Keep to the point! The pitcher's what concerns us.
Produce some proof – some proof that Rupert broke it!

MARTHA: Certainly, your grace! I'll prove it here
And then I shall investigate at home.

I shall produce a tongue to speak for me –
And counter every word that Rupert spoke;
Indeed, I would have brought that tongue to court
With me today, if I had had an inkling
That Eve's would fail to lend me its support!
But if you'll summon Mistress Bridget now –
She's Rupert's aunt – she'll do me just as well
For she'll contend the central point at issue.
At half past ten, she found him in the garden –
Note well: before the pitcher was destroyed –
She came upon him, arguing with Eve.
How far the testimony she will give
Explodes the fairy-tale that Rupert spun,
I'll leave it to yourselves, my lords, to judge.

RUPERT: Who found me?

VEIT: Sister Bridie?

RUPERT: Me and Eve?

MARTHA: Him and Eve – in the garden – half an hour
Before, as he related – at eleven –
He smashed the door and caught her unawares:
Their talk was sometimes tender, sometimes urgent,
As though he were attempting to persuade her.

ADAM: (*Aside.*) By Jupiter, the devil's on my side!

WALTER: Send for this woman.

RUPERT: Gentlemen, I beg you:
There's not a word of truth in what she says!

ADAM: You wait, you scoundrel! Hi, there, Beadle Hanfried!
Jugs do get smashed when thieves are put to flight!
You, Clerk, find Mistress Bridget; bring her here!

VEIT: You villain, Rupert! What were you about?
I'll tan that hide of yours!

RUPERT: Whatever for?

VEIT: You never told me that, at half past ten,
You and that girl were flirting in the garden.
Why keep it from me?

RUPERT: Keep it? Why? Because –
By all that's holy, father – it's not true!
If that's Aunt Bridie's tale, then you can hang me –
Upside down at that – for all I care!

VEIT: But if she says it, you watch out, my lad –
    You and that Eve of yours, so sweet and pure!
    If you stand trial, the pair of you will find
    Yourselves together in the self-same boat!
    There's still some shameful secret, known to her,
    Which she's been hiding for another's sake.
RUPERT: What secret's that?
VEIT: Why did you pack your clothes?
    Come, out with it! What made you pack last night?
RUPERT: My things?
VEIT: Your coats and trousers, underwear?
    The sort of bundle for a traveller's back?
RUPERT: Why? Because I'm going to Utrecht.
    To join my regiment! In heaven's name,
    You don't imagine –
VEIT: Yes, Utrecht! Utrecht!
    You couldn't wait to get there, it would seem!
    Two days ago, you still had no idea
    Whether you'd travel on the fifth or sixth.
WALTER: Have you, as father, something to contribute?
VEIT: My lord, I've nothing to declare as yet.
    I was at home, the time the jug was broken;
    Nor, in respect of other happenings,
    To tell the truth – all aspects having weighed
    Which seem to cast suspicion on my son –
    Can I make any observation now.
    Convinced completely of his innocence,
    I came here in the light of their dispute,
    Intending to revoke his pledge to marry
    And to reclaim for him the silver chain
    And coin which he bestowed upon the maiden
    Last autumn, when the pair became engaged.
    This talk of flight, desertion and betrayal –
    Affront to my grey hairs – is new to me,
    As, I don't doubt, it is to you, your lordships.
    If that's the way of it, the devil take him!
WALTER: Call Mistress Bridget quickly, Justice Adam!
ADAM: Will this affair not weary you, your grace?
    It looks like taking longer than expected.

Your grace has still to check my registry
Together with the safes...What time is it?
LICHT: It's struck the half past –
ADAM: Ten?
LICHT: No, past eleven.
WALTER: Never mind.
ADAM: The clock's gone mad – or you have.
   (*Looking at the clock.*)
I'll be damned! What is your lordship's wish?
WALTER: I favour –
ADAM: An adjournment? Good idea!
WALTER: Allow me – no! I'd sooner we continue.
ADAM: You'd sooner – yes, why not? But failing that,
   Nine sharp tomorrow morning, word of honour,
   I'll end it to your lordship's satisfaction.
WALTER: You know my wish.
ADAM: It shall be my command.
   Clerk, dispatch the beadle! He's to summon
   Mistress Bridget to the court without delay.
WALTER: And you yourself – to save my precious time –
   Could help by kindly getting on with things.
   (*Exit LICHT.*)

Scene 10

ADAM: Meanwhile, and may it please your grace,
   It might not hurt to stretch our limbs?
WALTER: Hmmm. Yes –
   But what I meant –
ADAM: Would you likewise permit
   Both parties, while awaiting Mistress Bridget –
WALTER: Both parties – what?
ADAM: Outside the door – that's if...
WALTER: (*Aside.*)
   Plague on him!
   (*Aloud.*)   Justice Adam, you know what?
   Give me a glass of wine to pass the time!
ADAM: With all my heart! Most gladly! Hi, there, Greta!
   You've made me very happy, sir. Hi, Greta!

(*Enter GRETA.*)

GRETA: Here, sir!

ADAM: What would you like? All of you – out!
  French? Into the anteroom! – or Rhein?

WALTER: Our Rhein!

ADAM: Of course! All out, until I call!

WALTER: Where?

ADAM: Greta, in the cupboard I keep locked –
  What? Oh, the field outside. Here, take the key!

WALTER: One moment!

ADAM: Out! Quick, Greta, off you go!
  Bring butter, freshly stamped, and Limburg cheese,
  With slices of plump, smoked goose from Pomerania!

WALTER: Hold hard a moment! Really there's no need
  To stand on ceremony, Justice Adam!

ADAM: Go to the devil, all of you! Do as you're told!

WALTER: You're sending them all away, are you?

ADAM: Your grace?

WALTER: Are you –

ADAM: They're just withdrawing, if they may,
  Till Mistress Bridget gets here – or perhaps –

WALTER: As you wish – but is it worth the trouble?
  You think it's going to take them all that time
  To find her in a village?

ADAM: Wood-day, sir!
  The womenfolk are mostly in the forest
  Gathering fuel. So –

RUPERT: Auntie is at home.

WALTER: At home. 'Tis well.

RUPERT: She'll be here right away.

WALTER: Oh, right away, will she? Then bring the wine.

ADAM: (*Aside.*)
  Blast it!

WALTER: Do hurry up! But never mind the meal!
  For me – a slice of bread, bone dry, with salt.

ADAM: (*Aside.*)
  Two minutes with that hussy on her own...
  (*Aloud.*) What? Just dry bread and salt? Come, come!

WALTER: That's all.

ADAM: A piece of Limburg? Surely, cheese at least?
  To prime the tongue, so's you can taste the wine.
WALTER: If you insist, some cheese, but nothing more.
ADAM: And spread the good white linen tablecloth!
  Poor fare maybe, but gently served.
  (*Exit GRETA.*)
                                    That's one
  Advantage bachelors, much-maligned, can boast:
  What others sparingly, with careworn hearts,
  Must daily share with hungry wife and children,
  We can at any given moment, with a friend
  Fully enjoy.
WALTER: I meant to ask you, Justice Adam:
  How came you by that injury of yours?
  That's quite a nasty head-wound you have there!
ADAM: I fell –
WALTER: You fell? Hmm…When was that? Last night?
ADAM: No, half past five this morning, very early,
  In fact, as I was getting out of bed.
WALTER: Fell over what?
ADAM: Why, over – well, your grace,
  To tell the truth, 'twas over me I fell;
  Stumbled and struck my head against the stove;
  Why? I'm still at a loss to understand.
WALTER: Backwards?
ADAM: How, backwards?
WALTER: Was it forwards, then?
  You've got two wounds: one front and one behind.
ADAM: Backwards and forwards…Greta!
  (*Enter GRETA and LISA with wine etc. They spread out the
  refreshments and leave.*)
WALTER: How do you mean?
ADAM: First one way, then the other. First the stove-edge
  Stove my forehead in, then falling backwards
  From the stove, I hit the floor and that
  Was how my head was struck again, behind.
  (*Pours the wine.*)
  That to your taste?

WALTER:　　　　　You know, if you'd a wife,
　　I might well think strange things about you,
　　Justice Adam.
ADAM:　　　　　　　How so?
WALTER:　　　　　　　　　Yes, indeed!
　　The way your face is scratched and cut about.
ADAM: (*Laughs.*)
　　Ah no, thank God, 'twas not a woman's nails!
WALTER: Quite! Another bachelor's advantage!
ADAM: (*Still laughing.*)
　　'Twas brushwood for the silkworms, set to dry
　　Upon the stove. It scratched me as I fell.
　　To your good health! (*They drink.*)
WALTER:　　　　　　　Besides, today of all days,
　　Too bad that you should somehow lose your wig.
ADAM: Alas, it never rains but what it pours.
　　Here, won't you have a slice?
WALTER:　　　　　　　　　Well, just a morsel...
　　From Limburg?
ADAM:　　　　　Yes, your lordship – all the way.
WALTER: But tell me, how the devil did it happen?
ADAM: What?
WALTER:　　　I mean, how *did* you lose your wig?
ADAM: Well, you see...Last night, I had a deed
　　To scan, but I'd mislaid my spectacles.
　　As I peered close, sunk deep in concentration,
　　My wig went up in flames, caught by the candle.
　　I thought at first that heaven must be heaping
　　Coals of fire upon my sinful head.
　　I grabbed the wig to tear it off, but even
　　Before I'd time to free the tape, the wig
　　Was blazing fierce as Sodom and Gomorrha;
　　All I could do to save a hair or two.
WALTER: Good Lord! And your spare wig was still in town –
ADAM: Under repair...But let's discuss the case.
WALTER: Time enough! Don't worry, Justice Adam.
ADAM: Time marches on. Let's have another drop...
　　(*Refills their glasses.*)

WALTER: This Lebrecht – if that fellow spoke the truth –
  He, too, had nasty injuries last night.
ADAM: I'm sure he had. (*Drinks.*)
WALTER: If, as I fear, this case
  Is not resolved, you'll easily recognise
  The culprit in the village by his wounds.
  (*Drinks.*)
  Niersteiner?
ADAM: What?
WALTER: Or good old Oppenheimer?
ADAM: Nierstein! Fancy that! You know your wines!
  Nierstein, sure as if I'd been to fetch it.
WALTER: I tried it at the press, three years ago.
  (*ADAM pours another glass.*)
  How high's your window – you there, Mistress Martha?
MARTHA: My window?
WALTER: Yes, the window of the room
  Where that young woman sleeps.
MARTHA: The room itself
  Is on the first floor, cellar underneath:
  Nine feet, at most, from windowsill to ground.
  However, its position, all considered
  Is very far from perfect for a jump.
  Two feet from the house wall is a vine
  Which thrusts its knotty branches through the trellis
  That runs the length entire of that same wall.
  Even the window's cluttered with the vine.
  A wild boar, armed with tusks, I'll guarantee,
  Would have its work cut out to struggle through.
ADAM: No one could hang there! (*Helps himself to wine.*)
WALTER: Really?
ADAM: Not a hope! (*Drinks.*)
WALTER: (*To RUPERT.*)
  Where did you strike the culprit? On the head?
RUPERT: (*Offering wine.*)
  Here.
WALTER: No thanks.
ADAM: Please!
WALTER: Still half-full.
ADAM: Let's fill it.

WALTER: You heard me.

ADAM: For good measure!

WALTER: Thank you, no!

ADAM: Come, come! According to Pythagoras...
   (*Fills WALTER's glass.*)

WALTER: (*Again to RUPERT.*)
   How many times was it you hit his head?

ADAM: One for the Lord; two for the murk of chaos;
   Three for the world; three glasses, I commend.
   The third contains the sun in every drop,
   And all the rest embrace the firmaments.

WALTER: How often did you strike the sinner's head?
   It's you I'm asking, Rupert!

ADAM: Answer him!
   How often did you strike the scapegoat? Speak!
   God help us! Has the fellow no idea?
   Forgotten?

RUPERT: With the latch?

ADAM: How should I know?

WALTER: When you attacked him, leaning out the window?

RUPERT: Twice, gentlemen.

ADAM: The scoundrel! He remembers! (*Drinks.*)

WALTER: Twice, was it? Two such blows, my word, could well
   Have killed the fellow...

RUPERT: Yes – and if I had,
   Then he'd be dead and serve the bastard right!
   And if his corpse were here, then I could say:
   That was the man – which proves I've not been lying!

ADAM: If he were dead, you could. But since he's not...
   (*Refills the glasses.*)

WALTER: Couldn't you recognise him in the dark?

RUPERT: Not for the life of me, your grace! How could I?

ADAM: You should have kept your eyes wide open, eh?

RUPERT: I did! I had them open till that devil
   Filled them full of sand.

ADAM: (*Aside.*)
                Yes, full of sand.
   Then more fool you for having opened them!
   (*Aloud.*) Just as we like it, eh, your grace? Good health!

WALTER: Here's to what's right and good and true,
Judge Adam!

(*They drink.*)

ADAM: One for the road, your grace, if you'll allow!
(*Pours wine.*)

WALTER: You call on Mistress Martha, now and then,
Judge Adam, do you not? I'd like to know:
Who else, apart from Rupert, visits her?

ADAM: Beg pardon, I'm not often there myself.
I couldn't tell you who goes in and out.

WALTER: The widow of a late-lamented friend?
Surely you visit her from time to time?

ADAM: I don't, in fact...Quite rarely!

WALTER: Mistress Martha!
You've fallen out, have you, with Justice Adam?
He says he doesn't see you much these days.

MARTHA: Fallen out, your grace? I wouldn't say so.
I think he still considers he's my friend.
However, as for visiting my home –
That is an honour I can rarely claim.
It's nine weeks now since last he called on me,
And then, sir, it was only just in passing.

WALTER: What's that?

MARTHA: What's what?

WALTER: Nine weeks, you say?

MARTHA: Yes – nine.
Ten, come Thursday. Seeds he asked me for –
Carnations and auricula, he wanted.

WALTER: And Sundays – when he's going to the farm?

MARTHA: Oh, yes! He does look in the window at me
And says good day to me and to my daughter.
He doesn't stop, though; just goes on his way.

WALTER: (*Aside.*)
Perhaps I ought to press the man...(*Drinks.*) I thought,
Since you occasionally seek the girl's
Advice, you might well, out of gratitude,
Call in and see Mama from time to time.

ADAM: How so, your grace?

WALTER: You told me, did you not,
    The maid had helped you with those hens of yours
    You said were sick. Today, I understood,
    She gave you more advice in this respect?
MARTHA: Why yes indeed, sir. That's quite right. She did.
    Day before yesterday, he sent us home
    A guinea fowl already at death's door.
    Last year, she saved one for him from the pip
    And this one, too, she'll salvage by force-feeding.
    But up to now, he's never come to thank me.
WALTER: (*Confused.*)
    Let's have another, Justice Adam – if you would!
    Please fill it up and we'll have just one more.
ADAM: Of course. I'd be delighted. Here we are! (*Pours.*)
WALTER: To your good health! I'm sure that Justice Adam
    Will call upon you by and by.
MARTHA: I doubt it.
    He might – if I could serve him Nierstein like
    The one you're drinking, or the watchman – my
    Late husband – sometimes fetched him from the cellar.
    That would make a difference, to be sure.
    These days, poor widow that I am, I've nothing
    In the house he'd find attractive.
WALTER: So much the better.

Scene 11

*Enter LICHT, MISTRESS BRIDGET, with a wig in her hand,
and GRETA and LISA.*

LICHT: Come in, Mistress Bridget.
WALTER: This is the woman, is it, Master Clerk?
LICHT: Yes, this is Mistress Bridget, by your leave.
WALTER: Well, let's get on and finish off this case.
    Please clear away, you maids!
    (*Exeunt LISA and GRETA, carrying glasses etc.*)
ADAM: (*Speaking meanwhile.*)
    Now listen, Eve!
    Take care the way you mix your pill for me:

If you do right by me, this very evening
I'll share a dish of carp with both of you.
That pill must pass the carrion's throat with ease;
If it's too big, then only death will feast.
WALTER: (*Catching sight of the wig.*)
    What is that wig that Mistress Bridget's got?
LICHT: Yes, your grace?
WALTER: I asked, what wig is that
    The woman's brought?
LICHT: Ahem!
WALTER: What's that?
LICHT: Forgive me –
WALTER: Am I not to know?
LICHT: Sir, if your grace
    Will kindly ask the woman – through the judge –
    I have no doubt the owner of the wig
    And much besides will quickly be revealed.
WALTER: I do not wish to know who owns the wig.
    How come she has it and where did she find it?
LICHT: She found it hanging, sir, upon the trellis
    At Mistress Martha's. It was like a bird's nest,
    Perched in the criss-cross branches of the vine –
    Just below the maiden's bedroom window.
MARTHA: What? On my trellis?
WALTER: (*Discreetly.*)   Look here, Justice Adam,
    Do you have something to confide to me?
    I ask you – for the honour of the court –
    If so, be good enough to tell me now.
ADAM: I – you – ?
WALTER: Have you not?
ADAM: Upon my word –
    (*Snatches the wig.*)
WALTER: Is not this wig here, Justice Adam, yours?
ADAM: Yes, gentlemen, this wig here is my own!
    Why bless me, if it's not the very wig
    I gave the lad eight days ago to take
    To Master Meal of Utrecht, did I not?
WALTER: To whom? What for?

LICHT: To Rupert?
RUPERT: Me?
ADAM: I gave it
  To this young scallywag eight days ago,
  In trust, as he was going to Utrecht,
  For him to ask the barber to restore.
RUPERT: Did he? Oh, yes. He gave me –
ADAM: Then why didn't
  You deliver it, you good-for-nothing?
  Why didn't you, as I expressly ordered,
  Convey it to the barber in his workshop?
RUPERT: Why didn't I? God's lightning strike me pink!
  I did! I took it to the barber's shop –
  To Master Meal himself!
ADAM: You gave it him?
  And now it's found in Mistress Martha's vine?
  Wait, you wretch! You'll not escape that lightly!
  I smell disguise behind all this, I do –
  And mutiny as well, for all I know! (*To WALTER.*)
  May I interrogate this woman now?
WALTER: You say you gave it –
ADAM: That's just it, your grace!
  When that lad there, last Tuesday, was about
  To leave for Utrecht with his father's ox,
  He came to me and asked me: 'Justice Adam,
  Can I do anything for you in town?'
  'My son,' said I, 'if you would be so good,
  You might get Meal to freshen up my wig.'
  I certainly did not say: Go, then keep it
  With you; wear it to disguise yourself,
  And leave it hung on Mistress Martha's vine!
BRIDGET: Gentlemen, by your leave, I wish to say
  It wasn't Rupert. For last night, as I
  Was going to my cousin's farm – she was
  In labour at the time – I heard Miss Eve
  Rebuking someone quietly in the garden,
  Fear and anger smothering her voice:
  'For shame, you villain! Go, or I'll call mother!'

I thought the Spanish troops were here again!
'Eve!' I shouted through the hedgerow, 'Eve!
What's wrong? What's going on?' Then, all was still.
'Why don't you answer?' – 'Aunty, what d'you want?'
'What are you doing?' 'Well, what do you think?'
'Is it Rupert?' 'Yes, of course, it's Rupert!
Off you go!' I thought, best leave them – though
It sounded more like quarrelling than love.

MARTHA: What then?

RUPERT:⠀⠀⠀⠀⠀⠀⠀What then?

WALTER:⠀⠀⠀⠀⠀⠀⠀⠀⠀⠀⠀Be quiet! Let her finish!

BRIDGET: Well, as I was returning from the farm,
⠀⠀Which must have been round midnight, I suppose,
⠀⠀Taking the path of limes by Martha's garden,
⠀⠀A man, bald-headed and with cloven hoof,
⠀⠀Shot past me, leaving in the air behind,
⠀⠀The stink of smoke, tar, singeing hair and sulphur.
⠀⠀I said a 'God-be-with-us' and turned round
⠀⠀In terror, just in time to see his pate –
⠀⠀Gleaming like rotten wood, your honours – flicker
⠀⠀Between the lime trees as the Demon fled.

RUPERT: What the blazes!

MARTHA:⠀⠀⠀⠀⠀⠀⠀Bridie must be mad!

RUPERT: She took him for the Devil?

LICHT:⠀⠀⠀⠀⠀⠀⠀⠀⠀Silence!

BRIDGET:⠀⠀⠀⠀⠀⠀⠀⠀⠀⠀⠀Sirs!
⠀⠀What I saw and what I smelt, I know!

WALTER: (*Impatiently.*)
⠀⠀Devil or not, ma'am, I am not concerned;
⠀⠀The Devil hasn't been accused so far!
⠀⠀If you can name another, well and good:
⠀⠀But I implore you, madam, spare us Satan!

LICHT: Perhaps your grace would let the woman finish?

WALTER: These stupid people!

BRIDGET:⠀⠀⠀⠀⠀⠀⠀As your lordship will!
⠀⠀But Master Licht, the clerk, can bear me out.

WALTER: The clerk, your witness?

LICHT:⠀⠀⠀⠀⠀⠀⠀⠀Yes, to some extent.

WALTER: Blest if I know –
LICHT: If I might humbly pray:
   Don't interrupt the woman's testimony.
   I cannot state as fact she saw the Devil,
   But cloven hoof, together with bald head
   And smoke behind – unless I'm much mistaken –
   Suggests she did. Continue, Mistress Bridget!
BRIDGET: Today, on hearing with astonishment
   What took place in Mistress Martha's house,
   I thought I'd try to trace that pitcher-breaker
   Who hurtled past me, through the limes last night:
   I went to check the place where he had jumped
   And in the snow, sir, I discovered tracks:
   What kind of tracks were they, you'd like to know?
   The outline of a right foot, still precise
   And sharp-defined – a normal human foot;
   The left foot, though, was formless, indistinct –
   The shape of some great, clumsy cloven hoof.
WALTER: (*Annoyed.*)
   That's crazy nonsense! Downright poppycock!
VEIT: Impossible!
BRIDGET: I swear it, sirs, on oath!
   Below the trellis, where the jump took place,
   A circle had been hollowed in the snow,
   As broad as if a sow'd been wallowing,
   And, leading from it, footprints – cleft-hoof, human;
   Cleft-hoof, human; cleft-hoof, human; all the way
   Across the garden, sirs, and out of sight.
ADAM: Can it be, the villain dared disguise
   Himself in devil's garb?
RUPERT: What, me?
LICHT: Be quiet!
BRIDGET: My triumph was as keen as any hunter's
   Who, seeking badger, stumbles on its tracks.
   'See, Master Clerk,' said I, when he appeared,
   The worthy man you sent to summon me –
   'No point in trying to conduct a hearing –
   You'll never judge the pitcher-breaker's guilt,

For he's already safely lodged in hell;
He's left his tracks to show the way he went.'
WALTER: You're quite convinced of that?
LICHT: Your grace,
The tracks corroborate the woman's story.
WALTER: A cloven hoof?
LICHT: A human foot, in fact,
But you could call it cleft, as she described.
ADAM: Upon my word, the case strikes me as grave.
There are no end of pertly phrased polemics
Which won't allow that there exists a God;
Yet, so far as I'm aware, no atheist
Has ever quite disproved that there's a Devil.
I think the case before us surely merits
The fullest ventilation. I submit,
Before we reach an ultimate conclusion,
That we request the Synod in the Hague
To rule on this court's competence to find
That it was Satan who destroyed the pitcher.
WALTER: That's just what I'd expect you to submit!
What's *your* opinion, Master Clerk?
LICHT: I think
Your grace will not require a Synod ruling.
If Mistress Bridget, pray, may end her story,
The facts, my lord, when taken in conjunction,
Will quite suffice to clarify the case.
BRIDGET: So then I said to Master Licht, the clerk:
'Let us pursue these tracks a bit and see
Whither the Devil made good his escape.'
'Why, Mistress Bridget, that's a great idea,'
Says he, 'and maybe we'd not go far wrong
Were we to head for Justice Adam's house.'
WALTER: So, then you found – ?
BRIDGET: Well, first, beyond the garden,
We found the place along the linden walk
Where, sulphur fumes emitting as he fled,
The Devil had to dodge me or collide:
The way dogs shyly circle to avoid
A spitting cat, which bars the way.

WALTER: What then?

BRIDGET: Not far beyond, beside a tree, we found
    A souvenir he'd left…Quite shocked, I was!

WALTER: What kind of souvenir?

BRIDGET: I hardly like –

ADAM: (*Aside.*)
    Confound my wretched bowels!

LICHT: That's quite enough!
    No need for details, thank you, Mistress Bridget.

WALTER: Where did these tracks *lead*, I would like to know.

BRIDGET: Where? Bless me, by the shortest route to you –
    Exactly as foretold by Master Licht.

WALTER: Here? To us?

BRIDGET: Yes – from the linden walk.
    Across the schoolfield, past the pond of carp,
    Over the ford and through the churchyard straight
    To Justice Adam's house here – as I say.

WALTER: To Justice Adam's house?

ADAM: What? Straight to me?

BRIDGET: To you, yes!

RUPERT: You don't mean to say the Devil
    Lives in the courthouse?

BRIDGET: Well, I couldn't say
    Whether he lives here, but the fact is, this
    Is where he stopped – you have my word.
    The tracks lead all the way to his back door.

ADAM: Could he perhaps have merely stopped in passing?

BRIDGET: He might have done. It's possible, at that.
    The tracks in front, though –

WALTER: Were there tracks in front?

LICHT: Beg pardon, sir, there were no tracks in front.

BRIDGET: In front, the path was trodden flat all over.

ADAM: Trodden flat. Passed through, or I'll be damned!
    Mark my words, the fellow left his card!
    My office is a mess – and that's the truth!
    If my accounts, as I have little doubt,
    Are found to be in uttermost confusion,
    Upon my word, I'll not be held to blame!

WALTER: Nor I! (*Aside.*) His left foot, was it? Or his right?
   I can't be certain. Surely, one of them –
   Lend me your snuffbox, will you, Justice Adam?
ADAM: My snuffbox?
WALTER: Please!
ADAM: (*To LICHT.*)
                        Just take it to his grace!
WALTER: Why so much fuss? A foot or two away!
ADAM: No fuss. It's done. Just hand it to his grace.
WALTER: I meant to whisper something in your ear.
ADAM: Perhaps we'll have occasion later…
WALTER: Good.
   (*After LICHT has resumed his seat.*)
   Tell me, gentlemen, in Huisum village,
   Has anybody got misshapen feet?
LICHT: Hmm…There is *one* man – right here, in Huisum.
WALTER: Who?
LICHT: I think that Justice Adam knows his name!
WALTER: Justice Adam?
ADAM: I have no idea.
   Ten years I've been the justice here in Huisum:
   As far as I'm aware, all feet are normal.
WALTER: (*To LICHT.*)
   Who do you mean?
BRIDGET: Why won't he show his feet?
   The way he hides them underneath the table,
   You'd almost think 'twas he who made the tracks.
WALTER: Who? Justice Adam?
ADAM: I who made the tracks?
   The Devil – me? Is that a cloven hoof?
   (*Showing his left foot which is, in fact, a club foot.*)
WALTER: (*Quickly, in embarrassment.*)
   The foot is perfect, on my word of honour!
   (*Sotto voce to ADAM.*)
   Best close the hearing now, without delay.
ADAM: If Satan had a foot like that, I warrant,
   He'd go to balls and dance the night away!
MARTHA: I quite agree, but how has Justice Adam –

ADAM: I? Why me?

WALTER: Conclude the hearing now!

BRIDGET: The only question unresolved, your honours,
    Concerns this ceremonial attire.

ADAM: What ceremonial – ?

BRIDGET: Why, this wig I'm holding!
    Whoever saw the Devil in such garb?
    So tall a wig, all nicely greased with tallow –
    Like some cathedral canon in his pulpit?

ADAM: We rustics, Mistress Bridget, can't be sure
    What fashions may be prevalent in hell!
    He's said to wear his own hair as a rule,
    But when on earth, I'm quite convinced that he'd
    Throw on a wig in order to be able
    To mix more freely with the upper classes.

WALTER: You good-for-nothing! You deserve to be
    Disgraced in public and expelled from court.
    All that protects you is the law's repute!
    Conclude this hearing!

ADAM: Sir, I hope you don't –

WALTER: Hope nothing! Just retire from this affair!

ADAM: Do you believe that I – a justice – would
    Have left my wig impaled on Martha's vine?

WALTER: No, God forbid! For we're assured that yours
    Went up in flames like Sodom and Gomorrha.

LICHT: Or rather – by your leave, sir – yesterday,
    The cat gave birth to kittens in his wig.

ADAM: Appearances condemn me, gentlemen,
    But I would ask you all to be less hasty:
    My honour or disgrace are in the balance.
    While Eve stays silent, I can't understand
    What right you have, your grace, to find me guilty.
    I sit here in the judgement seat of Huisum
    And lay this wig upon the table-top.
    Whoever dares assert that it is mine,
    I'll sue before Utrecht's Supreme Tribunal!

LICHT: The wig, however, fits you, I'll be bound,
    As neat as if you'd grown it on your skull.
    (Puts the wig on ADAM's head.)

ADAM: Slander!

LICHT: Well?

ADAM: Too wide to drape my shoulders,
    Let alone to wear upon my head!
    (*Looks at himself in the mirror.*)

RUPERT: A plausible rogue, if ever there was!

WALTER: Be silent!

MARTHA: Some justice! He's a villain – double-dyed!

WALTER: Will you conclude this hearing, or shall I?

ADAM: As you command!

RUPERT: (*To EVE.*)

                    Eve, tell us – was it him?

WALTER: How dare you interrupt, you shameless oaf!

VEIT: Hold your tongue!

ADAM: You wait, you lout! I'll get you!

RUPERT: You and your cloven hoof!

WALTER: Out with him, Beadle!

VEIT: Shut up, I said!

RUPERT: Today, I'll have your hide!
    This time, there'll be no blinding me with sand!

WALTER: Haven't you wit enough, man – ?

ADAM: If your grace
    Permits, I'll now pass sentence of the court.

WALTER: Alright. Do that.

ADAM: I find the case is proven:
    That rascal, Rupert, there's the guilty one.

WALTER: Right! Proceed!

ADAM: He's to be clapped in irons;
    And for his insubordinate behaviour
    To me, as magistrate, I sentence him
    To prison behind bars; the length of term
    Will be determined in due course by me.

EVE: Rupert – ?

RUPERT: Jail – me?

EVE: Rupert – you in irons?

WALTER: No need to worry, children! Have you finished?

ADAM: He can replace the jug – or not – at will.

WALTER: Very well. The hearing's at an end
    And Rupert has permission to appeal.

EVE: Has he to go to Utrecht to appeal?
RUPERT: What? Must I – ?
WALTER: Yes, by heaven! Until then –
EVE: Until then – ?
RUPERT: Have I to go to prison?
EVE: His neck in irons? Aren't you, too, a judge?
That shameless blackguard, sitting there – yes, him!
He was the one, himself –
WALTER: For God's sake, silence!
Until then, I say, he'll not be touched!
EVE: Rupert! 'Twas Justice Adam broke the pitcher!
RUPERT: You wait!
MARTHA: What, him?!
BRIDGET: Him, there?
EVE: Yes, Rupert! Yes!
'Twas him – that Adam! – with your Eve, last night!
Grab hold of him and beat him all you want!
WALTER: Stop that! Who sows disorder here –
EVE: No matter!
It's him deserves the irons! Catch him, Rupert!
Drag the scoundrel from his judge's seat!
ADAM: (*Trying to escape.*)
Excuse me!
EVE: Look out!
RUPERT: Grab him!
EVE: Quick!
ADAM: What's this?
RUPERT: You limping demon!
EVE: Got him?
RUPERT: Damn and blast!
He's left me with his coat!
WALTER: Quick! Call the beadle!
RUPERT: (*Punching the coat.*)
Take that! And that! And that! One more for luck!
Take that, you bastard! Wish it were your hide!
WALTER: You ill-bred fellow! Order! Order, please!
If you don't calm yourself at once, young man,
You'll find yourself in irons after all!
VEIT: Control yourself, you miserable fool!

Scene 12

ALL – less ADAM – move to front of stage.

RUPERT: Eve!
> How shamefully have I insulted you –
> Today and yesterday! By every means!
> My golden girl, my heart's desire! My bride!
> How can you ever in your life forgive me?

EVE: (*Throwing herself at WALTER's feet.*)
> If you don't help us now, your grace, we're lost!

WALTER: Lost? How so?

RUPERT: Great heaven! What's the matter?

EVE: Please save my Rupert, sir, from being conscripted!
> This latest batch – I heard from Justice Adam
> Who told me so in strictest confidence –
> Is bound for the East Indies, whence, you know,
> Of every three men sent, but one returns!

WALTER: East Indies? Bless my soul! You must be mad!

EVE: To Bantam – yes, your grace – you can't deny it!
> I've got the letter here, a secret order
> Affecting the militia, circulated
> By the government quite recently:
> As you can see, I'm very well informed.

WALTER: (*Takes the letter and reads it.*)
> Oh, what unheard of cunning! What deceit!
> This letter's forged!

EVE: It's forged?

WALTER: I stake my oath!
> Look, Master Licht, is that a government
> Order, recently received here from Utrecht?

LICHT: The order? This? The scoundrel! Why, he wrote it
> With his own hand! It's poppycock, your grace!
> The troops who're now being levied are reserved
> For service here at home; there's no intention
> Of sending those recruits to the East Indies!

EVE: What? Never?

WALTER: Never, on my word of honour!
> But just to make quite sure my word endures –
> If what you say prove true, I'll buy him free!

EVE: (*Standing up.*)
    Dear heaven, how that wicked man deceived me!
    That was the fearful prospect which he used
    To torture me. He came along at night
    And pressed me to accept an attestation,
    Falsely declaring Rupert was unfit
    And so excused all military service.
    Having assured me he would so declare,
    He crept to my bedroom, promising to write,
    But there made such a shameful proposition,
    As no good girl would ever dare repeat.
BRIDGET: The wicked, worthless, double-dyed deceiver!
RUPERT: Let's forget the cloven hoof, my darling!
    Had it been a goat that smashed the pitcher,
    I should be no less jealous than I am! (*They kiss.*)
VEIT: Kiss, make up – and love each other true!
    Come Whit, if you've a mind, we'll have the wedding!
LICHT: (*At the window.*)
    See, Justice Adam in full flight – up hill,
    Down dale, as though to flee the rack and rope –
    Stumping across ploughed meadows frozen hard!
WALTER: What? That's Justice Adam?
LICHT: Yes, indeed!
VOICES: Now he's reached the high road. Look at him!
    See how his pigtail's whipping him along!
WALTER: Make haste, good Master Licht, and bring
                                  him back!

    Lest, saving evil, he make matters worse.
    In any case, he's been removed from office
    And I appoint you, pending further notice,
    To exercise his functions in the village.
    But if the cash books tally, as I hope,
    I've no desire to force him to decamp –
    So off you go and kindly bring him back!
    (*Exit LICHT.*)
MARTHA: Beg pardon, could your lordship tell me please
    Where I can find the government in Utrecht?
WALTER: Why, Mistress Martha?

MARTHA: (*Testily.*)

> Why, indeed! Am I
To have no satisfaction for my pitcher?

WALTER: Forgive me! Yes, of course! The market square: Tuesdays and Fridays, hearings every week!

MARTHA: Good! A week from now, I shall be there!

The End.

ORDEAL BY FIRE

(Das Kätchen von Heilbronn
oder Die Feuerprobe)

Characters

THE EMPEROR

ARCHBISHOP OF WORMS

FRIEDRICH WETTER
Count vom Strahl

COUNTESS HELENA
his mother

LEONORA
her niece

FRANZ FLAMMBERG
vom Strahl's vassal

GOTTSCHALK
vom Strahl's orderly

BRIGITTE
housekeeper of Strahl Castle

KUNIGUNDE
the lady of Turneck

ROSALIE
her chambermaid

THEOBALD FRIEDEBORN
weaponsmith of Heilbronn

KATHRINA
his daughter, known as Katie

GOTTFRIED FRIEDEBORN
betrothed to Katie

MAXIMILIAN
Burgrave of Freiburg

GEORG VON WALDSTÄDTEN
his friend

THE RHINE-COUNT VOM STEIN
betrothed to Kunigunde

FRIEDRICH VON HERRNSTADT
friend of Rhine-Count

EGINHARDT VON DER WART
friend of Rhine-Count

COUNT OTTO VON DER FLÜHE
judge of secret court

WENZEL VON NACHTHEIM
judge of secret court

HANS VON BÄRENKLAU
judge of secret court

JAKOB PECH
innkeeper

THREE GENTLEMEN
of Turneck

TWO ELDERLY AUNTS
of Kunigunde

CHARCOAL-BURNER'S BOY

NIGHT-WATCHMAN

SEVERAL KNIGHTS

A HERALD

TWO CHARCOAL-BURNERS

MESSENGERS

ORDERLIES

PEASANTS

OTHERS

The action is set in Swabia (Schwaben), a medieval German duchy, seat of the Hohenstaufens in the twelfth and thirteenth centuries. The play was written between 1807 and 1808 and was first performed in Vienna in 1810.

ACT ONE

*An underground cavern, lit by lamps and decorated with the insignia
of the Vehmgericht – a secret, self-appointed tribunal of the 'great
and good', which once functioned in Westphalia.*

Scene 1

*The Tribunal: COUNT OTTO VON DER FLÜHE, chairman;
WENZEL VON NACHTHEIM and HANS VON BÄRENKLAU;
COUNTS, KNIGHTS and LORDS – all in disguise; ORDERLIES
and BODYGUARDS with torches etc. THEOBALD FRIEDEBORN,
plaintiff and citizen of Heilbronn and COUNT WETTER VOM
STRAHL, the accused, both standing at the bar of the court.*

COUNT OTTO: (*Stands up.*) We, judges of this high and
secret court – God's sentinels on earth and vanguard of his
winged, heavenly hosts, whose mission is to uncover
wickedness, wherever it lurks, beyond the reach of human
justice – like a salamander in the darkest recesses of the
soul – do call upon you, Theobald Friedeborn, honourable
and reputed weaponsmith of Heilbronn, to state your
complaint against Friedrich Count Wetter vom Strahl. In
response to the first summons of this holy Tribunal,
delivered by the court's herald, with a triple rap of his
sword hilt at the castle gate, the Count is here by your
request and now wishes to know what you want.
(*Sits down.*)

THEOBALD: Most holy, high and secret lords! As God is
my witness, had the accused ordered me to make him
a suit of armour, of silver or steel, chased with gold,
and then refused to pay me; or denounced me to my
superiors, or attacked me with sword and dagger, I don't
believe I would have brought a charge before you. In the
fifty-three years I've been alive, I've suffered so much
injustice that my soul is proof against pin-pricks.
Whereas I forge weapons for people who have been

bitten merely by midges, I myself can tell a scorpion to be off and let him go. But Friedrich Count Wetter vom Strahl has seduced my child, my only daughter, Kathrina, and therefore I now accuse him of sorcery, black magic and confraternity with Satan! Seize him, you earthly sentinels of God and deliver him to the armour-clad hosts brandishing their red-hot pikes at the gates of hell!

COUNT OTTO: Master Theobald! Think what you're saying! You are accusing Count vom Strahl, known to many of us and well vouched for, of having abducted your child. I trust you are not accusing him of black magic simply because he has won your daughter's affections? An impressionable girl could be charmed simply by being asked her name or by the sight of rosy cheeks beneath a visor, or by some other perfectly innocent artifice practised in broad daylight.

THEOBALD: It's true, gentlemen, I have not seen him at night trafficking with will-o'-the-wisps out on the moors or in reedy marshland or, indeed, anywhere men tread but seldom. Never seen him on a mountain peak, wand in hand, measuring the invisible realms of space, nor yet in underground caves where no ray of sunlight ever penetrates, weaving spells from the dust. Nor have I ever seen him fraternising with Satan and his cohorts, with their horns and tails and claws, as depicted over the altar in Heilbronn church. But, if you will just let me speak, I believe a straightforward account of what has occurred will bring you judges of this secret court to your feet, crying: 'We are 13 in number and the fourteenth present is the Devil.' And out you will race into the surrounding forest, sprinkling the earth for 300 yards around with your taffeta cloaks and feathered hats as you flee in terror!

COUNT OTTO: Well then, you unruly old plaintiff, speak!

THEOBALD: First, I must tell you that my Katie was 15 last Easter – as sound in body and soul as our first parents. A child truly after God's heart, rising heavenward from the desert in the restful evening of my life, fragrant as the smoke of myrrh and juniper. You

couldn't imagine a creature more gentle, pious and lovable, even if the wings of fantasy brought before you those dear little bright-eyed angels you see peeping out of the clouds from under God's hands and feet. When Katie went down the street in her Sunday best, with her straw hat gleaming yellow, her black velvet bodice and her little silver chain, there were whispers at every window. 'There she goes – Katie of Heilbronn!' Katie of Heilbronn, gentlemen, was as though begotten by the Swabian sky, impregnating with its kiss the town below, which then gave birth to her. At christenings and weddings, cousins and other kin who'd lost touch for generations made a point of greeting Katie...On her birthday, people thronged the market square in which we lived, vying with one another to present her with gifts. Somebody who perhaps had seen her only once and been greeted by her in passing, would include Katie in his prayers all the following week, as though she had done him an act of kindness. As the owner of an estate, willed to her – I myself being excluded – by a grandfather intent on spoiling his darling Katie, she was no longer dependent on me and was one of the richest young women in town. Five sons of worthy citizens had already asked to marry her. Knights who passed through town used to weep because she wasn't of noble birth. Indeed, if she had been, the whole Orient would have been sending baskets of pearls and diamonds, carried by Moors, to lay at her feet. But heaven preserved her, like myself, from pride.
And when young Gottfried Friedeborn, the farmer, proposed – his property adjoins the land left to her by her grandfather – and when I asked her would she have him and she said: 'Father, your will is mine!' I said: 'Lord bless you both!' and, weeping tears of joy, I decided that, come Easter next, they'd be wed. That was the situation, my lords, before he stole her away from me.

COUNT OTTO: How? By what means did he divert her from the path along which you had been leading her?

THEOBALD: My lords, if I knew the answer, I'd not be here
before you accusing him of hell's unfathomable horrors.
It's not as if he'd met her drawing water at the well and
asked her: 'What's your name?' – or stood by a pillar, as
she was coming away from matins and asked: 'Where do
you live, sweet maid?'– or crept to her window by night,
with a necklace for her, asking: 'Darling girl, where do
you sleep?' She'd have seen through all of that, as quick as
Our Saviour spotted the kiss of Judas. He wouldn't have
caught her that way, my lords! Fact is, she'd never set eyes
on him before. Why, she knew her own back and the
mole she had from her late mother better than she knew
him! (*Weeping.*)

COUNT OTTO: All the same, if he abducted her, it must
have happened sometime, somewhere.

THEOBALD: Whitsun eve, he dropped into my workshop
for a few minutes, as he said, to have me fix one of the
shoulder plates of his armour which had come undone.

NACHTHEIM: What?

BÄRENKLAU: In broad daylight?

NACHTHEIM: Called in for five minutes to get his
breastplate repaired?

(*Pause.*)

COUNT OTTO: Gather your wits and tell us what happened.

THEOBALD: (*Dabbing his eyes.*) Must have been about
eleven o'clock in the morning when he comes rattling up
to my workshop in full armour with a bunch of riders,
dismounts and marches in. Had to bend almost double to
get through the doorway with the plumes on his helmet.
'See here, master,' says he, 'I'm off to fight the Count
Palatine who means to tear down your city walls. I've
split my shoulder stays with excitement at the pleasure
of meeting him. Just get some iron and wire and patch
me up without my having to get undressed, will you?'
'Well,' says I, 'if you can burst your armour throwing out
your chest, we've nothing to fear from the Count
Palatine!' So I sat him down on a chair in the middle
of the room and called for wine and some fresh smoked

ham to give him a bite while I fetched my bench and
tools to fasten his plates. Then, with his charger
stamping about outside, raising clouds of dust as though
a cherub had come down from heaven, the door opened
ever so slow and in came the girl with a huge silver tray
on her head, loaded with bottles, glasses and food. If
God were suddenly to appear to me out of the clouds,
I might behave as she did. At sight of the knight, she
dropped the lot – cutlery, food, goblets and all. Then
deathly pale, hands clasped as if in prayer, she flung
herself down in front of him, breast and forehead kissing
the floor, like she'd been struck by lightning. 'Lord God,
what's come over her?' I cried and made to pick her up.
But she folds up like a pocketknife, throws her arm
around me and fixes her eyes on him, with flaming
cheeks, as though she'd seen a vision. Then the Count
vom Strahl, taking her hand, asks who the child belongs
to, while maids and apprentices come flocking in,
making a great to-do, calling out: 'Heaven help us!
What's happened to the girl?' and so on. But since she
seemed to recover after darting a few shy glances at him,
I thought the attack was probably over and set to work
with my straps and needles. 'There we are, Master
Knight!' says I. 'Now you're fit to meet the Count
Palatine. Plates all safely back. Next time your courage
won't blow them apart!' The Count stands up, looks
thoughtfully at the girl – no taller than his breastbone –
up and down from top to toe, bows, kisses her on the
forehead and says: 'God bless and keep you and His
peace be upon you, amen!' Then as we went upstairs,
thirty feet up, to watch the knight mounting his horse,
what does she do but throw herself out the window, arms
upraised and down she plunges on to the stones below,
like some poor wretched woman who's lost her wits.
Both her thighs she broke – her delicate little thighs just
above the ivory kneecaps and – pitiful old fool that I am,
as hoped she'd be the prop of my declining years – I had
to carry her on my shoulders, as though to the grave.

While he – God rot him! – on horseback, down there,
surrounded by a throng of people, calls out to know
what's happened...There she lay six endless weeks on her
deathbed, burning with fever and never making a move
or a sound. Not even delirium, that open sesame of
hearts, could open hers. Nobody could get her to say
a word about the secret that possessed her. But no sooner
does she slightly recover, than she ups and tries out
a step or two, fastens her bundle, and walks to the door
with the first ray of morning sunlight. 'Where are you off
to?' the maid asks her. 'To Count Wetter vom Strahl!' she
answers and with that she disappears.

NACHTHEIM: Not possible!

BÄRENKLAU: Disappeared?

NACHTHEIM: Left everything behind her?

BÄRENKLAU: Home and property as well as her betrothed?

NACHTHEIM: Without even asking your blessing?

THEOBALD: Gone – just like that! I was still asleep at the
time and she kissed my eyes. I only wish she'd closed
them for good.

NACHTHEIM: A strange occurrence, by heaven!

THEOBALD: From that day forth, she's been trailing about
after him from place to place in blind devotion, like some
camp-follower, drawn by the beam from his face, like
a five-strand rope about her soul – bare feet exposed to
every pebble, the little dress about her hips flapping in the
wind and only her straw hat to shield her from the searing
sun or the storm's angry lash. Wherever her feet follow
the path of his adventures, over misty precipices, through
deserts scalding in the noonday heat, through the darkness
of tangled forests; like a dog lured by the reek of its
master's sweat, she traipses after him. A girl who was used
to soft pillows; that sensitive, she could detect any careless
little knot she'd happened to spin in the fabric of her
bedsheet. Now she sleeps like a stable-maid, sinking
down exhausted at night on the straw they scatter for his
proud horses.

COUNT OTTO: Count Wetter vom Strahl, is this true?

VOM STRAHL: It is true, my lords. She dogs my footsteps.
I've only to look behind me, and what do I see? Two
things: my shadow and that girl.

COUNT OTTO: How do you account for this strange
circumstance?

VOM STRAHL: You nameless lords of this tribunal, if the
Devil is playing some game of his own with the girl, he's
using me as his cat's paw. I'll be damned if he's pulling my
chestnuts out of the fire! If you care to take my word for
that, as Holy Writ prescribes – well and good! If not, I'll be
off to Worms and ask the Emperor to summon Master
Theobald to a hearing. I challenge him, here and now!

COUNT OTTO: You're here to answer our questions! How
do you justify her sleeping under your roof – a girl that
belongs in the house where she was born and bred?

VOM STRAHL: It must have been about twelve weeks ago,
on my way to Strasburg, I fell asleep against a rock,
exhausted in the noonday heat. I hadn't even been
dreaming about the girl who jumped out the window in
Heilbronn, when I woke up to find her lying there like a
rose, asleep at my feet, as though she'd dropped from the
sky. I called out to the soldiers, sprawled around me in the
grass: 'What the devil! Why, that's young Katie from
Heilbronn!' With that, she opens her eyes and straightens
her hat which had slid down. 'Kathrina, girl,' I cried,
'where have you sprung from? We're a good fifteen miles
from Heilbronn!' 'Noble sir,' she replied, 'I've got business
in Strasburg but I was afraid of walking through the forest
on my own and thought I'd join you.' So I got my equerry
Gottschalk to give her a bite to eat and inquired how she
got on after the fall, what her father was doing and what
was taking her to Strasburg. However, she was not in the
mood for gossip, so I said to myself: 'What business is it
of yours, anyway?' ordered one of my men to see her
safely through the forest, remounted and rode off. That
evening, at the inn on the Strasburg highway, I was just
going to bed when Gottschalk came to tell me the girl

Katie was down below asking to spend the night in my
stables. 'With the horses?' I asked. 'Well,' I said, 'if it's soft
enough for her, no skin off my nose.' Then, turning over
in bed, I told him he'd better scatter some straw for her
and make sure she came to no harm. From then on, she'd
be up and about on the high road ahead of us each
morning and, every night, wherever our expedition took
us, she'd sleep in the stables, as though she belonged to
our party. And all of that I put up with for the sake of that
churlish old devil who now blames me for it. Gottschalk –
strange fellow that he is – had grown quite fond of the
girl, in fact, and was taking care of her like his own
daughter. If you ever happen to pass through Heilbronn,
I thought to myself, the old man will be grateful to you
for all this. But when we got to Strasburg and she was still
with us in the Archbishop's palace – obviously with
nothing to do but devote herself entirely to washing and
mending my clothes – I accosted her one day at the
stable-door and asked her straight out what she was doing
in Strasburg. 'Good master,' she said, blushing fit to set
fire to her apron, 'why do you ask? You already know!'
Hoho! I thought, so that's the way it is with you, eh? And
straight away, I sent a courier to her father in Heilbronn
to let him know that Katie was with me, that I was
looking after her and would take her back to my castle
at Strahl, where he could shortly collect her.

COUNT OTTO: So what happened then?

NACHTHEIM: Didn't the old man fetch her?

VOM STRAHL: When he arrived to collect her three weeks
later and I was showing him into the home of my
ancestors, I was not best pleased to see him dip his hand
in the baptismal font by the door and sprinkle me with
holy water. But guileless as I am by nature, I invited him
to sit down and gave him a full and frank account of
everything that had happened. Out of sympathy for him,
I even suggested what steps he might take to restore the
situation according to his liking. Then, attempting to
console him, and meaning to hand over Katie, I took

him down to the stables where she was cleaning the rust from one of my weapons. But the moment he walked through the door, with tears in his eyes, throwing his arms wide open to receive her, she turned deathly pale and flung herself at my feet, begging me by all the saints to protect her from him. He stood there like a pillar of salt at sight of her and, before I'd recovered my wits, he turned towards me with a look of terror in his eyes and shouted: 'You are the Devil incarnate!' Then he struck me in the face with his hat as though to banish some atrocious spectre, and rushed back to Heilbronn as if all the fiends of hell were after him.

COUNT OTTO: You strange old man! What curious fancies!

NACHTHEIM: What was blameworthy about the knight's behaviour? How can he help it if your foolish daughter's heart inclines towards him?

BÄRENKLAU: What is there to reproach him with in this whole affair?

THEOBALD: Reproach him, indeed? (*To VOM STRAHL.*) Why you…creature more hideous than word or thought can portray! Are you not standing there plain for all to see, as though the cherubim had undressed to clothe your soul in the brilliance of their May morning sparkle! What can I do but shudder before a being who could so pervert human instinct in the purest heart ever created, as to compel a daughter – chalk-white in the face – to shy away from a father, come to offer her his loving heart, and turn instead to the wolf about to devour her? So then, reign Hecate, princess of witchcraft, marsh-musty queen of the night! Sprout, you demonic powers which human society is normally at pains to weed out; blossom under the breath of witches and grow into forests whose treetops intermesh while the plants of heaven, budding on earth, moulder away. Run, you juices of hell, trickling from stalk and stem! Fall on the land like a cataract, so that the suffocating miasma of pestilence steams upwards to the clouds; pour and flow through all life's conduits, sweeping away virtue and innocence in a universal deluge!

COUNT OTTO: Did he get her to take poison?

NACHTHEIM: Do you think he gave her magic potions?

BÄRENKLAU: Opiates whose mysterious power can
enmesh the human heart?

THEOBALD: Poison? Opiates? Exalted lords, why ask me?
It wasn't I who uncorked the bottle he offered her as
refreshment when he was resting against the rock. I wasn't
at those inns where, night after night, she lay asleep in his
stables. How would I know whether he gave her poison?
Just wait nine months and you'll see what it was her
youthful body absorbed.

VOM STRAHL: Listen to the old fool! My only reply to
him is to cite my name! Send for the girl! If she should
say one word that hints in the slightest at anything of the
sort, then dub me Count of the Putrid Puddle – or
whatever you deem fit in your righteous revulsion!

Scene 2

*Enter KATIE, blindfolded, and led by two ORDERLIES who remove
the bandage and withdraw.*

KATIE: (*Gazes round at the assembly and, at sight of VOM
STRAHL, kneels down.*)
My noble lord!

VOM STRAHL: What do you want?

KATIE: I'm summoned to appear before my judge.

VOM STRAHL: I'm not your judge. Look yonder, there
he sits!
I stand accused before the court – like you.

KATIE: My noble lord! You mock me!

VOM STRAHL: No! But listen:
Why are you kneeling in the dust before me?
I am a sorcerer – as I've just admitted.
I hereby free your youthful spirit from
Every spell I cast upon you...(*Raises her up.*)

COUNT OTTO: Young woman, if you please – the court
is here!

BÄRENKLAU: We are your judges.

KATIE: (*Looking about her.*)
                              You would try me?
NACHTHEIM: This way! Step forward! You must
                                        speak to *us*!
(*KATIE stands beside VOM STRAHL and looks at the
JUDGES.*)
COUNT OTTO: Well?
NACHTHEIM: Will you – ?
BÄRENKLAU: Kindly stir yourself?
COUNT OTTO: Will you comply, miss, with your
                                   judges' order?
KATIE: (*Aside.*)
    They're calling me...
NACHTHEIM: Indeed!
BÄRENKLAU: What's that she says?
COUNT OTTO: (*Disconcerted.*)
    Gentlemen, what ails this curious creature?
    (*JUDGES exchange looks.*)
KATIE: (*Aside.*)
    Muffled from head to foot and masked they sit –
    As though this were the day of Final Judgement!
VOM STRAHL: (*Rousing her.*)
    You're dreaming, child! Don't you know where you are?
    You're standing here before the secret court!
    I'm charged with practising that wicked art,
    By which I gained your heart, as you're aware.
    Now go and tell the judges how this happened!
KATIE: (*Looks at him and crosses her hands on her breast.*)
    You torture me most cruelly; I could weep!
    Instruct your maiden, O my noble lord,
    How best she should behave in such a case.
COUNT OTTO: (*Impatiently.*)
    Instruct her?
BÄRENKLAU: In God's name! Whoever heard – ?
VOM STRAHL: (*Firmly but more gently.*)
    You should at once go stand before the bar
    And answer all the questions put to you.
KATIE: What's this? You say that you're accused?
VOM STRAHL: I am.

173

KATIE: And those men sitting there your judges?

VOM STRAHL: Yes.

KATIE: (*Stepping to the bar.*)

    My worthy lords, whoever you may be,

    Stand up and yield the judgement seat to him!

    For, by the living God, I warrant you

    His heart is spotless as his suit of mail;

    Beside it, yours and mine black as your cloaks!

    If sins have been committed, he should judge

    And you should all stand trembling at the bar!

COUNT OTTO: You foolish child, still wet behind the ears,

    Where did you gather this prophetic knowledge?

    Which Apostle was your confidant?

THEOBALD: Look at the hapless child!

KATIE: (*Sees her father and walks towards him.*)

                      My dearest father!

    (*Tries to take his hand.*)

THEOBALD: (*Sternly.*)

    That is the place where you belong, my girl!

KATIE: Don't cast me off! (*Takes his hand and kisses it.*)

THEOBALD: Do you still know these hairs,

    Grown newly grey with anguish at your flight?

KATIE: No day went past but in my thoughts I saw

    My father's falling locks. Have patience though;

    Do not surrender to unbounded grief!

    If joy can once more darken hair that's bleached,

    Then yours shall soon regain its youthful sheen!

COUNT OTTO: Seize her, you orderlies, and bring her here!

THEOBALD: Go where they tell you!

KATIE: (*To the JUDGES, as the ORDERLIES approach.*)

                      What do you want of me?

NACHTHEIM: Was ever child so stubborn seen as this?

COUNT OTTO: (*As she stands at the bar of the court.*)

    We want to hear your answers – short and simple –

    To all our questions, for in conscience we

    Are here to judge you and the punishment,

    If you have sinned, will tame your arrogance.

KATIE: Speak, your honours! What do you want to know?

COUNT OTTO: Why, on the day the Count vom
Strahl appeared
    In your father's house, did you prostrate yourself –
    As though before your God – fall at his feet?
    And why did you, as he rode off, then fling
    Yourself as though demented from the window
    Into the street and why, before your legs
    Were healed, pursue him everywhere he rode
    Come fog or fearsome dark by dead of night?
KATIE: (*Blushing deeply, to VOM STRAHL.*)
    What am I supposed to tell these men?
VOM STRAHL: The foolish child's bewitched, her
wits confused!
    Why ask me? Is it not enough that you're
    Commanded by those men to speak the truth!
KATIE: (*Falling to the ground ; to VOM STRAHL.*)
    My lord, if I've done wrong, then take my life!
    What happens in the spirit's silent realm –
    If God has sanctioned it – no man need know.
    And cruel is he who questions me about it!
    But if *you* wish to know, you've but to ask:
    For you, my soul's an ever-open book.
BÄRENKLAU: Who heard the like of it in all
his days?
NACHTHEIM: She lies before him in the dust –
BÄRENKLAU: She kneels!
NACHTHEIM: As we might prostrate lie before
our Saviour!
VOM STRAHL: (*To the JUDGES.*)
    My worthy lords, I trust you don't impute
    This maiden's folly to myself! It's clear
    That she's bewitched, though neither you
    Nor I can comprehend by what or whom.
    With your permission, I will question her;
    You may deduce from my interrogation
    Whether or not I'm guilty of offence.
COUNT OTTO: (*With a searching look.*)
    So be it, Count! Let's try. You may proceed.

VOM STRAHL: (*To KATIE, still on her knees.*)
 Katie, pay heed, are you prepared to share
 The deepest of those secret thoughts with me,
 That slumber in the cavern of your heart?
KATIE: My heart entire, my lord, if that's your wish –
 That you may know for sure what dwells inside.
VOM STRAHL: What was it then, quite simply – tell
          me straight –
 That drove you to desert your father's house?
 What forced you slavishly to dog my steps?
KATIE: My noble lord! You ask too much of me.
 Were I to lie – as now I do before you –
 Prone in the dust before my conscious mind,
 Upon a golden judgement seat, with all
 The instruments of torture close at hand
 And blazing furnaces in readiness,
 I still could utter only one reply
 In answer to your question: I don't know!
VOM STRAHL: Would you deceive me, maiden? Lie to me?
 To me, accused of having snared your heart?
 Me, at sight of whom, rose-like, you lay
 Opening your petals to the morning light?
 Now tell the court what I once did to you –
 What soul and body suffered at my hand!
KATIE: Where?
VOM STRAHL: Why, here or there.
KATIE: When?
VOM STRAHL: Then or later.
KATIE: Help me, my noble lord!
VOM STRAHL: I'm helping you,
 You curious creature – (*Pauses.*)
        Can you not recall?
(*KATIE hangs her head.*)
 Of all the places that you ever saw me,
 Which above all springs instantly to mind?
KATIE: The Rhine's the place that I remember best.
VOM STRAHL: Quite right. That's what I wished to know.
 The rocky outcrop by the riverbank

Where we lay resting in the noonday heat.
Don't you recall what happened to you there?

KATIE: I don't remember, sir.

VOM STRAHL: You don't? Quite sure?
What did I offer you to slake your thirst?

KATIE: Because, my lord, I scorned to drink the wine,
You bade your loyal retainer, Gottschalk, go
And fetch me clear spring water from the grotto.

VOM STRAHL: But didn't I take your hand and didn't I
Press something to your lips – no? Why not say?

KATIE: But when?

VOM STRAHL: Same time.

KATIE: Indeed not. No, my lord!

VOM STRAHL: Or was it later?

KATIE: Strasburg?

VOM STRAHL: Or before.

KATIE: You didn't ever take me by the hand.

VOM STRAHL: Kathrina!

KATIE: (*Blushing.*)
Oh, forgive me – once in Heilbronn...

VOM STRAHL: When?

KATIE: Father was refurbishing your armour.

VOM STRAHL: No other time?

KATIE: Why, no, my lord!

VOM STRAHL: Kathrina!

KATIE: By the hand?

VOM STRAHL: Why, yes – or any other way.

KATIE: (*Thinking hard.*)
Oh, once in Strasburg, when you touched my chin.

VOM STRAHL: When?

KATIE: As I sat weeping on the doorstep;
You asked me something and I didn't answer.

VOM STRAHL: And why was that?

KATIE: Because I was ashamed.

VOM STRAHL: Ashamed? And rightly so! At my suggestion,
Your cheeks flushed crimson and your neck as well.
What kind of proposition was it?

KATIE: Father,
You said, at home in Schwabenland,

Would be concerned about me and you asked
Wouldn't I like to travel home to him,
With horses you were sending to Heilbronn.
VOM STRAHL: (*Coldly.*)
    That wasn't it! Come on, now, think again!
    Where else was it I met you now and then?
    I used to pay you visits in the stables.
KATIE: Oh no, my lord!
VOM STRAHL: I didn't? Come, Kathrina!
KATIE: You never came to see me in the stables,
    Still less, my lord, did you lay hands on me!
VOM STRAHL: What, never?
KATIE: Never! No, my lord!
VOM STRAHL: Kathrina!
KATIE: (*With emotion.*)
    No, never! No, my noble lord – not once!
VOM STRAHL: Upon my oath, you're lying, girl. The truth –
KATIE: God banish me to hell, my lord, if ever
    You touched me –
VOM STRAHL: (*Pretending vehemence.*)
        How she swears, condemns herself
    To hell, the fickle trollop, and believes
    That God will pardon her a youthful lapse!
    What happened but five days ago, one evening,
    When we were in my stable – it was dusk –
    And I told Gottschalk that he needn't stay?
KATIE: Sweet Jesus, I'd forgotten that you came
    To see me in the stable at your castle.
VOM STRAHL: It's out at last! And she has sworn away
    Her soul's salvation! Yes, it was at Strahl
    I went to see her in my castle stables.
    (*KATIE weeps. Pause.*)
COUNT OTTO: You're torturing the child!
THEOBALD: Come, daughter!
    (*Tries to embrace her.*)
KATIE: Let me go!
NACHTHEIM: It isn't human to behave like that!
COUNT OTTO: It's clear that nothing happened in the stable.
VOM STRAHL: By heaven, gentlemen, if that's your view,
    It's mine, too! Say the word and we'll depart!

COUNT OTTO: We meant you to interrogate the child
    And not to mock her with barbaric triumph!
    Nature may well have lent you such a power,
    But as you wield it, it's more hateful still
    Than the satanic art with which you're charged.
VOM STRAHL: (*Raising KATIE.*)
    My lords, I acted as I did that I
    Might raise her up triumphant here before you.
    Not I, my lords –
    (*Pointing to the floor.*)   but this my gauntlet lies
    Before the court. If she's found innocent –
    As so she is – then let her now go free.
NACHTHEIM: No doubt you have your reasons

                           for that wish?
VOM STRAHL: Reasons? Compelling! You will not, I hope,
    Mock her with your barbaric...arrogance?
NACHTHEIM: (*Significantly.*)
    We still would like to know, if you'll allow,
    What happened in your stable at the castle.
VOM STRAHL: The court still wants to hear?
NACHTHEIM: Of course!
VOM STRAHL: (*Flushing with anger, turns to KATIE.*)

                         Kneel down!

    (*KATIE again kneels before him.*)
COUNT OTTO: You're very bold, I must say, Count

                         vom Strahl!
VOM STRAHL: (*To KATIE.*)
    So be it! Answer me and no one else!
BÄRENKLAU: We'll ask her, by your leave –
VOM STRAHL: (*To KATIE.*)

                     Stay where you are!
    For none shall judge you here, save he to whom
    Your spirit of its own free will submits.
NACHTHEIM: Count Friedrich, we have methods –
VOM STRAHL: (*With suppressed vehemence.*)

                       No, I say!
    The devil take me, if you try to force her!
    What do you want to know, my noble lords?
BÄRENKLAU: (*Indignantly.*)
    By heaven!

NACHTHEIM: Such audacity!

BÄRENKLAU: Hi, guards!

COUNT OTTO: (*Softly.*)

Friends, that will do! Remember who he is!

1ˢᵀ JUDGE: Although himself accused, he's questioned her
So far impartially.

2ᴺᴰ JUDGE: I quite agree;
I favour leaving him to carry on.

COUNT OTTO: (*To VOM STRAHL.*)

Then ask her what transpired five days ago
In the stable at Strahl Castle in the dusk,
When you instructed Gottschalk to withdraw.

VOM STRAHL: That evening, five days past, what happened in
The stable at my castle as dusk fell
And I instructed Gottschalk to withdraw?

KATIE: My lord, forgive me if I failed you – I
Will now recount the incident in full.

VOM STRAHL: Good. So I touched you – didn't I? Of course!
That you've admitted?

KATIE: Yes, my noble lord!

VOM STRAHL: Well?

KATIE: My lord?

VOM STRAHL: What do I want to know?

KATIE: What do you want to know?

VOM STRAHL: Yes, out with it!
I then caressed and kissed you, did I not?
And put my arm around you –

KATIE: No, my lord!

VOM STRAHL: What then?

KATIE: You thrust me from you with your foot!

VOM STRAHL: A kick? Not that! I wouldn't kick a dog!
For what? Why should I? What was it you did?

KATIE: Because I turned my back upon my father –
Who'd kindly come to fetch me home with horses –
And, terror-stricken, begged you to protect me,
Before collapsing senseless at your feet.

VOM STRAHL: You say I thrust you from me with a kick?

KATIE: You did, my noble lord!

VOM STRAHL: A knavish trick!
 Designed to fool your father, that was all.
 You went on living in my castle, didn't you?
KATIE: No, my noble lord.
VOM STRAHL: If not, then where?
KATIE: When you, with fiery cheeks, took down the whip
 That hung upon a beam, I ran outside
 Beyond the mossy gate and there lay down
 Among the ruins of the rampart wall,
 Close by the fragrant elder bushes where
 A twittering finch had built itself a nest.
VOM STRAHL: Then did I loose my hounds to drive you off?
KATIE: Why no, my lord!
VOM STRAHL: And when you fled –
 Pursued by yapping dogs – from my domain,
 Did I not call my neighbour, too, to chase you?
KATIE: No, no, my lord! I don't know what you mean!
VOM STRAHL: You don't? I fear the court will be displeased!
KATIE: Don't worry what these gentlemen may think.
 The third day, you sent Gottschalk out to say,
 That, notwithstanding I was dear to you,
 I must be sensible and go away.
VOM STRAHL: And how did you reply to him?
KATIE: I said
 You didn't mind the twittering finch
 That nested in the fragrant elder bush,
 So why not suffer Kate of Heilbronn, too?
VOM STRAHL: (*Lifting her up.*)
 So there, your lordships, she is yours to take –
 Do with her and with me as you see fit!
COUNT OTTO: (*Indignant.*)
 That dreaming dotard! Not the faintest inkling
 Of nature's most familiar sorcery!
 If, gentlemen, you too have reached your verdict,
 I'll close the case and put it to the vote.
NACHTHEIM: Yes, close it!
BÄRENKLAU: Vote!
ALL: Collect the votes!

1ˢᵀ JUDGE: Old fool!
> It's clear there wasn't any case to answer!

COUNT OTTO: Herald, take the helmet and collect.
> (*HERALD collects the balls in a helmet which he hands to*
> *COUNT OTTO.*)

COUNT OTTO: (*Standing.*)
> Friedrich Wetter, Count vom Strahl, you've been
> Unanimously found not guilty.
> You, Theobald, I now command
> To take your charge no further until you
> Have better proof to lay before the court.
> (*To the JUDGES.*) Rise, gentlemen; the hearing's at an end!
> (*JUDGES rise.*)

THEOBALD: My gracious lords, you find him innocent?
> Reputedly, God made the world from nothing;
> And he who now destroys it utterly –
> Plunging it into that primeval chaos –
> Is he not surely Satan in the flesh?

COUNT OTTO: Silence, you grey-beard fool! We are not here
> To straighten the disorder of your wits!
> Orderly, do your duty! Bind his eyes
> And lead him out again into the fields!

THEOBALD: Into the fields, you say? A poor old man!
> While she – my dear and only child – is –

COUNT OTTO: (*To VOM STRAHL.*)
>   Count!
> The court leaves that to you! You've given us
> So many strange examples of the power
> That you possess; pray, let us see one more –
> The greatest test of all – ere we depart –
> And give this father back his only child!

VOM STRAHL: My lords, if I can do so, then I shall.
> Maiden!

KATIE: My lord!

VOM STRAHL: You love me?

KATIE: That I do!

VOM STRAHL: Do me a favour then.

KATIE: What is it? Speak!

VOM STRAHL: Do not pursue me but go home to Heilbronn!
Will you do that?

KATIE: I promised you I would.
(*Falls in a faint.*)

THEOBALD: (*Catching her.*)
My child! My only one! Help! God in heaven!

VOM STRAHL: (*Turning.*)
A blindfold, orderly! (*Blindfolds himself.*)

THEOBALD: My curse upon you,
Basilisk whose glance is death! Must I
Endure this final sample of your art?

COUNT OTTO: (*Coming down from the bench.*)
What's happened, gentlemen?

NACHTHEIM: The girl collapsed.
(*All eyes are on KATIE.*)

VOM STRAHL: (*To the ORDERLIES.*)
Lead me outside!

THEOBALD: Go back to hell, you Satan!
And let the snake-haired porters at the gates
Lay hold of you, you wizard, and consign you
Ten thousand fathoms deeper than the pit
Where blaze the fiercest flames of your inferno!

COUNT OTTO: Be silent, you!

THEOBALD: (*Weeping.*)
My child, Kathrina!

KATIE: Oh!

NACHTHEIM: (*Gladly.*)
She's opening her eyes!

BÄRENKLAU: She's coming to!

COUNT OTTO: Take her to the porter's lodge at once!
(*Exeunt ALL.*)

End of Act One.

ACT TWO

Forest in front of the cavern where the secret court was in session.

Scene 1

Enter VOM STRAHL blindfolded, led by two ORDERLIES who then remove his blindfold and retire at once into the cavern. VOM STRAHL throws himself on the ground and weeps.

VOM STRAHL: Here let me lie down like a shepherd and lament. The sun's ruddy glow still shines through the trunks on which the forest treetops rest. If I get up again after a brief quarter of an hour, soon as the sun has sunk behind the hill, and then set off across the open country, keeping to the path where the ground is level, I should be able to reach Castle Strahl before lights out. I want to imagine that my horses down below, where the spring trickles, are sheep and goats, climbing among the rocks and tearing at tufts of grass and bitter shrubs; myself covered in a light linen garment with a red sash, while playful breezes flutter about me, carrying to the ears of the gods the sighs of grief that heave from my sore-afflicted breast. Really and truly! I shall comb through all my native tongue and so thoroughly plunder that whole rich chapter headed 'Emotion' that no rhyme-smith of the future will be able to find a new way of expressing his melancholy. I shall quote everything that's touching about sadness; joy and sadness unto death must alternate and my voice, like a skilled dancer, lead the way through all gyrations that enchant the soul. And if the trees remain in fact unmoved, failing to release the drizzle of their mild dew, as though it had just rained, then their hearts are wooden and everything the poets have told us about them nothing more than a delightful fairy tale. Dearest one, what am I to call you? Katie! But why can I not call you mine? Katie, girl – Katie! Why

can I not take you in my arms and carry you off to that
fragrant fourposter at home, which my mother installed
in my state apartment? Katie! Katie! Katie! You whose
young soul was bared before me in the court today,
dripping with sensuous beauty, like the bride of
a Persian shah, anointed all over with oils, sprinkling the
carpets as they lead her to his chamber. Katie, Katie,
girl! Why can I not? You who are more beautiful than
I could ever sing: I will invent an art of my own and
weep for you!...All vessels of perception, heavenly and
earthly I will open up and blend such a mixture of tears,
an infusion, so extraordinary – at once both salutary and
prolific that anyone upon whose neck I shed such tears
will immediately say they flow for Katie of Heilbronn!
But, stay, you grey-beard elders! What do you want?
Why leave your gilded frames, you portraits of my
ancestors in armour, who throng about me in unruly
assembly, shaking your revered locks? No, no, no!
I would not have her for my wife, although I love
her! For I intend to join your noble ranks. That was
a foregone conclusion, even before you appeared. But
I would ask you, Winfried – you the leader, first to bear
our name, whose godlike brow is that of Zeus – tell me:
was the mother of our clan more radiantly virtuous than
Katie, in body and soul more spotless, more generously
endowed with every lovable charm?...O greybeard
Winfried! I kiss your hand and thank you for my
existence...But had you pressed her to your breast of
steel, you would have bred a future race of kings and
every ruler on earth would bear the name Wetter vom
Strahl! I know I must control myself and this wound will
heal; what wound was ever beyond man's power to heal?
But, Katie, if I ever find your equal in a wife, I'll travel
through every land on earth, learn every language and
praise God in every tongue that's spoken!

Scene 2

GOTTSCHALK and VOM STRAHL.

GOTTSCHALK: (*Off.*) Hi, there! Count vom Strahl!

VOM STRAHL: What is it?

GOTTSCHALK: (*Enters.*) A messenger's arrived here from your mother!

VOM STRAHL: A messenger?

GOTTSCHALK: At full gallop, panting, breakneck all the way! I swear that if your palace were a bow and he the arrow, he couldn't have been shot here any quicker!

VOM STRAHL: But what has he to tell me?

GOTTSCHALK: Knight Franz, this way!

Scene 3

Enter KNIGHT FRANZ FLAMMBERG.

VOM STRAHL: Flammberg! What brings you here so swiftly?

FLAMMBERG: Most gracious lord! The order of your mother, the Countess! She bade me take the swiftest steed and ride to meet you.

VOM STRAHL: Well! What news have you brought me?

FLAMMBERG: War, upon my oath – it's war! The declaration of another feud – still warm, as she received it from the herald's lips!

VOM STRAHL: (*Downcast.*) Who is it this time? Not the Burgrave with whom I only recently made peace? (*Puts on his helmet.*)

FLAMMBERG: No, it's the Rhine-Count Junker von Stein, whose castle guards the vineyards on the Neckar.

VOM STRAHL: The Rhine-Count? But, Flammberg, what concern of mine is he?

FLAMMBERG: So help me, what concern is he of yours? What did so many another want from you, before you came up against the Burgrave? Unless you stamp out this little spark of Greek fire which is causing these wars,

you'll see the whole Swabian highland region go up in
flames against you, and the Alps and Houndsback, too.

VOM STRAHL: That's not possible! The lady Kunigunde –

FLAMMBERG: The Rhine-Count, in the name of the lady
Kunigunde of Turneck, wants to buy back your title to
Staufen – those three small towns, 17 villages and farms,
sold to your ancestor Otto von Peter by one of her
forebears, just as the Burgrave of Freiburg did, and – in
earlier times – some cousins of yours.

VOM STRAHL: She's a raging Fury! This is the third
knight she's set upon me, like a dog, in her efforts to
chase me off that bit of land. I think she's got the whole
realm eating out of her hand. Cleopatra found herself
a man and once he was done for, the others shied away.
But every creature with one rib less than herself seems
ready to serve Kunigunde! For every one I send her back
in pieces, another ten spring up against me...What
reasons did he give?

FLAMMBERG: Who? The herald?

VOM STRAHL: What were the reasons he gave?

FLAMMBERG: Not much he *could* say without blushing.

VOM STRAHL: I suppose he talked about Peter von
Turneck and the sale of the territory being invalid?

FLAMMBERG: Indeed he did – and the laws of Swabia.
Every second word of his speech was duty or conscience.
He also called on God to witness that nothing but the
purest of motives had induced his master the Rhine-Count
to take up Princess Kunigunde's cause.

VOM STRAHL: But he kept quiet about the lady's rosy
cheeks, eh?

FLAMMBERG: Not a word on that subject.

VOM STRAHL: A pox on her! I wish I could gather the dew
of the night in bucketfuls and pour it over her lily-white
neck! That accursed pretty face of hers is the real reason
for all these wars against me. Short of being able to poison
the March snow she uses to wash in, I'll have no peace
from any knight in this land. However, we must be
patient! Where is she at the moment?

FLAMMBERG: Stein Castle, where they've been celebrating her presence with such revels these past three days, the heavens are exploding and you can't see the sun, moon or stars. The Burgrave whom she recently got rid of is said to be plotting revenge. If you were to send him an emissary, I've no doubt he'd take up arms with you against the Rhine-Count.

VOM STRAHL: Very well! Bring the horses and let's away! I promised that young mischief-maker that if she didn't stop using her roguish good looks as a weapon against me, I'd play her such a trick, she'd have to wear a veil for the rest of her life! And sure as I raise my right hand, I'll keep my word! Follow me, friends! (*Exeunt ALL.*)

Scene 4

A charcoal-burner's hut in the mountains. Night, thunder and lightning. Enter the BURGRAVE OF FREIBURG and GEORG VON WALDSTÄDTEN.

FREIBURG: (*Shouting into the wings.*) Lift her down from the horse! (*Lightning and thunderclap.*) Strike anything you like, but not the powdered head of my dear betrothed, Kunigunde von Turneck!

A VOICE: (*Off.*) Ho, there! Where are you?

FREIBURG: Here!

WALDSTÄDTEN: Did you ever see such a night?

FREIBURG: The heavens are pouring, drowning treetops and mountain-peaks – like the start of a second flood! Lift her down from the horse!

A VOICE: (*Off.*) She can't move...

ANOTHER: She's lying there like a corpse by the horse's hooves.

FREIBURG: Play-acting! She's afraid of losing her false teeth! You tell her I'm the Burgrave of Freiburg, so I've already counted how many real ones she has left. Bring her here, then!

(*KNIGHT SCHAUERMANN appears, carrying the lady*
KUNIGUNDE on his shoulder.)
WALDSTÄDTEN: There's a charcoal-burner's hut over there.

Scene 5

The foregoing together with SCHAUERMANN, KUNIGUNDE,
KNIGHT WETZLAF and the BURGRAVE's SOLDIERS, together
with two CHARCOAL-BURNERS.

FREIBURG: (*Knocking at door of hut.*) Hi, there!
1ST BURNER: (*Inside.*) Who's knocking?
FREIBURG: Don't ask questions, you sluggard! Open up!
2ND BURNER: (*Inside.*) Not before I turn the key!
I suppose it's the Emperor, is it?
FREIBURG: You villain! If it isn't, it's someone who rules
hereabouts – as I'll show you, once I get hold of a stout
branch to use as sceptre.
1ST BURNER: (*Appears with lantern.*) Who are you? What
do you want?
FREIBURG: I am a knight and the lady they're carrying in,
mortally sick, is –
SCHAUERMANN: (*From behind.*) Get rid of that light!
WETZLAF: Knock the lantern out of his hand!
FREIBURG: (*Taking the lantern from him.*) You varlet! What
do you think you're doing with that light?
1ST BURNER: Seems to me, masters, I'm more use than any
of you! What do you mean by taking my lantern?
2ND BURNER: Who are you? What do you want?
FREIBURG: We're knights, you oaf! Told you already!
WALDSTÄDTEN: We're travelling knights, my good
fellows – surprised by the storm.
FREIBURG: (*Interrupting him.*) Crusaders on our way home
from Jerusalem. And that lady they're carrying –
wrapped in her cloak from head to foot – is –
(*Clap of thunder.*)
1ST BURNER: Go on, blast the clouds apart! From
Jerusalem, you said?

2ND BURNER: Can't understand a word you say with that
thunder making such a din!

FREIBURG: Yes, from Jerusalem!

2ND BURNER: And the woman they're carrying?

WALDSTÄDTEN: (*Pointing to FREIBURG.*) She's this
gentleman's sister. She's ill, my good man, and needs –

FREIBURG: (*Interrupting.*) She's his sister, you rogue, and
my wife; mortally ill, as you can see, half-dead from the
tempest and the hail. She can't say a word – but she seeks
shelter in this hut, till the storm's over and day dawns.

1ST BURNER: She wants some room in my hut?

WALDSTÄDTEN: Yes, good charcoal-burners, till the
storm's over and we can continue our journey.

2ND BURNER: You could have told us in fewer words!

1ST BURNER: Isaac!

FREIBURG: Will you help her?

2ND BURNER: We'd help the Emperor's hounds, my
masters, if they were howling at the door. Isaac! You
varmint! Can't you hear me?

BOY: (*In the hut.*) What's the matter?

2ND BURNER: Shake up the straw and put some blankets
over it. There's a sick woman here who needs
a bit of room in the hut, d'ye hear?

FREIBURG: Who's that inside?

1ST BURNER: It's a ten-year-old lad who gives us
a hand with things.

FREIBURG: Good. Come on, Schauermann – the gag's
worked loose.

SCHAUERMANN: Where?

FREIBURG: Never mind. Take her in and put her in the
corner. I'll call you at daybreak.

(*SCHAUERMANN carries KUNIGUNDE into the hut.*)

Scene 6

As before, less SCHAUERMANN and KUNIGUNDE.

FREIBURG: (*Jubilant.*) Let trumpets blare and cymbals
clash! We've got her, Georg! We've captured Kunigunde

von Turneck! Sure as I bear my father's name, not for
all the heavenly joys I used to pray for as a boy would
I exchange the delight that shall be mine at daybreak!
Why didn't you get here sooner from Waldstädten?

WALDSTÄDTEN: Because you didn't call me any sooner.

FREIBURG: You should have seen her, Georg, as she came
riding along, surrounded by her knights, like a fairy-tale
princess or the sun ringed by its planets. Thalestris,
Queen of the Amazons, riding down from the Caucasus
to beg a kiss from Alexander the Great, couldn't have
looked more divinely attractive!

WALDSTÄDTEN: Where did you catch her?

FREIBURG: Five hours away from Steinburg, where the
Rhein-Count had been entertaining her for the past three
days with feasting and revels. Her escort of knights had
barely left her when I fell upon her cousin Isidore who'd
stayed behind and tumbled him in the sand; then, up
with her on to my saddle-bow – and away!

WALDSTÄDTEN: But Max, Max – what are you – ?

FREIBURG: I'll tell you, my friend –

WALDSTÄDTEN: What's the point of this violent enterprise?

FREIBURG: My dear, good man! It's honey to refresh
a throat bone dry with the thirst for revenge! Why
should this artificial image, like some Olympian
goddess, continue to reign in splendour on her pedestal,
emptying Christian churches of people like ourselves?
Far better lay hold of the idol, fling it on the rubbish-
heap and turn the highest into the lowest – so that
everyone can see there's nothing divine about it!

WALDSTÄDTEN: But tell me, how do you come to be so
full of raging hate against her?

FREIBURG: Oh, Georg, a man can throw his personal
belongings to the winds, but not his feelings. I loved the
woman, Georg, and she wasn't worth it. I loved her and
she scorned me. She proved unworthy of my love. I'll
tell you something, Georg, though I pale at the thought
of it. When devils are lost for an idea, they ask a cock
who's been chasing after a hen in vain, only to find her
covered in scabs and so, unfit for what he has in mind.

WALDSTÄDTEN: I trust you're not planning some revenge unworthy of a knight?

FREIBURG: God forbid! I wouldn't ask a man-at-arms to have his way with her! I merely plan to take her back to the Rhine-Count at Steinburg, where I shall simply remove her neckerchief – and that will be my only vengeful act!

WALDSTÄDTEN: What? Remove her neckerchief?

FREIBURG: Yes, and call the people together.

WALDSTÄDTEN: And when you've done that, what then?

FREIBURG: I shall just philosophize a little regarding her. I will pronounce a metaphysical dictum about her, like Plato, and later elucidate my dictum, like merry old Diogenes: man is a…but, shush! (*He listens.*)

WALDSTÄDTEN: Well, come on! Man is what?

FREIBURG: Man, according to Plato, is a two-legged creature without feathers. You know how Diogenes proved as much? So far as I recall, he plucked a cock and threw it to the crowd…This Kunigunde, my friend, this Kunigunde of Turneck is, to my way of thinking – Shush, quiet! Sure as I'm alive, that's the sound of someone dismounting!

Scene 7

Enter VOM STRAHL and FLAMMBERG. Later GOTTSCHALK.

VOM STRAHL: (*Knocking at the door of the hut.*) Wake up there, good charcoal-burners!

FLAMMBERG: What a night! Enough to force the wolves to seek shelter in caves.

VOM STRAHL: May we come inside?

FREIBURG: (*Blocking his way.*) I'm sorry. Whoever you may be –

WALDSTÄDTEN: You can't come in here.

VOM STRAHL: Can't? Why not?

FREIBURG: Because there's no room – for you or for us. My wife is lying in there, mortally ill. She's occupying the only space to spare. You wouldn't want to turn her out.

VOM STRAHL: No, upon my oath! I only hope she'll soon recover in there! Gottschalk!

FLAMMBERG: Then we'll have to spend the night under heaven's roof.

VOM STRAHL: Gottschalk, I say!

GOTTSCHALK: (*Outside.*) I'm here!

VOM STRAHL: Bring the blankets! We'll camp under the trees.

(*Enter GOTTSCHALK and the charcoal-burners' BOY.*)

GOTTSCHALK: (*Bringing blankets.*) Devil knows what's going on in there! The boy says there's a man in armour guarding a lady, who's lying there bound and gagged like a calf ready for the slaughter.

VOM STRAHL: What's that? A lady bound and gagged? Who told you that?

FLAMMBERG: How do you know, boy?

BOY: Shush! By all the saints! What are you doing, masters?

VOM STRAHL: Come here!

BOY: I said 'shush'!

FLAMMBERG: Who told you, boy? Out with it!

BOY: (*Discreetly, after looking about him.*) I saw it, masters! Lay in the straw after they carried her in and said she were ill. Shone the lamp on her and saw she were quite well, cheeks as rosy as our Laura. She whimpered and pressed my hand and her eyes sparkled. It was as easy to understand her as a clever dog. 'Untie me, there's a good lad – untie me!' I could hear with me eyes and understand with me fingers.

VOM STRAHL: Well, then, flax-head, go and do it!

FLAMMBERG: What are you waiting for?

VOM STRAHL: Untie her and send her out here!

BOY: (*Nervously.*) Keep quiet, I tell you! Wish you could turn yourselves into mice. Otherwise those three will be coming over here to see what's going on. (*Blows out his lantern.*)

VOM STRAHL: Don't worry, my lad, they've not heard a sound.

FLAMMBERG: Not a thing.

VOM STRAHL: They're just changing places because of the rain.

BOY: (*Looking round.*) Will you protect me?

VOM STRAHL: On my word of honour as a knight!

FLAMMBERG: You can count upon it!

BOY: I'll tell my father that. Wait a moment and watch what I do. (*Speaks to the OLD MEN standing round the fire then goes into the hut.*)

FLAMMBERG: Odd folk by the sound of it! Knights of Beelzebub, cloaked in darkness. Married couples on the highway, conjugally bound with cords and fetters?

VOM STRAHL: Ill, they said!

FLAMMBERG: Mortally ill and most grateful for all help.

GOTTSCHALK: Just wait! We'll separate them! (*Pause.*)

SCHAUERMANN: (*Inside the hut.*) Hey, what's this! God's teeth!

VOM STRAHL: On your feet, Flammberg! Get up! (*Both rise.*)

FREIBURG: What's the matter? (*FREIBURG's men also rise.*)

SCHAUERMANN: Someone's tied me up! I'm bound! (*KUNIGUNDE appears.*)

FREIBURG: Ye gods! What's this I see?

Scene 8

KUNIGUNDE in travelling costume, hair loose.

KUNIGUNDE: (*Throws herself at the feet of VOM STRAHL.*) My saviour! Whosoever you may be,
Have pity on a maiden much despised
And deep dishonoured! If your knightly oath
Enjoins protection of the innocent,
Then here lies one who claims it as of right!

FREIBURG: Drag her away, you men!

WALDSTÄDTEN: No, listen, Max!

FREIBURG: Drag her away, I say! Don't let her talk!

VOM STRAHL: Hold, gentlemen! What is it?

FREIBURG: What, you ask?
I want my wife, by God! Grab hold of her!

KUNIGUNDE: Your wife? You lying villain!

VOM STRAHL: (*Sternly.*)

Do not touch her!
If you're demanding something of this lady,
Then tell me what it is, for now she's mine,
Since she commends herself to my protection.
(*Raises KUNIGUNDE up.*)

FREIBURG: Who are you, insolent ruffian, that you dare
To interfere 'twixt man and wife? What right
Have you to keep my spouse from me by force?

KUNIGUNDE: Your spouse? You false rapscallion! That
I'm not!

VOM STRAHL: And who are you, ignoble reprobate,
To claim her as your spouse, accursed knave –
To call a maiden yours, vile rapist, only
By Satan wed to you with gag and fetters?

FREIBURG: How? What? Who?

WALDSTÄDTEN: Please, Max!

VOM STRAHL: Who are you?

FREIBURG: You're much mistaken if –

VOM STRAHL: I said, who are you?

FREIBURG: If you believe, my lords, that I –

VOM STRAHL: Fetch torches!

FREIBURG: That woman there, I brought with me, she is –

VOM STRAHL: Light over here, I said! Make haste!

(*GOTTSCHALK and CHARCOAL-BURNERS with torches and flares.*)

FREIBURG: I am –

WALDSTÄDTEN: (*Quietly to FREIBURG.*)
You're raving mad! Quick, let's away at once!
Or you'll disgrace your coat-of-arms for ever!

VOM STRAHL: Come here, brave charcoal-burners! Shine
your light!

(*FREIBURG lowers his visor.*)
Now, we shall see! Who are you? What's your name?

FREIBURG: I am –

VOM STRAHL: Raise your visor!

FREIBURG: Just you listen!

VOM STRAHL: You crafty knave! You think you can reject
My challenge and escape unpunished?
(*Tears his helmet off; FREIBURG staggers.*)
SCHAUERMANN: The insolent cur! Have at him! Bring
him down!
WETZLAF: Quick! Draw your sword!
FREIBURG: You madman! You shall pay!
(*Rises, draws his sword and slashes at VOM STRAHL who
dodges the blow.*)
VOM STRAHL: You specious bridegroom! Do you dare resist?
(*Fells him with a blow.*)
Then, back to hell with you, where you belong,
And celebrate your honeymoon down there!
WETZLAF: Oh horror! See, he's swaying, he's collapsed!
FLAMMBERG: (*Pressing forward.*)
Quick, friends!
SCHAUERMANN: Away! Escape!
FLAMMBERG: Have at the dogs!
Come on, let's put this scurvy crew to flight!
(*FREIBURG's party take to their heels, except for
WALDSTÄDTEN, busy with the fallen man.*)
VOM STRAHL: (*To FREIBURG.*)
It's Freiburg! O ye gods! What's this I see?
Can it be really you?
KUNIGUNDE: (*Stifled voice.*)
Ungrateful hell-hound!
VOM STRAHL: What were you doing with this
maiden, wretch?
What did you want with her?
WALDSTÄDTEN: He cannot speak.
Blood, welling from his scalp, is choking him!
KUNIGUNDE: Then let him drown in it!
VOM STRAHL: I must be dreaming!
A man like him, reputed brave and good!
Come help him, all of you!
FLAMMBERG: Let's lift him up
And carry him inside the hut to rest.
KUNIGUNDE: Bury him! Fetch shovels! He's no more!

VOM STRAHL: Madam, compose yourself! The state he's in,
    Even unburied, he can't harm you now!

KUNIGUNDE: Water, I beg you!

VOM STRAHL: Do you feel unwell?

KUNIGUNDE: It's nothing – nothing – help me – to a seat…
    I'm feeling faint…(*Swaying on her feet.*)

VOM STRAHL: By all the heavenly powers! Here,
    Gottschalk, help!

GOTTSCHALK: Bring torches, quick!

KUNIGUNDE: No, never mind!

VOM STRAHL: (*Having led her to a seat.*)

                               It's passing?

KUNIGUNDE: The sight's returning to my darkened eyes.

VOM STRAHL: What was it overcame you of a sudden?

KUNIGUNDE: Oh, my courageous knight and liberator,
    What shall I call it – that unspeakable,
    Inhuman horror which awaited me?
    The very thought of what, without your aid,
    I might have suffered, caused my hair to bristle
    And robbed my limbs of all remaining strength.

VOM STRAHL: Who are you? Tell me what it was befell you.

KUNIGUNDE: I'm overjoyed that I can tell you all!
    She for whom you did this noble deed
    Is worthy of it: I am Kunigunde,
    The lady of Turneck, may it please your grace.
    This precious life that you have saved for me
    Shall soon, in Turneck, not by me alone
    But by my kith and kin, be recompensed.

VOM STRAHL: You are – It cannot be! You're Kunigund'
    Of Turneck?

KUNIGUNDE: That is so. Why so surprised?

VOM STRAHL: (*Rising.*)
    Because, upon my oath, I'm sad to say,
    You've quit the frying-pan to brave the fire!
    For I am Friedrich Wetter, Count vom Strahl!

KUNIGUNDE: What? Is that your name – my saviour's name?

VOM STRAHL: Friedrich Count vom Strahl.

                            I much regret,
    My lady, I can offer you none better.

KUNIGUNDE: You heavenly powers! How sorely I'm
being tried!

GOTTSCHALK: (*Quietly.*)
    Of Turneck, did she say?

FLAMMBERG: (*Astonished.*)
She did, by God!

KUNIGUNDE: So be it! But that shall not quench the flame
    Of gratitude now burning in my heart!
    I'll think no thought and nothing feel but life,
    Honour, innocence, salvation and
    Protection from that wolf now lying dead!
    Come here to me, you darling, golden boy –
    My rescuer! Accept this ring from me;
    It's all that I can give you, for the moment:
    Reward more fitting for a hero later
    Shall grace your deed: the loosing of my bonds,
    Your bravery in saving me from shame –
    A deed that turned my misery to bliss!
    (*Turning to VOM STRAHL.*)
    You are my master: all that I possess
    Belongs to you! Speak! What is your decision?
    For I am in your power! What is your will?
    Am I to follow you to Castle Strahl?

VOM STRAHL: (*Somewhat embarrassed.*)
    My lady, it is not that far away.
    If you can ride, my mother – the Countess –
    Will welcome you as guest to pass the night.

KUNIGUNDE: Bring me a horse!

VOM STRAHL: (*After a pause.*)
I hope you'll pardon me
    If in the circumstances, your reception –

KUNIGUNDE: Don't mention it! You'll make me
feel ashamed;
    I'd not object to sleeping in your dungeon!

VOM STRAHL: My dungeon! No, my lady, rest assured –

KUNIGUNDE: Don't crush me with your magnanimity!
    Give me your hand, pray!

VOM STRAHL: Torches! Light our way!
    (*Exeunt ALL.*)

Scene 9

A chamber in Castle Strahl.

Enter KUNIGUNDE half-dressed in period costume; she sits down at the dressing table.

ROSALIE and the old housekeeper BRIGITTE behind her.

ROSALIE: (*To BRIGITTE.*) Be seated, mother! The Count vom Strahl has sent my lady word to say he's here. She just wants me to tidy her hair and would like to chat with you while I'm about it.

BRIGITTE: (*Seated.*) So you are the lady Kunigunde of Turneck?

KUNIGUNDE: Yes, old woman – that I am.

BRIGITTE: And you're a daughter of the Emperor?

KUNIGUNDE: Of the Emperor? No, who told you that? I don't know the present emperor at all. I'm the great-granddaughter of one of the emperors who sat on the German throne centuries ago.

BRIGITTE: Lord! Is it possible? The great-granddaughter –

KUNIGUNDE: Why, yes!

ROSALIE: What did I tell you?

BRIGITTE: So I can go to my grave in peace! Count vom Strahl's dream has come true!

KUNIGUNDE: What dream was that?

ROSALIE: Just you listen! It's the strangest story you ever heard. But keep it short, mother! Leave out the first part. As I told you, we haven't got much time.

BRIGITTE: Well, towards the end of the year before last, the Count fell ill with a strange depression. What caused it, nobody could say. He lay there exhausted, in delirium, his face red-hot. After trying everything, the doctors finally gave him up for lost. Now, in the delirium of his fever, his tongue gave voice to all the closest secrets of his heart. He was happy to depart this world, he said, for the only girl who could love him was nowhere to be found. Life without love, he said, was death. The world was his grave, he said, and the grave his cradle, meaning he was only now about to be born. On three successive nights, during which his mother never left his bedside, he told her an angel had appeared, crying out to him: 'Have faith! Faith! Faith!' When the Countess asked him whether he hadn't felt strengthened by this heavenly appeal, he replied: 'Strengthened? No!' adding with a sigh, that he would be, once he had seen the girl. 'And will you be seeing her?' asked the Countess. 'Certainly I shall,' was his reply. When and where, the Countess wanted to know. 'On New Year's Eve,' he said, 'he'll lead me to her.' 'Who will and to whom?' asked the Countess. 'The angel will lead me to my girl,' he replied and with that he turned over and fell asleep.

KUNIGUNDE: What a lot of nonsense!

ROSALIE: Just wait till you hear the rest!

BRIGITTE: Well, on New Year's Eve – at the very moment the year changed – he sat up in bed and stared into the room as though he beheld a vision. Then, pointing a finger, he called out: 'Mother! Mother! Mother!' 'What is it?' she asked. 'There! There!' – 'Where?' 'Quick!' he said. 'What?' 'My helmet! My armour! My sword!' 'Where are you going?' his mother asked. 'To her!' he said, 'to her!' Then he sank back in bed, muttering 'Farewell, mother,' stretched out his limbs and lay there, as though dead.

KUNIGUNDE: Dead?

ROSALIE: Yes, dead!

KUNIGUNDE: She means looking like a corpse.

ROSALIE: She said 'dead'. Don't interrupt her. Well – go on!

BRIGITTE: We listened to his chest. Quiet as an empty room. We held a feather to his mouth to test his breathing. It didn't move. The doctor thought his spirit had indeed passed away. He called his name anxiously into his ear; tried to revive him with smelling salts; scratched him with sticks and needles; pulled out one of his hairs so that he bled. All in vain! He didn't stir a limb and lay there as though dead.

KUNIGUNDE: So then? What next?

BRIGITTE: Well, after he'd been lying like that for some
time, he started up, turned towards the wall with
a look of dismay and said: 'Now they're bringing
candles and I can't see her any more!' He seemed to
be flinching from the gleam. And as the Countess bent
over him and raised his head to her breast, asking:
'Friedrich, where have you been?' he answered
joyfully: 'With her! With the girl who loves me – the
bride that heaven means me to wed! Mother, go and
have them pray for me in all the churches, for now
I wish to live!'

KUNIGUNDE: And he really did recover?

ROSALIE: That was the miracle.

BRIGITTE: Hour by hour, lady, from then on, he started to
regain his strength, as though healed by some heavenly
salve and, before the new moon, he was as sound as ever.

KUNIGUNDE: Did he speak about it? What did he say?

BRIGITTE: As to that, he was never done talking about it:
how the angel took his hand and led him through the
darkness, softly opened the girl's bedroom door,
lighting the walls with his radiance. How they went in
and saw this lovely girl lying there, clad only in her
nightdress; how she opened her eyes wide at sight of
him, calling out in a voice hoarse with astonishment
'Marianna!' who must have been somebody asleep in
the next door room. How she then got out of bed,
blushing all over with joy, knelt down before him with
bowed head and whispered, 'O my noble lord!' How the
angel then told him that she was an emperor's daughter
and showed him a reddish birthmark on the child's
neck and how he, trembling with infinite delight, took
her by the chin, to look at her face and how the
wretched maid, Marianna, came running with a candle
and the whole vision disappeared as she entered
the room.

KUNIGUNDE: And now you think I'm this emperor's
daughter?

BRIGITTE: Who else?

ROSALIE: I agree.

BRIGITTE: As soon as you arrived and they heard who
you were, everyone in the castle clapped their hands and
cried: 'She's the one!'

ROSALIE: It only needed the bells to loosen their tongues
and ring out: 'Yes! Yes! Yes!'

KUNIGUNDE: (*Rises.*) Thank you, old woman, for your
story and please accept these earrings as a keepsake.
Now – be off with you!
(*Exit BRIGITTE.*)

Scene 10

KUNIGUNDE and ROSALIE.

KUNIGUNDE: (*Looks at herself in the mirror, then wanders
abstractedly to the window and opens it. Pause.*)
Have you put everything in order for me,
Rosalie? The things to show the Count –
The documents, certificates and letters?

ROSALIE: (*Standing behind at the table.*)
They're all together in this envelope.

KUNIGUNDE: Then give me –
(*Picks up a limed twig from outside.*)

ROSALIE: What, ma'am?

KUNIGUNDE: Look here! Isn't this
A sign some bird has surely passed this way?

ROSALIE: (*Walking towards her.*)
What's that you've got?

KUNIGUNDE: A limed twig which
Somebody must have fastened to the window.
I'd say a bird had perched here, wouldn't you?

ROSALIE: Oh yes, it's left a trace! A finch, perhaps?

KUNIGUNDE: No doubt the cock finch I was trying to lure
All morning but with no success at all.

ROSALIE: Look, there's a little feather left behind!

KUNIGUNDE: (*Thoughtfully.*)
Just give me…

ROSALIE: What, my lady? All the papers?
KUNIGUNDE: (*Laughs and gives her a smack.*)
   No, you silly goose! The bowl of birdseed!
   (*ROSALIE laughs and fetches the birdseed.*)

Scene 11

Enter a FOOTMAN.

FOOTMAN: Count Friedrich and his mother, Countess Helena!
KUNIGUNDE: (*Quickly dropping everything.*)
   Everything out of sight! Be quick about it!
ROSALIE: Of course, my lady – right away!
   (*Closes the dressing-table and leaves the room.*)
KUNIGUNDE: (*To FOOTMAN.*)
                              They're welcome!

Scene 12

Enter COUNTESS HELENA and VOM STRAHL.

KUNIGUNDE: O, mother of my saviour! Most revered!
   To whom am I indebted for the pleasure
   Of seeing you and for the privilege
   Of being allowed to kiss your cherished hands?
COUNTESS: My lady, you embarrass me. I've come
   To kiss your brow in welcome and to ask
   If you are being well cared for in my house.
KUNIGUNDE: Most amply. I have everything I need.
   Though I've done nothing to deserve your favour,
   You've treated me as though I were a daughter.
   If anything disturbed my peace of mind,
   'Twas feeling shamed by your solicitude;
   However, I required a moment only
   To resolve this minor struggle in my heart.
   (*Turning to VOM STRAHL.*)
   And how is your left hand today, Count Friedrich?
VOM STRAHL: My hand? My lady, your inquiry pains me
   More than the trifling injury itself.

I scratched it on the saddle, that was all,
In helping you dismount when we arrived.
COUNTESS: You hurt your hand, did you? I'd no idea.
KUNIGUNDE: 'Twas as we reached the castle that I noticed
Your hand was dripping blood upon the ground.
VOM STRAHL: If so, the hand's forgotten it already.
I must say, if 'twas Freiburg whom I paid
In blood, while I was fighting him for you,
The price he sold you for was low indeed.
KUNIGUNDE: That's your assessment of its worth –

not mine!
(*Turning to the COUNTESS.*)
But will you not be seated please, your grace?
(*She and VOM STRAHL fetch chairs and all sit down.*)
COUNTESS: And what about your future plans, my lady?
Have you yet weighed the situation which
Fate has assigned to you? Have you decided
How you'll react in view of what's befallen?
KUNIGUNDE: (*With emotion.*)
Countess most revered and bountiful,
All my remaining days, I shall devote
To praise and gratitude, recalling ever
The Count's heroic deed on my behalf;
In never-failing reverence for yourself
And for your family, till my final breath,
If I may be most graciously allowed
To pass those days in Turneck with my kin.
(*In tears.*)
COUNTESS: When are you thinking of returning home?
KUNIGUNDE: My aunts are waiting, so – if possible –
I'd like to be escorted there tomorrow;
If not, at least within a day or two.
COUNTESS: But have you pondered on the obstacles?
KUNIGUNDE: There'll be none, gracious lady, if I may,
With your permission, tell you my intent.
(*Stands up, kisses her hand and fetches the papers.*)
Accept these from my hand, pray, Count vom Strahl!
VOM STRAHL: (*Rising.*)
But, may I know, my lady, what they are?

KUNIGUNDE: These documents relate to the dispute
    About your Staufen properties. They form
    The basis of my claim to those domains.
VOM STRAHL: You make me feel ashamed, indeed, my lady!
    If, as you think, these papers constitute
    A rightful claim, then I'll defer to you –
    Even should I forfeit my last shack!
KUNIGUNDE: Take them, dear Count! These letters
                              seem to me
    Ambivalent. The title to redemption
    Which they confer on me has now expired.
    But were my right to Staufen crystal-clear,
    I could no longer urge it against *you*!
VOM STRAHL: Ah no, my lady! That can never be!
    Gladly, indeed, will I accept from you
    The gift of peace, but if there still remains
    The slightest doubt about your right to Staufen,
    I'll not accept the deed on which it rests.
    Present your case to Emperor and State
    And let the law determine who's mistaken.
KUNIGUNDE: (*To the COUNTESS.*)
    Then, honoured Countess, pray deliver me
    From these ill-omened documents. You take them.
    They burn my hands; their content's out of tune
    With my new-found emotions, nor could I
    Ever, in God's wide world, make use of them –
    Even were I to live until I'm ninety!
COUNTESS: (*Standing up.*)
    I fear, my lady, that your gratitude
    Has carried you away. You can't forswear,
    When in the throes of transient emotion,
    Something which may belong to all your family.
    Accept my son's proposal and agree
    To let your claim be ruled upon in Wetzlar:
    And rest assured, whatever they decide,
    You shall remain as dear to us as ever!
KUNIGUNDE: (*Deeply moved.*)
    This claim, in fact, is my own property!
    I need consult no brother, aunt or cousin,

And to my son I shall bequeath my heart!
I'd sooner not disturb the lords in Wetzlar:
So, here and now, my eager heart decides!
(*Tears up the papers and drops the scraps.*)

COUNTESS: My dear, young woman! Oh, you
                                    headstrong child!
What have you done? But never mind, come here!
What's done is done! Come here and let me kiss you!
(*Embraces her.*)

KUNIGUNDE: I wish that nothing further should impede
Those feelings newly kindled in my breast!
Down with the barrier which separates
Me from him whose valour saved my life!
I want to spend my days, without distraction,
Praising and loving him with all my heart!

COUNTESS: (*Moved.*)
There, there, my little one! All will be well!
You're too distressed, my dear!

VOM STRAHL: I only hope
That you will have no cause to rue your deed! (*Pause.*)

KUNIGUNDE: (*Drying her eyes.*)
When may I return to Turneck, please?

COUNTESS: Now, if you want! My son himself will guide you.

KUNIGUNDE: So be it – till tomorrow!

COUNTESS: As you wish,
Though I was hoping you would stay a little longer.
I trust you'll honour us today at table?

KUNIGUNDE: (*Bowing.*)
As soon as I collect myself, I'll join you.
(*Exit KUNIGUNDE.*)

Scene 13

The COUNTESS and VOM STRAHL.

VOM STRAHL: As sure as I'm a man, she is the wife
For me!

COUNTESS: Now, now! Keep calm!

VOM STRAHL: Not her?
You want to see me choose myself a bride;
But not her? Why not her?
COUNTESS: What ails you, son?
I've not said she displeases me entirely.
VOM STRAHL: Nor have I said I want to wed today.
Her ancestors were Saxon emperors…
COUNTESS: Your dream on New Year's Eve is in her favour:
That's what you feel?
VOM STRAHL: Why hide it? Yes, I do!
COUNTESS: Well then, my son, let's think the matter over.
(*Exeunt.*)

End of Act Two.

ACT THREE

Some weeks later. A monastery set amid mountains and forest.

Scene 1

THEOBALD and GOTTFRIED FRIEDEBORN, Katie's fiancé, leading KATIE down from a rock.

THEOBALD: Be careful, Katie. There's a crevice in the path here. Rest your foot on that mossy stone. If I knew where you could find a rose, I'd tell you…(*Helping her.*) That's it!

GOTTFRIED: Didn't you even tell God about the journey you had in mind for today? I was thinking that – once we reached that crossroads with the picture of the Virgin Mary, two angels would appear – tall young men with snow-white wings on their shoulders, who'd say: 'Farewell, Theobald! Farewell, Gottfried! You go back where you came from; we'll take Katie the rest of her journey to God.' Not a bit of it! We've had to see you all the way to the convent.

THEOBALD: These oaks scattered about the mountain are so quiet, you can hear the woodpeckers tapping. The trees must know that Katie's coming. They're listening out for her thoughts. If only I, too, could learn them by merging myself with nature! The sound of harps could hardly be sweeter than Katie's emotions. Israel, they say, was captivated by David and taught new psalms to sing…Well, Katie dear?

KATIE: Father, dear!

THEOBALD: Say something…

KATIE: Are we there yet?

THEOBALD: We are. In that delightful building with the towers, wedged among the rocks, are the silent cells of the pious Augustine monks and, here, their hallowed place of prayer.

KATIE: I'm exhausted.

THEOBALD: Let's sit down. Give me your hand and
I'll support you. There, in front of that grille, there's
a grassy bank to rest on. I never saw a pleasanter spot!
(*They sit down.*)

GOTTFRIED: How do you feel?

KATIE: Very well.

THEOBALD: You're looking pale. There's sweat on
your forehead.
(*Pause.*)

GOTTFRIED: You used to be so sturdy. You could walk
miles through field and forest. All you needed was a stone
and the bundle on your back for a pillow and you'd
recover your strength in no time. But today, you're so
tired out, you look as though all the beds the Empress
ever slept in wouldn't suffice to put you back on your feet.

THEOBALD: Would you like some refreshment?

GOTTFRIED: Shall I fetch you a drink of water?

THEOBALD: Or pick you some fruit?

GOTTFRIED: Speak, Katie dear.

KATIE: No, thank you, dear father.

THEOBALD: You refuse us?

GOTTFRIED: You scorn all offers?

THEOBALD: All you want is for me to get it over: to go in
and tell my old friend, Prior Hatto, that old Theobald is
here, waiting to bury his only daughter?

KATIE: Father dear!

THEOBALD: Very well! So be it! But before we take that
decisive, irrevocable step, let me tell you something that
occurred to Gottfried and myself on the way. It seems to
us we ought to get it straight before we talk things over
with the Prior. Would you like to hear what it was?

KATIE: Tell me.

THEOBALD: Very well! Listen carefully and make quite
sure of your feelings! You want to enter the Ursuline
Convent which is hidden away in a lonely pine-clad
wilderness. This world and life's pleasures no longer
attract you. Remote and pious contemplation of God's
countenance will be your substitute for father, marriage,
a child and the kisses of your grandchildren as they grow.

KATIE: Yes, father dear.

THEOBALD: (*After short pause.*) How would it be if you were to spend another couple of weeks – while it's still fine – back there by the castle walls, just to give the matter a bit more thought?

KATIE: What?

THEOBALD: If you were to go back to Castle Strahl, I mean, and camp in the elder bushes, where the finch built its nest, under the cliff, you know – from where the castle, sparkling in the sunlight, looks out across the surrounding countryside?

KATIE: No, father dear!

THEOBALD: Why not?

KATIE: The Count – my lord and master – forbade me to.

THEOBALD: He forbade it, did he? I see. What he forbids, you may not do. But what if I were to go there and ask him to let you?

KATIE: What's that you say?

THEOBALD: If I were to ask him to grant you that little spot you were so fond of, and let me supply you with everything you need?

KATIE: No, my dear father!

THEOBALD: Why not?

KATIE: (*Uneasily.*) You wouldn't do it. Even if you did, the Count would not allow it – and even if he did, I wouldn't use his permission.

THEOBALD: Katie, my dear Katie! I will do it. I'll lie down in front of him, as I now do before you, and I'll say: 'My noble lord, please allow Katie to dwell beneath the sky above your castle. When you go riding, please let her follow you at a distance – say, a bow-shot – and, at nightfall, give her a spot to lie in the straw they scatter for your noble steeds. That would be better than letting her die of grief.'

KATIE: (*Lying down in front of him.*) Oh, God in the highest! You're destroying me! Your words cut into my breast like knives! I don't want to enter the convent any more! I'll go home to Heilbronn with you, forget the

Count and marry anyone you like – even if my bridal
bed be a grave eight feet deep!

THEOBALD: (*Standing up and raising her.*) Are you angry
with me, Katie?

KATIE: No, no! Why should I be?

THEOBALD: I'll take you to the convent.

KATIE: No, never! I'm not going – either to Castle Strahl
or the convent! Just arrange with the Prior for me to
spend the night here and recover my strength, and
tomorrow, at daybreak, if possible, let us go home.
(*Weeping.*)

GOTTFRIED: (*To THEOBALD.*) What have you done?

THEOBALD: I've upset her!

GOTTFRIED: (*Ringing the doorbell.*) Is Prior Hatto at home?

PORTER: (*Opening door.*) Praised be Jesus Christ!

THEOBALD: For ever and ever, amen!

GOTTFRIED: Perhaps she'll come to her senses!

THEOBALD: Come, daughter!

(*Exeunt ALL.*)

Scene 2

*An inn. RHINE-COUNT VOM STEIN and FRIEDRICH VON
HERRNSTADT; later, JAKOB PECH, the innkeeper, and SOLDIERS.*

RHINE-COUNT: (*To his followers.*) Unsaddle the horses!
Post sentries at 300 paces from the inn. Nobody's to be
allowed in or out! Fodder the animals and stay in the
stables. Don't let yourselves be seen more than you can
help. I'll give you fresh orders when Eginhardt gets back
from his reconnaissance in Turneck. (*Exeunt SOLDIERS.*)
Who's living here?

PECH: If it please you, sir, my wife and I.

RHINE-COUNT: And here?

PECH: The animals.

RHINE-COUNT: What?

PECH: Animals. A sow with her litter, by your leave! It's
a pigsty, covered with laths on the outside.

RHINE-COUNT: Right. Who lives here?

PECH: Where?

RHINE-COUNT: Behind this third door?

PECH: Nobody, by your leave.

RHINE-COUNT: Nobody?

PECH: Nobody, my lord, cross my heart. Or rather,
I should say, anybody. It leads to an open field.

RHINE-COUNT: Good; what's your name?

PECH: Jakob Pech.

RHINE-COUNT: Then go about your business, Jakob
Pech! (*Exit PECH.*) I'm going to curl myself up here like
a spider, so that I look like a harmless little pile of dust.
Then as soon as this Kunigunde strays into my web, I'll
go for her and plunge the sting of my revenge deep into
her treacherous bosom! Kill! Kill! Kill! And her skeleton
I'll preserve, nailed to the timbers of Stein Castle, in
memory of an arch-whore!

HERRNSTADT: Easy there, Albert! Eginhardt, whom you
sent to Turneck, is still not back with confirmation of
what you suspect.

RHINE-COUNT: You're right, my friend. Eginhardt has still
to return. It's true, the slut wrote in that note she sent me
that I needn't worry about her any more: Staufen had been
ceded to her by Count vom Strahl as a result of friendly
mediation. By my immortal soul, if this turns out to be
correct, I'll swallow it and disband the armed forces I've
rallied on her behalf. But if Eginhardt comes back and
confirms the rumour that she is now his betrothed, then
I'll tuck my courtesy away like a pocketknife and insist on
making her reimburse me for the military expenses I've
incurred – even if I have to turn her upside down and
shake the cash from her pockets, coin by coin!

Scene 3

Enter EGINHARDT VON DER WART.

RHINE-COUNT: Welcome, friend! And how did you find
things at Turneck?

VON DER WART: Just as rumour led us to believe! The pair of them are running before the wind on the ocean of love and, come new moon, they'll tie up in the harbour of marriage.

RHINE-COUNT: Lightning shatter their masts before they get there!

HERRNSTADT: Are they betrothed?

VON DER WART: Not in so many words, perhaps. But if looks could speak, manners write and handshakes seal, the marriage contract is as good as signed.

RHINE-COUNT: Tell us what's happened about the transfer of the Staufen domain!

HERRNSTADT: When did he make her a present of it?

VON DER WART: The day before yesterday, on her birthday morning. Her cousins had arranged a brilliant celebration but the sun's rosy gleam had barely lit her bedroom, when she woke up to find the document already lying on her coverlet. Wrapped in a letter from her lovesick Count, it was, with the assurance that this would be her wedding present, if she would decide to give him her hand.

RHINE-COUNT: Did she accept? Of course she did! Stood in front of the mirror, curtsied and accepted?

VON DER WART: The document? Naturally!

HERRNSTADT: But what about the hand he asked for in exchange?

VON DER WART: She didn't refuse it.

HERRNSTADT: She didn't?

VON DER WART: No, God forbid! When would she ever refuse her hand to a suitor?

RHINE-COUNT: But, when the time comes, will she keep her word?

VON DER WART: That's another question.

RHINE-COUNT: How did she reply to the letter?

VON DER WART: She was so moved, her eyes gushed like a couple of fountains, drowning the script! The language she used to express her emotion was sheer humbug. Even without this sacrifice, she wrote, the

Count's right to her eternal gratitude was etched in her heart, as with a diamond. In short – a letter full of equivocation, changing colour like shot silk, and saying neither yes nor no.

RHINE-COUNT: Well, friends, that artifice will be her last piece of witchcraft! She deceived me, sure enough, but she won't live to trick another! I am the last of that long line of fools she's led by the nose. Where are the two dispatch-riders?

HERRNSTADT: (*Calling indoors.*) Hey, there!

Scene 4

Enter two DISPATCH-RIDERS.

RHINE-COUNT: (*Taking two letters from his jerkin.*) Each of you, take one of these letters: this one to Prior Hatto at the Augustine monastery saying I'll visit him about seven this evening to seek absolution; and this one to Peter Quanz, chief steward of Turneck Castle to let him know that, on the stroke of midnight, I shall be outside the castle with a party of armed men, ready to break in. Don't go into the castle yourself before dark and don't let anyone see you! Understood? You'll have nothing to fear once it's light. Is that quite clear to you both?

RIDERS: Quite clear. Yes, sir.

RHINE-COUNT: (*Taking the letters back again.*) You haven't mixed the letters, have you?

RIDERS: No, no.

RHINE-COUNT: Sure? Damn and blast it!

VON DER WART: What's wrong?

RHINE-COUNT: Who sealed them?

HERRNSTADT: The letters?

RHINE-COUNT: Yes!

HERRNSTADT: For heaven's sake! You yourself sealed them!

RHINE-COUNT: (*Handing the letters back to them.*) So I did! Here, take them! I'll be waiting for you at the mill by the waterfall. Come, friends, let's be off! (*Exeunt ALL.*)

Scene 5

Turneck – a room in the castle.

VOM STRAHL, deep in thought at a table with two candles. He plays a few chords on a lute. In the background, GOTTSCHALK is busy with his clothes and weapons.

KATIE: (*Off.*)
Let me in! Let me in!
GOTTSCHALK: Hello! Who is it, please?
KATIE: (*Off.*) Gottschalk, it's me! Dear Gottschalk, let me in!
GOTTSCHALK: Who?
KATIE: (*Off.*) Me!
GOTTSCHALK: You?
KATIE: (*Off.*) Yes!
GOTTSCHALK: Who?
KATIE: (*Off.*) Me!
VOM STRAHL: (*Laying aside the lute.*)
I know that voice!
GOTTSCHALK: By all the saints, I've heard it somewhere, too!
KATIE: (*Off.*) Please, Count vom Strahl, I beg you – let me in!
VOM STRAHL: By heaven, that's –
GOTTSCHALK: As sure as I'm alive –
KATIE: (*Off.*) It's Katie! Who else could it be, but me?
Young Katie of Heilbronn!
VOM STRAHL: (*Standing up.*)
Who? What the devil?
GOTTSCHALK: (*Dropping everything.*)
You Katie, is it! Dearest child! (*Opens the door.*)
VOM STRAHL: Who ever heard the like of it?
KATIE: (*Entering.*)
It's me!
GOTTSCHALK: Just look at her, by God! The girl herself!

Scene 6

KATIE with a letter in her hand.

VOM STRAHL: Get rid of her at once! I will not see her!
GOTTSCHALK: You cannot mean it!

KATIE: Where's the Count vom Strahl?

VOM STRAHL: Throw her out! I will not have her here!

GOTTSCHALK: (*Taking her by the hand.*)
  Sir, won't you grant – ?

KATIE: (*Holding out the letter.*)
                              Please, take the letter, Count!

VOM STRAHL: (*Turning to her suddenly.*)
  What do you want? What are you doing here?

KATIE: Nothing! God forbid! This letter – please!

VOM STRAHL: Take it away! What sort of letter is it?
  Where did it come from? What is it about?

KATIE: This letter is –

VOM STRAHL: I don't care what it is!
  Get out and hand it to the guards below!

KATIE: My noble lord! I beg you – it's important –

VOM STRAHL: (*Furious.*)
  Leave me alone! Get out, you shameless tramp!
  Be off with you and don't come here again!
  Go back to Heilbronn now – where you belong!

KATIE: Lord of my life, I'll leave you right away!
  Just for a moment, though I beg you, condescend
  To take this urgent letter from my hand!

VOM STRAHL: But I don't want it and I will not have it!
  Get out at once! This instant – go!

KATIE: My lord!

VOM STRAHL: (*Turning.*)
  Where's my whip? Which nail's it hanging on?
  I'll show you how a slattern can be taught
  To leave a man in peace when he's at home!
  (*Taking down the whip.*)

GOTTSCHALK: Oh, good my lord, what's this? You'll
                              surely not –
  Why not just kindly take the letter from her?
  After all, it wasn't she who wrote it!

VOM STRAHL: Be quiet, you old idiot!

KATIE: (*To GOTTSCHALK.*)
                              Let it be!

VOM STRAHL: I'm here in Turneck now! I know my mind!
  I won't accept a letter from the girl!
  Now, will you go?

KATIE: (*Quickly.*)
                              Oh yes, my noble lord!
VOM STRAHL: Then, go!
GOTTSCHALK: (*Quietly to KATIE, who is trembling.*)
                              Don't be afraid!
VOM STRAHL: Go on, be off!
    Give the sentry at the gate the letter,
    And you go back at once to where you came from!
KATIE: I will, I promise. I'll obey, my lord!
    But pray don't whip me, till I've talked to Gottschalk!
    (*Turning to GOTTSCHALK.*)
    You take the letter!
GOTTSCHALK: Give it me, dear child!
    What kind of letter is it? What's it say?
KATIE: It's from the Count vom Stein, you understand?
    It says inside, there'll be a raid tonight –
    Attack upon the castle, here in Turneck:
    To seize the lovely lady Kunigunde –
    The Count, my noble lord's, intended bride!
GOTTSCHALK: Attack upon the castle! Can't be true!
    By Count vom Stein? Where did you get this letter?
KATIE: The letter was received by Prior Hatto,
    When I and my father, by the will of heaven,
    Were visiting his peaceful monastery.
    The Prior could not understand the contents
    And wanted to return it to the envoy,
    Instead, I tore it from the Prior's hand,
    Then hastened here to Turneck to alert you
    And urge you all to arm yourselves in time,
    For, on the stroke of midnight, they are due
    To carry out this murderous assault.
GOTTSCHALK: How came Prior Hatto by the letter?
KATIE: That I don't know. It doesn't signify.
    As you can see, the letter is addressed
    To someone living here in Turneck Castle.
    I've no idea how that concerns the Prior.
    But it's a fact: they're planning an attack;
    That much I saw myself, for on my way,
    I met the Count approaching with his men.

217

GOTTSCHALK: Like as not, 'twas ghosts you saw!
KATIE: Some ghosts!
    I tell you, no! As true as Kate's my name!
    The Count lies hid no distance from the castle.
    Were you to take a horse and ride about
    You'd see the mighty forest, far and wide,
    Alive with all his troopers, fully armed!
GOTTSCHALK: Look at the letter, Count! See for yourself!
    I really don't know what to make of it.
VOM STRAHL: (*Puts the whip away, takes the letter and*
    unfolds it.)
    'Upon the stroke of midnight, I'll be there –
    Outside the castle. Leave the main gates open
    And, as the lantern flickers, I'll march in.
    I mean no harm to anyone save two –
    The lady and her bridegroom, Count vom Strahl.
    You'll be on hand to guide me to their rooms.'
GOTTSCHALK: That's dastardly! Who was it signed the letter?
VOM STRAHL: No name. Three crosses only. (*Pause.*)
    How many troopers at a guess, Kathrina?
KATIE: Sixty or seventy, my noble lord.
VOM STRAHL: And did you see the Count himself?
KATIE: Not him.
VOM STRAHL: Then who was leading them?
KATIE: Two knights, my lord,
    But neither of them did I recognise.
VOM STRAHL: And now, you say, they're halted near
                          the castle?
KATIE: Yes, my noble lord!
VOM STRAHL: How far away?
KATIE: Three thousand paces, scattered in the forest.
VOM STRAHL: Right of the high road?
KATIE: Left, among the firs,
    Near where they've built a bridge across the torrent.
    (*Pause.*)
GOTTSCHALK: A raid at night! Unheard of villainy!
VOM STRAHL: (*Pocketing the letter.*)
    Summon the lords of Turneck here at once!
    What time is it?

GOTTSCHALK: Just half an hour to midnight.

VOM STRAHL: Be quick! Ye gods, we've got no time to spare!
   (*Puts on his helmet.*)

GOTTSCHALK: Right away! I'm going now! Come, Katie,
   You're exhausted! Some refreshment…
   We're deeply in your debt, by God, for running
   So far by night, through forest, hill and dale –

VOM STRAHL: And you, girl, have you something else to
                                               tell me?

KATIE: Why, no, my noble lord!

VOM STRAHL: What have you lost?

KATIE: (*Clutching her bosom.*)
   The envelope. It may still be important.
   I think I've got it – here –
   (*Looking round.*)

VOM STRAHL: The envelope?

KATIE: Yes, here it is!
   (*She hands it to him.*)

VOM STRAHL: Let's see! Your cheeks are blazing!
   Wrap something round your shoulders, don't catch cold,
   But wait till you've cooled down before you drink.
   You've got no cape?

KATIE: No, sir.

VOM STRAHL: (*Takes off his scarf; turns sharply, throws
   it on the table.*)
                      Then, take my scarf!
   (*Drawing on his gloves.*)
   If you are going home to father, then
   I hardly need to say that I – (*He pauses.*)

KATIE: That you?

VOM STRAHL: (*Catching sight of the whip.*)
   Why is my whip – ?

GOTTSCHALK: You took it down yourself!

VOM STRAHL: (*Fiercely.*)
   For what? Have I got dogs that need a beating?
   (*Throws the whip through the window, breaking the glass,
   then addresses KATIE.*)
   I'll give you horse and carriage, my dear child,
   To see you safely home again to Heilbronn.
   When would you like to go?

KATIE: (*Trembling.*)

At once, my lord!

VOM STRAHL: (*Stroking her cheek.*)

Not now, my dear. Stay at the inn tonight.

(*Tearful.*) What are you staring at? Pick up those splinters!
(*GOTTSCHALK clears the broken glass from the window.*
VOM STRAHL takes the scarf from the table and hands it
to KATIE.)

When you've cooled down a bit, I'll have it back!

KATIE: (*Tries to kiss his hand.*)

My noble lord!

VOM STRAHL: (*Turns away from her.*)

Farewell, farewell, farewell!

(*Noise of tumult and bells ringing outside.*)

GOTTSCHALK: Good God Almighty!

KATIE: What's all that? What's wrong?

GOTTSCHALK: They're taking us by storm!

KATIE: By storm?

VOM STRAHL: Stand to!

By the living God! The Rhine-Count's here already!
(*Exeunt ALL.*)

Scene 7

Night; square in front of the castle which is ablaze. Noise of bells
sounding alarm. Enter a NIGHT-WATCHMAN who blows his
trumpet.

NIGHT-WATCHMAN: Fire! Fire! Fiii-re! Men, women and
children of Turneck, rouse yourselves! Throw off the
slumber that weighs upon you like a giant! Arise, collect
your wits, arise, wake up! Fire! Violence has crept in
softly through the gates! Death's busy in our midst with
bow and arrow! The torches of destruction light his way,
setting the castle's every room ablaze! Fire! Fire! Would
I had lungs of brass and knew a word that I could shout
more lustily – Fire! Fire! Fire!

Scene 8

VOM STRAHL, three KNIGHTS OF TURNECK, FOLLOWERS and NIGHT-WATCHMAN.

VOM STRAHL: Heaven and earth! Who set fire to the castle? Gottschalk!

GOTTSCHALK: (*Off.*) Here!

VOM STRAHL: My shield! My lance!

KNIGHT: What's happened?

VOM STRAHL: Don't ask! Seize any weapons to hand, race to the walls and hack and slash all round you, like wild boars attacked!

KNIGHT: Is the Rhine-Count at the gates?

VOM STRAHL: He was inside before you shot the bolts! Some traitor in the castle opened them for him!

KNIGHT: A murderous conspiracy! Incredible! Come on!

(*Exit with FOLLOWERS.*)

VOM STRAHL: Gottschalk!

GOTTSCHALK: (*Off.*) My lord!

VOM STRAHL: My sword, my shield and lance!

Scene 9

Enter KATIE.

KATIE: (*Carrying sword, shield and lance.*) Here they are!

VOM STRAHL: (*Girding on sword.*) What do you want?

KATIE: I've brought you your weapons.

VOM STRAHL: It wasn't you I called!

KATIE: Gottschalk's gone to the rescue!

VOM STRAHL: Why couldn't he send the page? Are you pushing your way in again?

(*NIGHT-WATCHMAN sounds his trumpet again.*)

Scene 10

Enter FLAMMBERG with TROOPERS.

FLAMMBERG: Blow till your cheeks burst! By now, even
the fishes and moles know the castle's on fire! Who
needs your blasphemous music to alert us?

VOM STRAHL: Who's there?

FLAMMBERG: Friend of Strahl!

VOM STRAHL: Flammberg?

FLAMMBERG: The very same!

VOM STRAHL: Come in! Wait here a moment till we find
out where the battle's raging!

Scene 11

As before; enter the AUNTS OF KUNIGUNDE.

1ST AUNT: God help us!

VOM STRAHL: Easy now! Keep calm!

2ND AUNT: We're done for! They'll impale us!

VOM STRAHL: Where is your niece, the lady Kunigunde?

1ST/2ND AUNT: The lady? Our niece?

KUNIGUNDE: (*From somewhere in the castle.*) Help,
someone! Help me, anyone!

VOM STRAHL: God in heaven! Wasn't that her voice?
(*He hands shield and lance to KATIE.*)

1ST AUNT: She's calling! Hurry! Quickly!

2ND AUNT: There she is, by the main gate!

1ST AUNT: Quick! By all the saints! She's staggering, she's
collapsing!

2ND AUNT: Hurry, she needs help!

Scene 12

KUNIGUNDE. Others as before.

VOM STRAHL: (*Catching her in his arms.*)

My Kunigunde!

KUNIGUNDE: (*Weakly.*)
    The portrait that you gave me recently,
    Count Friedrich, and its case –
VOM STRAHL: Where is it then?
KUNIGUNDE: In the fire! Quick! Save it! 'Twill be burnt!
VOM STRAHL: What of it, dearest? Won't you still have me?
KUNIGUNDE: The portrait in its case, good Count
                                    vom Strahl!
    Portrait and case!
KATIE: (*Stepping forward.*)
                    Where did you see it last?
    (*Hands shield and lance to FLAMMBERG.*)
KUNIGUNDE: 'Twas in my writing-desk, my precious!
    Here's the key!
    (*KATIE takes a few paces.*)
VOM STRAHL: Listen, Katie!
KUNIGUNDE: Hurry!
VOM STRAHL: Wait, child!
KUNIGUNDE: Fly!
    Why are you trying to stop her?
VOM STRAHL: But, my lady,
    I'll give you ten more paintings in its place!
KUNIGUNDE: (*Interrupting him.*)
    That is the only one I want – none other!
    It's neither time nor place to tell you why!
    Away, girl! Save my picture and the case
    And you shall have a diamond as reward!
VOM STRAHL: Go on, then – do it! Serves the
                                    nitwit right!
    What did she mean by coming here at all?
KATIE: Your room is to the right?
KUNIGUNDE: The left – upstairs;
    You see the balcony above the gate?
KATIE: It's in the centre room?
KUNIGUNDE: That's it – the centre!
    You cannot miss it! Quick! The danger's great!
KATIE: I'll go! God willing, I shall bring it back!
    (*Exit KATIE.*)

Scene 13

As before, less KATIE.

VOM STRAHL: A purse of gold, you men, for him who dares
　　To follow her inside!
KUNIGUNDE:　　　　　But why? What for?
VOM STRAHL: Veit Schmidt! Hans, you! Karl Bötticher!
　　　　　　　　　　　　　　　　Fritz Töpfer!
　　Will no one dare to go?
KUNIGUNDE: (*To VOM STRAHL.*)
　　　　　　　　　　　What's wrong with you?
VOM STRAHL: My lady, it's a task, I must confess –
KUNIGUNDE: Why are you showing such intense concern?
　　What makes the child so special?
VOM STRAHL:　　　　　　　That's the girl
　　Who showed such zeal in warning us tonight!
KUNIGUNDE: What if she were the Emperor's only daughter?
　　There's nought to fear. The house may be in flames,
　　But stands rock-steady on its timbers still!
　　She'll be quite safe along the corridor,
　　Nor has the stairway yet been touched by fire:
　　Smoke is the only menace facing her!
KATIE: (*Appears at burning window.*)
　　God help me! I can't breathe! The smoke, my lady!
　　The key is wrong! It doesn't fit!
VOM STRAHL:　　　　　　Damnation!
　　Can you not teach your hand to choose with care?
KUNIGUNDE: Not the right key?
KATIE: (*Voice weak.*)
　　　　　　　　　God help me! Help me, pray!
VOM STRAHL: Come down, my child!
KUNIGUNDE:　　　　　　No, leave her!
VOM STRAHL:　　　　　　　Down, I say!
　　Why stay without the key? Come down, at once!
KUNIGUNDE: One moment, please!
VOM STRAHL:　　　What's that? But why the devil – ?
KUNIGUNDE: The right key, darling, as I now recall,
　　Is hanging on the pivot of the mirror
　　So neatly set above my dressing-table!

KATIE: The mirror-pivot?

VOM STRAHL: How I wish, by God,
That he who painted me had never lived!
Likewise, the one who sired me in this world!
Search, then!

KUNIGUNDE: My dressing-table, love – you hear?

KATIE: Where is that? The smoke's too thick! Can't see!

VOM STRAHL: Search!

KUNIGUNDE: The right-hand wall!

KATIE: The right?

VOM STRAHL: Look hard!

KATIE: God help me! I can't see!

VOM STRAHL: I told you: look!
Confound your doglike readiness to serve!

FLAMMBERG: Unless she's quick, the castle will collapse!

VOM STRAHL: Someone fetch a ladder!

KUNIGUNDE: What, my love?

VOM STRAHL: Bring me a ladder quick! I'm going up!

KUNIGUNDE: My dear, you don't intend –

VOM STRAHL: Let go of me!
Out of my way! I'll get your precious portrait!

KUNIGUNDE: No, wait a moment longer, I entreat you.
She'll bring it down with her.

VOM STRAHL: Let go, I say!
Mirrors, dressing-tables and the rest
Are quite unknown to her but not to me;
I'll find the chalk-and-oil on canvas picture
And bring it to you here since that's your wish.
(*Enter four LABOURERS carrying a ladder.*)
Here, set the ladder up!

1ST LABOURER: (*Front man looking round.*)
Hey, there, behind!

2ND LABOURER: (*To VOM STRAHL.*)
Where?

VOM STRAHL: Against the open window.

LABOURERS: (*Lifting the ladder up.*) Ho! Ha!

1ST LABOURER: Not so fast! Keep back, you men behind!
Too long, this ladder!

LABOURERS: Push it in the window!
Knock out the crossbar! That's the way to do it!
FLAMMBERG: (*Who has been helping.*)
The ladder's steady now, won't shift about.
VOM STRAHL: (*Throwing off his sword.*)
Then up I go!
KUNIGUNDE: Just listen to me, love!
VOM STRAHL: I won't be long! (*Puts foot on ladder.*)
FLAMMBERG: (*Yelling.*)
Hold hard! For God's sake, stop!
KUNIGUNDE: What's wrong?
LABOURERS: The house is caving in! Stand back!
ALL: Have mercy, Lord! It's just a heap of rubble!
(*The house collapses. VOM STRAHL turns away, both hands pressed to his brow; all on stage shrink back and turn away at the same time. Pause.*)

Scene 14

KATIE, carrying a roll of paper, steps quickly from between two portals which have remained standing. Behind her is a CHERUB in the form of a young, fair-haired man, radiating light and with white wings on his shoulders and a palm-sprig in his hand.

KATIE: (*Turns as soon as she is clear of the portals, throws herself at his feet.*)
What's happening to me? Heaven grant protection!
(*The CHERUB touches her forehead with the tip of the palm-sprig and disappears.*)

Scene 15

KUNIGUNDE: (*After looking about her.*)
Now, by the living God! I must be dreaming!
My friend, look here!
VOM STRAHL: (*Distraught.*)
Oh, Flammberg! (*Falls on his shoulder.*)

KUNIGUNDE: Cousins! Aunts!
　Oh, listen to me, Count!
VOM STRAHL: Go, go! I pray you!
KUNIGUNDE: Fools! Pillars of salt, the lot of you?
　All's ended happily!
VOM STRAHL: I'm in despair!
　No beauty left on earth! Just leave me! Go!
FLAMMBERG: (*To the LABOURERS.*)
　Quick, brothers! Hurry!
1ST LABOURER: Shovels, hatchets, spades!
2ND LABOURER: Let's search the rubble! See if she's alive!
KUNIGUNDE: (*Sharply.*)
　A lot of grey-beard oafs! The girl they think
　Was burnt to ashes in the conflagration
　Is lying there before them, safe and sound,
　Sniggering in her apron at them all!
VOM STRAHL: Where?
KUNIGUNDE: Here!
FLAMMBERG: Come, that's not possible!
1ST/2ND AUNT: You say the girl – ?
ALL: By heaven! Look! There she lies!
VOM STRAHL: (*Walks over and looks at her.*)
　Then God is watching you with all his angels!
　(*Lifts her off the ground.*)
　Where did you come from?
KATIE: I don't know, my lord!
VOM STRAHL: There stood the house with you inside,
　　　　　　　　　　　　　　　I think?
　Is that not so?
FLAMMBERG: Where were you when it fell?
KATIE: My lords, I've no idea at all what happened.
VOM STRAHL: She even brought the picture, too!
　(*Takes the roll of paper from her.*)
KUNIGUNDE: (*Grabbing hold of it.*)

　　　　　　　　　　　　　　　Where?
VOM STRAHL: Here!
　It *is* the picture, isn't it?
1ST/2ND AUNT: Amazing!
FLAMMBERG: Tell us who gave it to you!

KUNIGUNDE: (*Slapping her in the face with the roll.*)
                           Stupid goose!
  I told you what I wanted was the case!
VOM STRAHL: As God is just, my lady! I must say –
  The *case* was what you wanted!?
KUNIGUNDE: Nothing else!
  You had inscribed it for me with your name;
  I valued it, as I made clear to her.
VOM STRAHL: Well, really, if that's all it was –
KUNIGUNDE: You think?
  That is for me to say, my friend – not you!
VOM STRAHL: My lady, I am dumbstruck by your kindness!
KUNIGUNDE: (*To KATIE.*)
  Why did you remove it from its case?
VOM STRAHL: Why, my child?
KATIE: The picture?
VOM STRAHL: Yes, indeed!
KATIE: I didn't take it out, my noble lord.
  It lay, half-rolled, in a corner of the desk,
  Which I had opened – and the case beside it.
KUNIGUNDE: Be off, you monkey-face!
VOM STRAHL: Come, come, my lady!
KATIE: Should I then have put it back again
  Inside the case – ?
VOM STRAHL: No, no, my dearest Katie!
  I praise your deed and what you did was right;
  How could you guess the case itself was precious?
KUNIGUNDE: Her hand was devil-driven!
VOM STRAHL: Do not fret!
  My lady doesn't mean it! Best go now!
KATIE: If only you'll not whip me, noble lord!
  (*She walks towards FLAMMBERG and merges with
  LABOURERS in the background.*)

Scene 16

Enter the KNIGHTS OF TURNECK.

1ST KNIGHT: A triumph, gentlemen! We beat them off!
  The Rhine-Count's homeward bound with bloody nose!

FLAMMBERG: He got away?
ALL: Hurrah, hurrah!
VOM STRAHL: To horse!
    If we can reach the waterfall in time,
    We'll cut the villains off, before they flee!
    (*Exeunt ALL.*)

End of Act Three.

ACT FOUR

In the mountains, with waterfall and bridge. The RHINE-COUNT, on horseback, crossing the bridge with a party of soldiers on foot. They are later followed by VOM STRAHL on horseback; then FLAMMBERG with soldiers and troopers on foot. Finally, GOTTSCHALK on horseback with KATIE beside him.

Scene 1

RHINE-COUNT: (*To his men.*) Over the bridge, men! Straight across! This Wetter vom Strahl is tearing after us like a hurricane! The bridge must be destroyed, or we'll all perish! (*Rides across.*)

RHINE-COUNT's MEN: (*Behind him.*) Tear down the bridge! (*They do so.*)

VOM STRAHL: (*Appears on stage, horse wheeling.*) Clear off! Leave that ford alone!

RHINE-COUNT's MEN: (*Shooting arrows at him.*) There's your answer! Take that!

VOM STRAHL: (*Turning his horse.*) Murderers! Hey, there, Flammberg!

KATIE: (*Holding a cylindrical object above her head.*) My noble lord!

VOM STRAHL: (*To FLAMMBERG.*) Archers forward!

RHINE-COUNT: (*Shouting across the river.*) Fare you well, Count! Swim across, if you can! You know where to find us – Stein Castle, this side of the bridge! (*Rides off with his men.*)

VOM STRAHL: Thank you, gentlemen! If the river will carry me, I shall keep the appointment! (*Rides into the water.*)

1ST SOLDIER: (*One of FLAMMBERG's.*) Hold hard! For God's sake, take care!

KATIE: (*Staying behind on the bank.*) Count vom Strahl!

2ND SOLDIER: (*One of FLAMMBERG's.*) Bring boards and beams!

FLAMMBERG: Who do think you are? Noah?

ALL: Plunge in! Straight across!

VOM STRAHL: Follow me! It's just a trout stream – neither broad nor deep! Let's get after them and cut the swine to ribbons!

(*Rides on with his followers.*)

KATIE: Count vom Strahl! Count vom Strahl!

GOTTSCHALK: (*Turns his horse.*) What are you screaming and shouting about? What do you want running after us in the middle of all this confusion?

KATIE: (*Clinging to a tree trunk.*) O heaven help me!

GOTTSCHALK: (*Dismounting.*) Come along, hitch up your petticoats! I'll lead the horse and see you across.

VOM STRAHL: (*Off.*) Gottschalk!

GOTTSCHALK: Right away, sir! At your command!

VOM STRAHL: I want my lance!

GOTTSCHALK: (*Helping KATIE into the stirrup.*) You shall have it, right away!

KATIE: The horse is skittish!

GOTTSCHALK: (*Pulling the reins.*) Stand still, you wretched nag! Off with your shoes and stockings!

KATIE: (*Sitting on a stone.*) Won't be a moment!

VOM STRAHL: (*Off.*) Gottschalk!

GOTTSCHALK: Right away, sir! Just bringing your lance! What's that you're holding?

KATIE: It's the case that was missing yesterday!

GOTTSCHALK: What? The one that was lost in the fire?

KATIE: The one I was scolded about! Early this morning, I went searching for it in the ruins and with God's help – here it is! (*Pulling at her stocking.*)

GOTTSCHALK: Well, I'll be damned! (*Takes case from her hand.*) And not the least bit damaged! Might have been made of stone! What's in it?

KATIE: I don't know.

GOTTSCHALK: (*Takes out a sheet of paper and reads.*) 'Act concerning the gift of Staufen by Friedrich Count vom Strahl.' Well, damn my eyes!

VOM STRAHL: (*Off.*) Gottschalk!

GOTTSCHALK: Coming, sir! Right away!

KATIE: (*Standing up.*) I'm ready!

GOTTSCHALK: You must give this to the Count! (*Hands her back the case.*) Come on, give us your hand and follow me! (*Leads her and the horse across the stream.*)

KATIE: (*As she steps into the water.*) Ah!

GOTTSCHALK: Hitch up your dress!

KATIE: No, that I won't! (*Stands still.*)

GOTTSCHALK: Only as far as the clock on your stocking, Katie!

KATIE: No, I'd sooner find a ford! (*Turns round.*)

GOTTSCHALK: (*Holding her back.*) Just up to the ankle, child! The sole of your foot, then – for heaven's sake!

KATIE: No, no, no! I'll be with you in a moment! (*Breaks free and runs away.*)

GOTTSCHALK: (*Walks back out of the stream and calls after her.*) Katie! Come here! I'll turn my back! Close my eyes! Katie! There isn't a ford for miles! As though her virtue were at risk! There she goes – tearing along the bank all the way back to the source, up in those snowy peaks! Unless some ferryman takes pity on her, by God, that'll be the end of her!

VOM STRAHL: (*Off.*) Gottschalk! In heaven's name! What the devil? Gottschalk!

GOTTSCHALK: Go on, you! Shout your head off! Coming now, sir! (*Leads his horse sulkily across the stream and exits.*)

Scene 2

The gounds of Castle Strahl. A glade of trees, along the dilapidated outer wall of the fort. In the foreground a clump of elders, forming a natural bower in which is a seat made of stones covered with straw matting. Petticoat and stockings etc. hung out to dry in the bushes. KATIE is lying asleep. Enter VOM STRAHL.

VOM STRAHL: (*Thrusting the case, which had contained the portrait, into his jerkin.*) Just as Gottschalk told me, when he brought me the case! She's here again, sure enough! No sooner does Kunigunde move into my castle, now her

own's in ruins, than along comes Gottschalk with the news
that Katie's back again, out in the elder bushes, fast asleep
and he begs me with tears in his eyes, to let him make
room for her in the stable. I said I'd book her a room at
the inn, till her father, Theobald, comes to fetch her. But
I'd like to know why I'm condemned to put up with her
trailing after me everywhere like a camp-follower. It's
more than just a natural inclination on her part. This is
some hellish obsession. Whenever I ask her why she was
so frightened at first sight of me in Heilbronn, she looks
confused and then replies: 'You know very well why.'
To look at her lying there with her rosy cheeks and hands
clasped, I feel as sentimental as a woman. Tears in my
eyes. I'll die if she hasn't forgiven me for threatening to
whip her. Wouldn't be surprised if she fell asleep praying
for me, who treated her so badly. But I must hurry, or
Gottschalk will come and disturb me! Three things he's
told me about her: first, she sleeps as soundly as a mole;
second, she dreams all the time, like a hunting-hound;
and third, she talks in her sleep. With that in mind, I want
to carry out a little experiment. God forgive me if I'm
committing a sin!

(*Kneels down in front of her, putting both arms gently round
her body. KATIE moves slightly as though about to wake up,
then lies quite still again.*)

VOM STRAHL: Katie! Are you asleep?

KATIE: Why, no, my lord!

VOM STRAHL: How so? So far as I can see, your eyes
                                                                    are closed.

KATIE: My eyes?

VOM STRAHL: Yes, child, they're both of them shut tight.

KATIE: Far from it!

VOM STRAHL: No? You mean to say they're open!

KATIE: Wide open, dearest – far as they will go!
    I see you sitting there astride your horse.

VOM STRAHL: Is it the roan you see?

KATIE: No, no! The grey!
    (*Pause.*)

VOM STRAHL: Where are you then, dear heart? I'd like
                                                                    to know.

KATIE: A lush, green meadow, that is where I am,
Where everything is bright and flowers bloom.
VOM STRAHL: Lovely forget-me-nots, sweet camomile!
KATIE: And here are violets! What a pretty clump!
VOM STRAHL: I think I'll just dismount, if you don't mind,
And rest beside you, Katie, on the grass.
May I?
KATIE: That you may, my lord!
VOM STRAHL: (*As though calling.*)

                              Hey! Gottschalk!
Where can I leave the horse? Gottschalk, where are you?
KATIE: Leave her where she is! She'll not run off!
VOM STRAHL: You think not? Then so be it! (*Smiles.*)
(*Pause – rattles his armour.*)
(*Takes her hand.*)   Dearest Katie!
KATIE: My noble lord!
VOM STRAHL: You're well-disposed towards me?
KATIE: With all my heart!
VOM STRAHL: But I – what do you think?
I'm not?
KATIE: (*Smiling.*)
        You rascal!
VOM STRAHL: Rascal?
KATIE: Oh, come on!
Head-over-heels in love with me, you are!
VOM STRAHL: Head-over-heels? What me? I think you're –
KATIE: What?
VOM STRAHL: (*Sighing.*)
Your faith is firmly rooted as a tower!
Then I resign myself! But, Katie, even if
It's as you say –
KATIE: Well, then? Go on –
VOM STRAHL: What future would there be?
KATIE: What future?
VOM STRAHL: Have you thought?
KATIE: No question!
VOM STRAHL: Meaning what?
KATIE: A year from now, at Easter, you will wed me.
VOM STRAHL: (*Stifling a laugh.*)

Me wed you? Bless my soul! I didn't know!
Kathrina, look! Who was it told you that?
KATIE: Marianna was the one who told me.
VOM STRAHL: Did she, indeed? Who's Marianna, pray?
KATIE: She was the maid who used to sweep our house.
VOM STRAHL: And she? She came to hear of it from whom?
KATIE: She saw it, pouring lead in my direction,
On New Year's Eve – the way soothsayers do.
VOM STRAHL: So that was it! She poured, then prophesied –
KATIE: A tall and handsome knight would marry me –
VOM STRAHL: And you assumed straight off it must be me!
KATIE: Yes, my noble lord!
(*Pause.*)
VOM STRAHL: (*Touched.*)
Then let me tell you,
I think, my child, that it will be another:
Flammberg, or someone like him – what say you?
KATIE: No! No!
VOM STRAHL: Not him?
KATIE: No, no!
VOM STRAHL: Why not? Explain!
KATIE: Because just after that, I went to bed
On New Year's Eve and prayed to God that, if
What Marianna told me was the truth,
He'd show me who the knight was, in a dream.
And so he did. At midnight, you appeared –
As plain as I can see you now before me;
And tenderly you hailed me as your bride!
VOM STRAHL: You say I – ? Dearest, I know nothing of it!
When am I supposed – ?
KATIE: On New Year's Eve –
Two years ago 'twill be, next time it falls!
VOM STRAHL: Where was it? In Castle Strahl?
KATIE: No. 'Twas in Heilbronn;
At home – the little room in which I slept.
VOM STRAHL: That's nonsense, my dear child! For then, I lay
Asleep at Strahl and gravely ill, besides!
(*Pause. KATIE sighs, stirs and whispers something.*)
VOM STRAHL: What did you say?

KATIE: Who?
VOM STRAHL: You!
KATIE: I didn't speak!
(*Pause.*)
VOM STRAHL: (*Aside.*)
    Strange, all the same! It was that New Year's Eve...
    (*Falling into reverie.*)
    Tell me some more about it, Katie dear!
    Was I alone?
KATIE: Why no, my noble lord.
VOM STRAHL: Then who was with me?
KATIE: Need you ask?
VOM STRAHL: Who was it?
KATIE: You can't remember?
VOM STRAHL: Not to save my life!
KATIE: A cherub, noble lord, was at your side,
    With wings as white as snow upon his shoulders;
    So radiant! The way he shone and twinkled!
    He led you by the hand to where I lay.
VOM STRAHL: (*Staring at her.*)
    True as I hope for heaven, I believe,
    You're right, my child!
KATIE: I am, my noble lord!
VOM STRAHL: You lay there, Katie, on a hair-filled pillow,
    The bedsheets white; on top, a crimson blanket.
KATIE: That's how it was!
VOM STRAHL: You wore a flimsy shirt!
KATIE: A shirt? Oh no!
VOM STRAHL: You didn't?
KATIE: Flimsy shirt?
VOM STRAHL: You called for Marianna!
KATIE: Yes, I did!
    Christine as well – I bade them come at once!
VOM STRAHL: Did you not look at me with staring eyes?
KATIE: I did; I thought it was a dream...
VOM STRAHL: Then, slowly,
    Trembling in every limb, climbed out of bed,
    And sinking at my feet –
KATIE: I whispered faintly –
VOM STRAHL: You whispered, didn't you? 'My noble lord' –

KATIE: (*Smiling.*)

    Now, don't you see? And then, the angel showed you –

VOM STRAHL: The birthmark! Heavenly powers above!

                                   You have it?

KATIE: Of course!

VOM STRAHL: (*Tearing off KATIE's neckerchief.*)

               Where? On the neck?

KATIE: (*Stirring in her sleep.*)

                         Please look and see!

VOM STRAHL: O you eternal ones! And as I then

    Lifted your chin, examining your face –

KATIE: Unfortunately, in came Marianna

    Holding a candle and I saw no more!

    I woke up in my nightshirt on the floor

    With Marianna making fun of me!

VOM STRAHL: Support me, O ye gods! I have a double –

    My spirit-self who sleepwalks in the night!

    (*He lets go of KATIE and jumps up.*)

KATIE: (*Waking up.*)

    Lord of my life! What has become of me?

    (*Stands and looks around.*)

VOM STRAHL: What seemed to me a dream, but real as day!

    While I was lying at death's door in Strahl,

    A cherub came and led my spirit forth

    To visit her where she lay sound asleep

    At home in Heilbronn in her little room!

KATIE: My God! The Count!

    (*Puts on her hat and straightens neckerchief.*)

VOM STRAHL: Now what am I to do and how behave?

    (*Pause.*)

KATIE: (*On her knees.*)

    My noble lord! I'm on my knees before you,

    Remembering the threat you made to me;

    You've found me by your castle wall once more,

    In spite of being forbidden all too clearly!

    I only meant to rest awhile, I swear –

    And now, this instant, I'll be on my way!

VOM STRAHL: Woe me! My mind, astonished by a miracle,

Sways on the edge of lunacy's abyss!
How can I comprehend the revelation
Whose silver voice still echoes in my ear,
That she's the daughter of my Emperor?
GOTTSCHALK: (*Off.*)
Hey, Katie! Are you there?
VOM STRAHL: (*Helping her up.*)

Quick, up you get!
Straighten your neckerchief! You look a sight!

Scene 3

Enter GOTTSCHALK.

VOM STRAHL: I'm glad to see you, Gottschalk! You
were asking
If you might put this maiden in the stable?
For various reasons, that would not be proper:
Instead, she'll join my mother in the castle.
GOTTSCHALK: What's that? Where? Up, inside the castle?
VOM STRAHL: Yes, right away! Take all her things up there!
And follow her along the castle drive!
GOTTSCHALK: By all that's holy, Katie! Did you hear?
KATIE: (*With an elaborate bow.*)
My noble lord! I gratefully accept
Till I can find out where my father is.
VOM STRAHL: Good! I'll have inquiries made at once.
(*GOTTSCHALK gathers her things; KATIE helps him.*)
So! All in order?
(*Picks up a cloth and hands it to her.*)
KATIE: (*Blushing.*)

Please! You mustn't trouble!
(*GOTTSCHALK picks up her bundle.*)
VOM STRAHL: Give me your hand!
KATIE: Most honourable lord!
(*VOM STRAHL leads her over a stony patch, then lets her go
ahead and follows her. Exeunt ALL.*)

Scene 4

A garden. In the background is a grotto in the Grecian style. Enter KUNIGUNDE, wrapped from head to foot in a fiery red veil, and ROSALIE.

KUNIGUNDE: Where did the Count vom Strahl ride off to?

ROSALIE: My lady, the whole castle's at a loss. Three envoys from the Emperor came late last night and woke him up. They closeted themselves in long discussion, then at daybreak, the Count jumped on his horse and disappeared.

KUNIGUNDE: Open the grotto for me.

ROSALIE: It's already open.

KUNIGUNDE: I hear the noble Flammberg's courting you. At midday, when I've bathed and dressed, I'll ask you what's behind all this.

(*Exit into grotto.*)

Scene 5

Enter LEONORA, niece of the COUNTESS, and ROSALIE.

LEONORA: Good morning, Rosalie!

ROSALIE: Good day, my lady! What brings you here so early?

LEONORA: The air is so warm, I thought I'd take Katie, the Count's delightful young guest, for a bathe in the grotto.

ROSALIE: Beg pardon, my lady Kunigunde's just gone in.

LEONORA: Kunigunde? Who gave you the key?

ROSALIE: The key? The grotto was already open.

LEONORA: But didn't you find Katie inside?

ROSALIE: Why, no my lady! Nobody at all!

LEONORA: I'm absolutely certain Katie's there.

ROSALIE: In the grotto? That's not possible!

LEONORA: Oh, yes, it is – in one of those adjoining

caverns. They're rather dark and well hidden. She went
in ahead of me because, when we got to the entrance,
I said I'd go back and fetch a towel from the Countess.
Why, here she comes!

Scene 6

KATIE emerges from the grotto.

ROSALIE: (*Aside.*)
    Dare I believe my eyes?
KATIE: (*Trembling.*)
               It's Leonora!
LEONORA: Katie, you were quick! You've bathed already?
    Just look at her! Asparkle and agleam!
    Like some fair swan that struts and preens herself,
    Fresh from the crystal waters of a lake!
    Are your young limbs now quite restored to vigour?
KATIE: Leonora! Come away!
LEONORA: What's wrong?
ROSALIE: (*Deathly pale.*)
    Where have you come from? Were you in the grotto,
    Hiding in one of those gloomy passages?
KATIE: Leonora, I entreat you! Come!
KUNIGUNDE: (*From inside the grotto.*)
    Rosalie!
ROSALIE: My lady! (*To KATIE.*) Did she see you?
LEONORA: What is it? You're so pale!
KATIE: (*Collapsing in her arms.*)
                Leonora!
LEONORA: Merciful heavens, Katie! What's the matter?
KUNIGUNDE: (*In the grotto.*)
    Rosalie!
ROSALIE: (*To KATIE.*)
        Better for you, by all the saints,
    To scratch your eyes out, than let them confide
    What they've just seen to your unguarded tongue!
    (*Goes into the grotto.*)

Scene 7

LEONORA: What happened, child? Why was she
                                          scolding you?
   Why are you trembling so in every limb?
   If Death himself had faced you in the grotto
   Complete with scythe and hourglass in his hand,
   You couldn't be more terrified, I'm sure!
KATIE: I'll tell you – (*Unable to speak.*)
LEONORA: Pray go on! I'm listening!
KATIE: But you must promise never, Leonora,
   Never to tell a soul what I reveal!
LEONORA: I promise, Katie! You can count on me!
KATIE: The grotto's splendour I found overpow'ring,
   So, through a hidden door, I made my way
   Into a smaller cavern at the side.
   The bath refreshed me, so, light-heartedly,
   I then returned to try the centre one,
   Where you, I thought, were splashing in the water.
   But just as I was entering the basin,
   My eye caught sight –
LEONORA: What? Who?
KATIE: What can I say?
   Leonora, you must find the Count –
   Immediately – and tell him everything!
LEONORA: If only I knew what it was you saw!
KATIE: Don't tell him – no, for pity's sake –
   Don't say *I* told you! I would sooner he
   Should never know this horror, than suspect –
LEONORA: These riddles are beyond me, Katie dear!
   What kind of horror, child? What did you see?
KATIE: Oh, Leonora, now I feel 'twere best
   That I should not say anything at all!
   He cannot, must not learn the truth from me!
LEONORA: Why not? Why should you hide the truth
                                          from him?
   If you'd just tell me –
KATIE: Shush!

LEONORA: What's wrong?
KATIE: She's coming!
LEONORA: Her ladyship and Rosalie – that's all!
KATIE: Quick! Let's escape!
LEONORA: Why?
KATIE: Madness to delay!
LEONORA: Where to?
KATIE: Away from here! Out of this garden!
LEONORA: Are you insane?
KATIE: Come, Leonora, quick!
    If she should find me here, then I am lost!
    I'm fleeing to the arms of the Countess!
    (*Exeunt.*)

Scene 8

KUNIGUNDE and ROSALIE emerge from the grotto.

KUNIGUNDE: (*Handing key to ROSALIE.*)
    Take it! In the drawer below my mirror,
    The powder's to the right – a small black box.
    Sprinkle in wine, in water or in milk
    And urge her: 'Katie, come, take a drink' –
    Or manage it however you think best:
    Poison, death, revenge! Do it your way:
    But just make sure she swallows it, that's all!
ROSALIE: My lady –
KUNIGUNDE: Poison, plague and putrefaction!
    Silence her! There's nothing to discuss!
    Once she is poisoned, dead and in her coffin,
    Buried, decayed, and dry as myrtle dust,
    And what she saw is whispered by the wind –
    Then talk to me of kindness and forgiving,
    Of duty and the law – of God, hell, Satan,
    Remorse and qualms of conscience – not before!
ROSALIE: She knows the truth already! What's the point?
KUNIGUNDE: Poison! Dust and ashes! Night and chaos!
    That powder would suffice to blight the castle –
    Cats and dogs included! Do as I say!

I heard she was my rival for his heart:
May I drop dead if her accursed monkey-face
Has not infatuated him already!
Dust to dust! Away with her, I say!
The world's not wide enough for both of us!

End of Act Four.

ACT FIVE

An open square in front of the EMPEROR's palace at Worms. Throne to one side. In the background, the lists where jousts take place.

Scene 1

The EMPEROR sits on his throne, at his side the ARCHBISHOP OF WORMS, COUNT OTTO, judge of the secret court, and other KNIGHTS, LORDS and GENTLEMEN-AT-ARMS. VOM STRAHL in light helmet and armour; THEOBALD, KATIE's father, in full armour from head to foot, both facing the throne.

EMPEROR: Count vom Strahl, when you – three
                               months ago –
  Were riding through Heilbronn, it seems you chanced
  To captivate a foolish maiden's heart.
  Since then, the girl has left her aged father
  And you, instead of sending her straight home,
  Have sheltered her in your ancestral castle.
  To mitigate so heinous an offence,
  You've spread a ludicrous and godless tale,
  To wit: a cherub you beheld one night
  Informed you that the girl now living with you
  Is progeny of my imperial loins.
  So tasteless a prophetic declaration
  I naturally treat with high disdain!
  Crown her, if you like, for all I care –
  But Swabia she never shall inherit,
  Nor shall she ever grace my court at Worms!
  However, here's a craftsman bent with age,
  Whose daughter you've seduced – and not content –
  Whose late wife you have branded as a trollop!
  Though he, for his part, found her ever-faithful;
  And prides himself as father of their child.
  In view of his most grievous accusations,
  We've summoned you before our throne today,

For having so defamed his spouse's tomb.
Take up your arms, friend of the cherubim,
For you are here to prove this claim of yours
With words of steel – by combat in the lists!
VOM STRAHL: (*Flushing with indignation.*)
My lord and Emperor, behold my arm
In prime of strength, these muscles, girt in steel
And fit to best the Devil in a duel!
Were I to strike that grizzled head a blow
I'd flatten it, as though it were Swiss cheese,
Fermenting on the dairy-farmer's shelf.
I beg you, noble lord and Emperor,
Absolve me from confirming in this way
A childish rumour, crazy and confused,
Which gossips, misconstruing two events –
Together strange – have joined with idle skill,
As one might patch two halves to make a ring.
I beg you, in your wisdom, to dismiss
That incident on New Year's Eve as just
A feverish fancy! Pray let my delirious
Claim, that this man's daughter was the child
Of my most honoured Emperor, trouble you
No more than I would be dismayed, my liege,
Had you, sir, dreamt that I was born a Jew!
ARCHBISHOP: My lord and master, surely that's enough
To set the worthy plaintiff's mind at ease?
Strahl claims no secret knowledge of the wife,
And what he may have gossiped privately
He's now disclaimed, admitting 'twas a dream.
Punish him not for momentary confusion
In this world's labyrinth of mysteries.
An hour ago, good Theobald, he gave me
His hand upon it, that if you will call
At Strahl, your Katie he'll return at once...
Be comforted, go there, reclaim your daughter –
And having done so, let the matter rest!
THEOBALD: You cursed hypocrite! You dare deny
Your evil soul is totally suffused,
From tip to toe, with this insane belief:

My daughter, Katie, is the Emperor's love-child?
Did you not search the parish register
To check her day of birth, then calculate
The hour at which she would have been conceived?
And did you not, with your atrocious guile,
Discover His Imperial Majesty
Tarried in Heilbronn, sixteen Easters past?
You arrogant demon, offspring of some god's
Hot kiss, imprinted on a Fury's avid lips;
Flamboyant, patricidal spirit, you!
Heaving and rattling every granite pillar
Of ageless Nature's sempiternal temple –
Scion of hell! My trusty sword will now
Unmask you or – turned back upon myself –
Dispatch me to the darkness of my tomb!
VOM STRAHL: God damn you for a venomous persecutor
Of one who never has insulted you
But who, by right, should have your sympathy!
So be it! Let your death-wish be fulfilled!
A cherub, girt in radiance, appeared
To me by night as I lay dying,
And – why should I deny it any longer? –
Confided knowledge drawn from heaven's well.
Before God's august countenance I stand
And thunder his pronouncement in your ear:
Katie of Heilbronn, whom you claim to've fathered,
Is the Emperor's child, in fact! Come, if you must,
And try convince me of the opposite!
EMPEROR: Let trumpets sound! The slanderer be slain!
(*Blasts on a trumpet.*)
THEOBALD: (*Drawing his sword.*)
Were this my sword no stouter than a reed,
Its handle loose and slippery, or cast
In yellow wax – no matter, I would still
Split you apart, I vow, from head to foot
Like a poisonous toadstool, sprung upon the heath,
To show the world that you're a fiendish liar!
VOM STRAHL: (*Takes off his sword and hands it to someone.*)
And were my helmet and the brow beneath it
Transparent, knife-edge thin and fragile

As an empty eggshell, still, I vow your sabre –
Spraying sparks – would slither off and shatter,
Sending fragments flying far and wide,
As though it were a diamond you had struck:
To show the world that I have spoken true!
Have at me and let's see whose cause is just!
(*Takes off his helmet and stands right in front of THEOBALD.*)
THEOBALD: (*Shrinking back.*)
   Put on your helmet!
VOM STRAHL: (*Advancing.*)
                Thrust!
THEOBALD: Put on your helmet!
VOM STRAHL: (*Sends THEOBALD sprawling with a push.*)
   The lightning from my eyes has crippled you?
   (*Twists the sword from THEOBALD'S grasp, stands over
   him and places a foot on his chest.*)
   What's there to stop me, in the righteous flush
   Of victory, from trampling your skull? No, live!
   (*Throws the sword in front of the throne.*)
   May time – that ancient sphinx – enlighten you!
   But Katie is – as I have already said –
   The daughter of His Peerless Majesty!
BYSTANDERS: (*To one another.*)
   By heaven, look! Count Friedrich is the victor!
EMPEROR: (*Turns pale and rises.*)
   My lords, disperse!
ARCHBISHOP: Where to?
A KNIGHT: What's wrong? What is it?
COUNT OTTO: Heavens above! What ails His Majesty?
   Follow, my lords! He seems to be unwell!

Scene 2

A room in the EMPEROR's palace.

EMPEROR: (*Turning in the doorway.*) Away! Don't follow me!
   Only admit the Burgrave of Freiburg and the knight,
   Georg von Waldstädten. I wish to speak to no one else.
   (*Slams the door shut.*)…That angel of God who assured the
   Count vom Strahl that Katie is my daughter…on my

honour as emperor, I believe he's right! The girl's 15, so
I hear. It's certainly a fact that sixteen years ago less a few
months, to be exact, I was here in Heilbronn attending a
great tourney in honour of the Countess Palatine, my sister.
It must have been about eleven in the evening and Jupiter
with his sparkling light just rising in the east – when,
weary with dancing, I went out through the palace gate,
for a refreshing stroll in the gardens close by, thinking to
move about among the common people without being
recognised. I don't doubt a star like that one – mild and yet
powerful – shone as she was conceived. Gertrude, as far as
I can recall, was the name of the girl I was with in one of
the less frequented parts of the garden, while the lamps
were burning low and the sound of dance music from the
distant ballroom, wafting towards us mid the scent of linden
blossom. So Katie's mother was called Gertrude!
I know that, to comfort her since she wept a lot, I took off
a medallion I was wearing with a portrait of Pope Leo on it
and gave it to her as a keepsake. She thrust it into her
bodice, not knowing whom it represented any more than
she knew who *I* was. I'm told that Katie of Heilbronn has
a similar trinket in her possession! O heaven! The world is
out of joint! If the Count vom Strahl, this confidant of the
elect, can free himself from that courtesan he's attached to,
I'll make the prophecy come true by persuading Theobald,
on some pretext or other, to surrender the child to me and
then make sure they marry. If not, I have reason to fear
the cherub may descend to earth a second time and make
known to all the secret I have just confided to these
four walls! (*Exit.*)

Scene 3

*Enter FREIBURG and WALDSTÄDTEN, followed by
FLAMMBERG.*

FLAMMBERG: (*Astonished.*) Lord Burgrave von Freiburg!
Can it really be you – or is it your ghost? Don't hurry
away, I entreat you!

FREIBURG: (*Turning.*) What do you want?

WALDSTÄDTEN: Who are you looking for?

FLAMMBERG: My pitiful master, the Count vom Strahl! The lady Kunigunde, his betrothed – oh, would that we had never won her from you! – has tried to bribe the cook to poison Katie. Poison, my lords, and for the appalling, incomprehensible and mysterious reason, it would seem, that the child eavesdropped on her while she was bathing!

FREIBURG: And that, you don't understand?

FLAMMBERG: No, I don't!

FREIBURG: Well, I'll tell you. She's a piece of mosaic, assembled from all three realms of nature. Her teeth belong to a girl from Munich. Her hair was ordered from France. Her cheeks have a healthy glow, thanks to the Hungarian mines, and her figure, which you so much admire, she owes to a corset of Swedish steel, made for her by a blacksmith. Now, do you understand?

FLAMMBERG: What?

FREIBURG: My compliments to your master!

WALDSTÄDTEN: Mine, too! The Count has already returned to Castle Strahl. Tell him from me that, if he'd care to take the master key, early one morning and surprise her when her charms are laid out on chairs, he will at once turn into a statue of himself, which he can then have erected outside the charcoal-burner's hut in everlasting memory of his heroism!

(*Exeunt ALL.*)

Scene 4

Castle Strahl: KUNIGUNDE'S room. ROSALIE is busy at the dressing-table. KUNIGUNDE has just got out of bed. No make-up. Later, VOM STRAHL.

KUNIGUNDE: (*Sitting down at the dressing-table.*) Did you see to the door?

ROSALIE: It's locked, my lady!

KUNIGUNDE: Locked? Is it bolted, too, I want to know! Lock and bolt it every time I dress!

(*ROSALIE goes to bolt the door but meets VOM STRAHL walking towards her.*)

ROSALIE: (*Shocked.*)

Oh God! But how did you get in, my lord?
My lady!

KUNIGUNDE: (*Looks round.*)

Who?

ROSALIE: Pray look, ma'am!

KUNIGUNDE: Rosalie!

(*Stands up quickly and hurries out.*)

Scene 5

VOM STRAHL: (*Thunderstruck.*)

Tell me, who was that unknown lady?

ROSALIE: Where?

VOM STRAHL: Rushed past, as crooked as the Tower of Pisa!
I hope, not –

ROSALIE: Who?

VOM STRAHL: My lady Kunigunde?

ROSALIE: Oh no! You're joking! That was Sybil, sir!
My aged stepmother –

KUNIGUNDE: (*Off.*)

Come, Rosalie!

ROSALIE: The mistress, still abed, is calling me.
Forgive me if I...

(*Brings over a chair.*)

Won't you please sit down?

(*Gathers make-up box, clothes etc. and hurries out.*)

Scene 6

VOM STRAHL: (*Shattered.*)

Oh, heavenly powers! What is this soul of mine?
A thing no longer worthy of the name!
False is the scale by which it rates the worth
Of what's on offer in the world's bazaar!
Atrocious wickedness, my soul has bought –

Spurning the glory of sweet innocence!
What can I do to flee my wretched self?
If thunderstorms were raging over Swabia,
I would bestride my horse and, in my frenzy,
Gallop until the lightning struck me dead!
What's to become of me? What shall I do?

Scene 7

*Enter KUNIGUNDE now brilliantly arrayed as usual; ROSALIE
and old SYBIL, unsteady on her crutches, leave by the centre door.*

KUNIGUNDE: There you are, Count Friedrich! And what
brings you,
So early in the day, to my apartment?
VOM STRAHL: (*Eyes fixed on SYBIL as she leaves.*)
What! Are there two witches?
KUNIGUNDE: (*Looking round.*)
Who?
VOM STRAHL: Forgive me, pray!
I wanted to make sure that you were well.
KUNIGUNDE: Is everything in order for the wedding?
VOM STRAHL: (*Approaching her with a searching look.*)
Apart from the highlight – ready, more or less.
KUNIGUNDE: (*Shrinking away.*)
The date's been fixed?
VOM STRAHL: It was to be...tomorrow.
KUNIGUNDE: The day that I have yearned so long to see!
You don't seem happy...not in merry mood?
VOM STRAHL: (*Bowing.*)
Forgive me! I'm the luckiest of men!
ROSALIE: (*Sadly.*)
Is it true that yesterday, young Katie –
Whom you had sheltered here –
VOM STRAHL: The devil!
KUNIGUNDE: (*Surprised.*)
What ails you?
ROSALIE: (*Aside.*)
Blast it!

VOM STRAHL: (*Controlling himself.*)
        Destiny of man!
 She is already resting in the churchyard.
KUNIGUNDE: What's that you say?
ROSALIE: But not yet buried, surely?
KUNIGUNDE: First, I must see her lying in her shroud!

Scene 8

Enter a SERVANT.

SERVANT: A messenger from Gottschalk's here, my lord,
 Who'd like to see you in the anteroom.
KUNIGUNDE: Gottschalk?
ROSALIE: Where from?
VOM STRAHL: The bier of the deceased!
 Let us, I pray you, not disturb your toilet!
 (*Exeunt VOM STRAHL and the SERVANT.*)

Scene 9

KUNIGUNDE: (*Outburst.*)
 He knows! It's all in vain! No remedy!
 He saw me as I am! I am undone!
ROSALIE: He doesn't know!
KUNIGUNDE: He does!
ROSALIE: No, no, my lady!
 You grieve, but I could almost jump for joy!
 He's under the illusion that the woman
 Sitting here was Sibyl, my stepmother –
 Who, by the luckiest of chances ever,
 Was in your bedroom at that very moment,
 Filling your basin with fresh gathered snow,
 Brought from the mountains, for mylady's wash.
KUNIGUNDE: You saw the way he looked me up and down?
ROSALIE: He couldn't believe his eyes, my lady! I'm
 As happy as a squirrel in the pines!
 Even supposing he'd the slightest doubt,
 Once you appeared – tall, slim, magnificent –

Any such hint was instantly dispelled.
Strike me dead, if he'd not fling his gauntlet
At anyone who dared deny that you,
My gracious lady, are the queen of women!
Take courage! Come along now, time to dress;
Tomorrow's sunbeams, I'll be bound, will hail you:
Countess Kunigunde of Castle Strahl!
KUNIGUNDE: Would that the earth might swallow me entire!
(*Exeunt.*)

Scene 10

Inside a cave, with view of landscape. KATIE, disguised, sits sadly on a stone, head resting against the wall. COUNT OTTO, NACHTHEIM, BÄRENKLAU, wearing robes of Imperial Counsellors, and GOTTSCHALK; members of their retinue; the EMPEROR and THEOBALD, muffled in cloaks, in the background.

COUNT OTTO: (*Roll of parchment in his hand.*)
Young maid of Heilbronn, why have you sought shelter,
Here in this lonely cavern, like a sparrow?
KATIE: (*Standing up.*)
Dear God, who are these lords?
GOTTSCHALK: Don't frighten her!
An enemy's attempt to kill the maid
Forced us to seek her safety in the mountains.
COUNT OTTO: Where's Count vom Strahl, the master
whom you serve?
KATIE: I do not know.
GOTTSCHALK: He'll be here presently!
COUNT OTTO: (*Hands her the parchment.*)
Take you this scroll; it is a document
Signed by His Imperial Majesty.
Cast your eye over it and follow me!
This is no place for maiden of your rank:
The castle of the Emperor awaits you!
EMPEROR: (*In the background.*)
She looks so charming!
THEOBALD: Truly, she's an angel!

Scene 11

Enter VOM STRAHL.

VOM STRAHL: (*Astonished.*)
  Imperial Counsellors in all their splendour!
COUNT OTTO: Our greetings, Count vom Strahl!
VOM STRAHL: What brings you here?
COUNT OTTO: A royal communication for this maid!
  Ask her and she'll explain to you, herself!
VOM STRAHL: (*Aside.*)
  My heart is pounding!
  (*To KATIE.*)   Child, what have you there?
KATIE: My lord, I know not!
GOTTSCHALK: Give it him, dear child!
VOM STRAHL: (*Reading the document aloud.*)
  'Know you that heaven has disposed my heart
  To realise the angel's prophecy.
  The maiden Katie is no longer Theobald's,
  The weaponsmith's; he's ceded her to me.
  I recognise her henceforth as my daughter –
  Kathrina, she'll be called, of Swabia.'
  (*Leafs through the other papers.*)
  'Be it known,' and here: 'of Schwabach Castle'...
  (*Short pause.*)
  So let me kneel before our Mother Mary,
  Here in the dust, embrace and bathe her feet
  With scalding tears of humble gratitude!
KATIE: (*Sits down.*)
  Gottschalk, lend me your arm! I'm feeling faint!
VOM STRAHL: (*To KATIE.*)
  Where are the Emperor and Theobald?
EMPEROR: (*Both throw off their cloaks.*)
  They're here!
KATIE: Good God in heaven! Father!
  (*Hurries to his embrace.*)
GOTTSCHALK: (*Aside.*)
  The Emperor! As true as I'm alive!

VOM STRAHL: Speak, holy one! What may I call you?

Speak –

Did I read aright?

EMPEROR: You did, by God!

An emperor is proud to be the father
Of one who has an angel for her friend!
Katie for me is now the first of mortals,
As long she was for God! Who seeks her hand
Must prove to me his worthiness to woo her.

VOM STRAHL: (*Bending knee before him.*)

Then, on my bended knee, pray make her mine!

EMPEROR: I don't know what you mean, Count!

VOM STRAHL: Make her mine!

How else am I to understand your action?

EMPEROR: Then you're in earnest! Only death is free,
So I set one condition.

VOM STRAHL: Tell me, pray!

EMPEROR: (*Gravely.*)

That you'll accept her father in your house!

VOM STRAHL: You mock me!

EMPEROR: You refuse?

VOM STRAHL: Far from it, sire!

My hands and heart shall welcome him with joy!

EMPEROR: Good Theobald, you heard him?

THEOBALD: (*Leading KATIE to the EMPEROR.*)

Give her to him!

Whom God has joined, let no man put asunder!

VOM STRAHL: (*Stands up and takes KATIE's hand.*)

You've made of me the blessedest of men!
Fathers, let me imprint a kiss – one only –
Upon those lips of hers – so heavenly sweet!
Had I ten lives beyond our wedding night,
Gladly I'd sacrifice them for you both!

EMPEROR: Away then! You explain it all to her!

(*Exit.*)

Scene 12

VOM STRAHL and KATIE.

VOM STRAHL: (*Taking her by the hand as he sits down.*)
    Come, Katie! Come to me, my darling girl!
    My lips have something to confide to you.
KATIE: My noble lord! I fail to understand –
VOM STRAHL: First, dear girl, let me assure you now,
    I love you! Love – unspeakable, eternal –
    With all my senses, I devote to you!
    A stag tormented by the noonday heat
    Who with his pointed antlers scrapes the earth,
    Is tempted no less grievously to plunge
    From the rocks and breast the foaming rapids,
    Than I am longing – now that you are mine –
    To steep myself in all your youthful charms.
KATIE: (*Blushing.*)
    My lord! What are you saying? I'm confused!
VOM STRAHL: Forgive me if my words from time to time
    Offended or insulted you; if my rough manners
    Now and then, my sweet, caused you to suffer.
    When I recall how, loveless, once I strove
    To drive you from me – and now see you here,
    Standing before me full of gentle virtue,
    I'm overcome, dear Katie, by remorse
    So keen that I cannot restrain my tears.
    (*Weeps.*)
KATIE: (*Anxiously.*)
    Heavens, what is it? Why are you so moved?
    You never harmed me – not that I'm aware.
VOM STRAHL: O Katie, when the sun once more is shining,
    Then I shall sheath that foot in gold and silk
    That once bled freely running in my wake.
    A canopy shall shield that gentle brow,
    Once scorched by noonday, following my trail.
    And Araby shall send its finest steed,
    Caparisoned in gold, to bear my dear one,
    When trumpets summon me to take the field.
    There, where the twittering finch once built its nest,
    Among the elder bushes, I'll construct

A summer house with cheerful, roomy chambers,
To greet my darling girl when I return!
KATIE: O Friedrich, whom I have so long adored,
What am I to make of this fine speech?
You want – ? You say that – ? (*Moves to kiss his hand.*)
VOM STRAHL: (*Withdrawing it.*)

No, no, sweet child.

(*Kisses her forehead.*)
KATIE: No?
VOM STRAHL: Not yet. I thought it was tomorrow.
What did I mean to ask you? Yes, I know!
I wanted to request a little service. (*Brushing away tears.*)
KATIE: (*Softly.*)
What kind of service? You have but to name it!
VOM STRAHL: Well, as you know, tomorrow I'll be wed;
And everything is ready for the feast.
At midday, the procession of the bride
With all her retinue will reach the altar.
Now I was thinking we might stage a masque,
In which you'd play the goddess, Katie dear.
So, for your master's sake, would you tomorrow,
Instead of what you're wearing now, put on
A fine embroidered dress of silk and satin
Already set aside for you by Mother.
Would you do that for me?
KATIE: (*Holding apron to her eyes.*)

It shall be done.
VOM STRAHL: You must look beautiful – in

modest splendour –
As your own nature and your style require.
You'll be supplied with emeralds and pearls:
I'd like you to outshine all ladies present –
Including even lady Kunigunde.
Why are you crying?
KATIE: I don't know, my lord!
I think there's something in my eye.
VOM STRAHL: Let's see!
(*Kisses the tears from her eyes.*)
We'd best go now and all will soon be clear.
(*Leads her away.*)

Scene 13

The castle square. In the foreground on the right, entrance gateway.
On the left, some distance back, the castle with ramp leading up to it.
Church in the rear. March and procession, led by a HERALD, then
GENTLEMEN-AT-ARMS. Canopy carried by four MOORS. In the
middle of the castle square the EMPEROR, VOM STRAHL,
THEOBALD, COUNT OTTO, the RHINE-COUNT, FREIBURG
and other followers waiting to meet the canopy. Under the palace portico,
right, KUNIGUNDE in bridal costume, with her aunts and cousins,
waiting to join the procession. In the background, spectators including
GOTTSCHALK, FLAMMBERG, ROSALIE etc.

VOM STRAHL: Halt here, with the canopy! Herald, do
  your duty!

HERALD: (*Reading.*) Be it known to all that Count
  Friedrich Wetter vom Strahl, is today celebrating his
  marriage to Kathrina, Princess of Swabia, daughter of
  our most illustrious lord and Emperor. May heaven bless
  the bridal pair and, from the clouds above, upon their
  beloved heads, shower its cornucopia of happiness.

KUNIGUNDE: Rosalie, is this man possessed, or what?

ROSALIE: If not, by heaven, what's happening is fit to
  make us so!

FREIBURG: Where is the bride?

TURNECK KNIGHT: Here, my most worthy lords!

FREIBURG: Where's that?

TURNECK KNIGHT: Here stands my lady cousin – under
  this portico!

FREIBURG: We're looking for the bride of Count vom
  Strahl. My lords, about your business! Follow me, we'll
  go and fetch her.
  (*FREIBURG, WALDSTÄDTEN and the RHINE-COUNT*
  mount the ramp and enter the castle.)

TURNECK KNIGHTS: Hell! Death and devil! What is the
  meaning of all this?

Scene 14

KATIE in the imperial wedding gown, escorted by the COUNTESS and LEONORA, her train carried by three PAGES; behind her FREIBURG and the rest descending the ramp.

COUNT OTTO: Hail, my lady!

FLAMMBERG: Hail, Katie of Heilbronn, Imperial Princess of Swabia!

PEOPLE: Long live Katie! Hurrah! (*etc.*)

VON HERRNSTADT/VON DER WART: (*Friends of the RHINE-COUNT who have remained on the square.*) Is this the bride?

FREIBURG: It is.

KATIE: Me, my noble lords? Whose bride?

EMPEROR: The bride of him the cherub chose for you. Will you exchange this ring with him?

THEOBALD: Do you agree to give the Count your hand?

VOM STRAHL: (*Embraces her.*) Katie! My bride! Will you accept me?

KATIE: May God and all his saints protect me!
(*She sinks down and is supported by the COUNTESS.*)

EMPEROR: Then take her, Count vom Strahl, and lead her to the altar!
(*Bells begin to peal.*)

KUNIGUNDE: Plague, death and vengeance! You shall pay dearly for this insult!
(*Storms off with her retinue.*)

VOM STRAHL: Poisoner!
(*March. The EMPEROR beside KATIE and VOM STRAHL under the canopy, followed by KNIGHTS and LADIES. GENTLEMEN-AT-ARMS bring up rear of procession. Exeunt ALL.*)

The End.

Also Published by Oberon Books

Wyspianski
THE WEDDING
Translated by Noel Clark
ISBN: 1 84002 041 5   Price £6.99

Fredro
THREE PLAYS
Revenge, The Annuity, Virgin's Vows
Translated by Noel Clark
ISBN: 0 948230 64 9   Price £7.95

van den Vondel
LUCIFER
Translated by Noel Clark
ISBN: 0 948230 37 1   Price £5.95

Corneille
THREE PLAYS
Le Cid, Cinna, Polyeuct
Translated by Noel Clark
ISBN: 0 948230 57 6   Price £7.95